The Sea, the
and the Passage

Graham Durrant

SESAME SEES

Copyright © 2020, Graham Durrant.

The author has asserted his rights under the Copyright Design and Patents Act, 1988, to be identified as the author of his work.

Sesame Sees, Hull, Yorkshire HU5 3TG, UK.

All Rights Reserved.

No part of this publication may be reproduced, stored in a retrieval system, or transmitted in any form or by any means, electronic, mechanical, photocopying, recording or otherwise without the prior written consent of the publisher or a licence permitting copying in the UK issued by the Copyright Licensing Agency Ltd, 90 Tottenham Court Road, London W1P 9HE.

ISBN 978-1-71659-206-5

2 3 4 5 6 7 8 9

*To Sesame Sky Durrant Fox
with love.*

Contents

MV Trebartha 7
Las Palmas and the Canary Islands 29
Australia 59
Missed the Boat 72
The Panama Canal 91
MV Pacific Stronghold 118
MV Douro 122
Back aboard MV Douro 152
MV Lock Loyal 169
MV Pacific Ranger 174
MV Oroya 183
MV Essex 231
MV Rio Cobre 243
Back To School 251
Barge Diction and Barge Blatence 256
MV Westminsterbrook 268
MV Trewidden 276
MV Trecarne 282
Epilogue 286

Acknowledgements

To Holly Bidgood, author, for proofreading the manuscript and providing inspiration.

To the members of Whitby Writers Group, who generously listened to extracts from my manuscript and offered welcome encouragement plus many helpful comments.

To Ian Clark, and several other proofreaders, who have worked countless hours for little reward to make this book possible.

And lastly, to Jude Fox, for her great faith in human nature! I'm unable to thank her enough.

About the Author

Graham Durrant was born in Watford in 1953. Unable to gain any qualifications on account of his profound dyslexia (an undiagnosed condition in the 1960s) he left school at the age of 15, shortly after his parents' marriage had broken up. But perseverance in hardship, plus a chance meeting on a train, gained him a real-life education in the British Merchant Navy, sailing as a deck hand on many different ships out of the Royal Docks, London.
Since leaving the Merchant Navy he has done many things in many places. He now lives in Hull with his partner Jude and their 7 year old daughter, to whom this book is dedicated.

Ship illustrations are by the author.

MV Trebartha

MV Trebartha

I walked up to the top of the gangway. There was a framed black board wedged in the taff rail and chalked upon it were the words:

Depart 18:00 hours 5 January 1970 leaving for Las Palmas

I didn't have a clue where that was. But it sounded wonderful. A superb trigger for a great adventure, it sent my mind reeling with images of sun, sea and palm-fringed beaches.

The *MV Trebartha* was moored alongside F shed, Royal Albert Dock, in the East End of London. She had just finished being loaded with every sort of ship's cargo you can imagine: consumables of all kinds – trucks, engine parts – 5,000 tons of consignments filled with products packed in everything from cardboard boxes to huge wooden cases. They were all bound for Australia, and stencilled on them were a host of addresses in Adelaide, Melbourne, Sydney and Brisbane. The Blue Peter flying from the foremast flag halyard announced that we sailed tomorrow with the tide.

It was around 7 o'clock on a chilly evening. I had to report to the chief officer. After enquiring from the night watchman, I found him in his cabin on the boat deck just below the bridge. I knocked and was commanded to enter.

Inside was a dark-haired medium-sized man with a short beard. He seemed a calm and friendly but slightly aloof man, who lived up to my first impression throughout the trip. I announced myself and said that I was there to take up one of the two vacant positions of deck boy, and that I'd been told to report to the ship by the marine superintendent for the Hain-Nourse shipping company. The chief officer welcomed me aboard and informed me that the rest of the crew would arrive later, when we'd all sign on to ship's articles in the morning. I was then sent off to find my cabin.

The crew's accommodation was situated at the after end of the ship, between the steering gear flat and the poop deck. The officer explained that there had been a skeleton crew working by the dock, and two JOS (junior ordinary seamen) had already taken the deck-boy double cabin, as they were both from Devon and good friends. He left me to sort it out with them as to who would have which cabin for the duration of the trip. I thanked the chief officer and headed down to the stern of the boat, not knowing what I'd find.

The walk was most memorable. Just 16 years of age, and after years of waiting, plus the difficulties of the past 6 months, I thought I was finally at the beginning of my dream. I was signed on a merchantman, all set to head off around the world across the ocean deep.

—oOo—

I went down the companionway stairs from the boat deck and out past the officers' saloon, then onto the cargo deck on the starboard side (the shore side).

The ship was built in the late 1950s. It was one of the last of its type, with five cargo hatches, three on the forward part plus two on the after part, with accommodation for officers, engineers and catering crew, plus the bridge, boat deck, mess room and engine situated amidships. The deck department's cabins on the other hand were at the stern of the ship.

It was a dark cold January evening as I walked past 4 and 5 holds' hatch coamings and saw the eight aft castle derricks reaching up into the sky. I paid no attention to the cold. Here was a boy living his dream. I picked my way around the mess of ropes, wires, strops, pallets, circular ropes for lifting cargo, and huge bundles of 4"×2" timber known as dunnage. This was used by the carpenter to shore up the cargo in the holds to stop it moving whilst at sea. It was a very important job, shoring up the cargo – paramount for the stability of the ship at sea. If the load shifted, it could cause a permanent list, risking the ship foundering in heavy seas.

I stopped for a while and looked out over the side of the ship. Presently I became aware of the sound of generators powering the lights flickering on the long lines of ships doubled-up on either side of the Albert Dock. I knew that at the far end of the Victoria Docks was a swing bridge to be passed through, then a small basin to enter the sea lock leading to the River Thames, and from there downstream to the sea.

I stood looking out over this scene and took a deep breath, recalling that the year before I'd stood at dusk on the other side of the swing bridge in question during my many Sunday ship-spotting expeditions. For these I needed to travel from Hertfordshire on three trains plus a bus to get to all the London docks, or to the Gravesend pilot and tug station on the lower reaches of the River Thames.

One evening a large passenger cargo ship came through the lock to enter the dock. It was the *Akaroa*, formerly the *Amazon*, one of three Royal Mail Lines passenger cargo liners employed on the East Coast of South America run. I was to become closely acquainted with that trade route in the years ahead. I had gazed up at this huge white ship, knowing nothing of her at the time. But the rust streaks below her starboard anchor told its tale of long voyages in heavy seas and foul weather.

I turned around and looked up the dock, seeing all the ships from various countries, at their myriad lights glowing in the slight mist, and I savoured the smells and sensed the romance of those many fragrances from all over the world. I was on the other side now, looking back at a shadow of myself on the dockside, dreaming of possibilities which were now becoming a reality. A feeling of achievement flooded through me. After relishing the moment I came back to the here-and-now, and continued on aft to find my berth.

Inside the crew's accommodation I began to look for the deck boys' cabin. I was conscious of some most improbable noises. How could it be? Yes, I was not mistaken: it was definitely rock-&-roll – heavy rock in fact.

I traced the music to a door with a small ivory plaque above it saying "Deck Boys" and knocked several times. Getting no answer I tried the door: it opened.

I couldn't believe my eyes.

Inside the cabin was dimly lit. There was a small record player on the table from which the music was coming. Sitting around it, in a haze of smoke, were eight or so young men, smoking, drinking, chatting and laughing away. They were dressed very strangely, their hair varying from shoulder-length to down to their backsides. I didn't know what to think. I just stood there.

A thin red-faced young man with a broad Devon accent said "Hiya, I'm Chris. This is the other JOS, John."

"Hi," said John. "This is a great party cabin. So could we keep it? You and the other deck boy can have our single berths below, if you like."

I said okay and he replied, "Sit down and have a drink, man," and gave me a can of lager. I sat there for a while in total bewilderment.

The person sitting next to me was a bit older than the others. He had a Che Guevara T-shirt, and a huge head of long wavy hair parted in the middle. He turned to me with a smile on his heavy features and a big cigarette streaming dense smoke and said in a broad Scottish accent, "Here, get some of this doon your neck, son."

I stared at the cigarette, back up at him, and all around the room. I'd never smoked before, not even ordinary tobacco. Under the circumstances this was a testing moment. So I said okay, took it from him, closed my eyes and, to coin a phrase, took my first blast of marijuana. Figuratively however I had my eyes wide open. Things would never be the same again, in all sorts of ways.

The next morning I woke up in what was to be my cabin for the rest of the voyage. A voice on the other side of the door shouted "Turn to! Breakfast."

I lay there for a while, coming-to, taking in the 12×8 ft cabin and its contents. I sat up and peered round the rim of a small porthole. Across the room there was a built-in wardrobe, a chest of drawers with a slide-out table mirror, and a daybed. The bed I was in ran the length of the room. It had a blue counterpane with the blue and white emblem of the Hain-Nourse shipping company. The bare walls and pipe leading to an air conditioning vent were painted magnolia.

I leapt out of bed and stared through the round porthole at the wonderful sight of the dockside, with its ship's cranes all working away. Then I became aware of all sorts of noises rattling round the ship.

I left the cabin. There was a communal washroom for the crew. I used it, got dressed, went upstairs and went out on deck.

The ship was a hive of activity. I picked my way back past the two after holds. The deck was swarming with dockers directing the crane drivers lowering the last few strops of goods into the hold. The cranes were huge ones on the dockside, running on rails.

Down in the hold, a team of men were placing the goods in position while others nailed timbers up. The sound of hammers hitting nails was like gunfire.

I found my way to the mess room, which was situated aft of the centre accommodation on the main deck, starboard side, and collected my breakfast. A lot of the crew had still to arrive, so as yet the mess was fairly quiet. It had rows of tables and chairs, a fridge, and at one end a serving hatch in the wall through from the galley.

Behind the hatch a hot press was being loaded by a caricature of a man with long red hair and a gaucho moustache. He turned out to be from Dublin and his name was George. George the Messman. He was a lively fellow, though he kept himself to himself. He spoke at top speed, always ending with "d'you know what I mean", and called everyone "boss" the whole time.

I took my breakfast tray to a vacant table and sat down. Just then John, Chris and some others came in and sat down with their breakfasts too. They were brilliant company, just as they had been the night before. We had our "scran", and they "told me the score" about everything. After that I knew what we'd be doing for the day, right up until the time we were due to set sail: 4 PM. Or rather: 16:00 hours, ship's time (the 24 hour clock is always used at sea).

Then the bo's'un came in and put us to work.

The first part of the morning was taken up by lowering and stowing away all the derricks into their crutches and lashing them on the foredeck. Hatches 1, 2 and 3 were complete with their McGregor hatches (known informally as "tin lids") closed and dogged down. These hatches were opened and closed by a series of wires leading to the winches on top of the mast housing between the hatches.

The derricks however were in a total mess. Each hatch had four derricks, with a separately operating electric winch for each two. Whenever the ship came into port all these derricks would be lifted if they were needed, or to gain access to the hold. However, if there were shoreside cranes, as there were in most docks, the derricks were lifted and then let go and swung outboard so as not to get in the way. Each derrick had a wire topping lift plus a wire runner for working, two rope blocks-and-tackle for positioning, and a preventer wire for additional safety. So the next three hours were spent lowering the derricks into their housing, lashing them, and leaving all associated rigging either coiled or stowed away. It was confusing to start with, but okay once we had a system going.

—oOo—

In no time at all it was 12 o'clock, time for dinner. A huge three-course meal awaited us: it tasted good and there was plenty of it. There were crowds more people around as by now the rest of the crew had arrived. They had all manner of accents, shapes, sizes and ages.

After lunch we all made our way up to the officers' saloon to sign on ship's articles. This is a standard procedure on all British ships. It is a contract valid for 6 months, governed by what was then the Board of Trade. After 6 months, wherever you were in the world, the company would be obliged to fly you home unless you chose to sign on again for another 6 months. Up until this requirement was introduced it used to be that you remained on the ship until you landed at a UK port. The change came about because it was found that men who didn't get along naturally, being confined to the one ship for so long, got claustrophobic. This could result in serious disruption among the crew, with gang-like divisions appearing among crew members, ending up in arguments, fights, or even murders.

After signing on, plus saying a sincere thank-you to the Company's shipping superintendent, who had helped me a lot in the past two months, we went back to work. This time we made ready-for-sea the last two hatches, 4 and 5, on the after part of the ship.

—oOo—

"Smoko," bellowed the bo's'un. ("Smoko" is ship's slang for tea break). He was a stocky, unemotional but fair-minded man from Hull named Billy Applegate. In his 30s, he was surprisingly young for a bo's'un, but extremely confident. He instantly earned everyone's respect.

It was around 15:00 hours, so our instructions were to stand by our sailing stations at 16:00. Sure enough, we heard the whistles of the two tugs that would tow us down the dock stern-first. At the same time the bo's'un called out, "Right – turn-to for stations, lads".

The crew were split into two gangs of six men each, fore and aft, for letting-go shorelines and making-fast the tugs. These gangs were led by the second officer, aft, and on the foredeck (my station) by the chief officer. The order was then given to *single up*. This meant that all bar one head rope, one quarter rope and the "spring", that led aft from the quarterdeck – were taken-in.

At the same time a heaving line – a long lightweight line with a lead-weighted knot on the end known as a monkey's fist – was thrown to the now-positioned tug, made fast on their towing line, which was a large cable, part-rope, part-wire, then brought up through the fair lead, turned around the drum of the winch, and taken down to two large bollards, where it was made fast by placing the eye over the two large bollards.

Then the Tannoy shouted "okay, let go". We quickly slackened the remaining ropes, and the watermen onshore slipped the eyes [of the ropes] off the bollard and we winched them in, coiling them down as they came in.

Then there was one very loud blast from our ship's horn, with two higher pitched corresponding blasts in answer from the tugs. As their engines roared, the lines from the tugs became tight. There was a vibration through the hull as our engine picked up, and the 10,000 tons of the *MV Trebartha* started to move away from its berth. It gave me a feeling of exhilaration and excitement, plus slight apprehension, as this huge boat set off into the unknown.

We all stood for a while waiting for our next order. I looked around at the faces waiting there like me, and I knew that they were all feeling the same as I, as we slowly moved down the dock.

It was nearly dark, and as some stood by the tug lines, we generally tidied up the foredeck, making fast anything that could move and stowing ropes down in the fore peak. This was a space above the anchor chain locker and under the fo'c's'le head locker, where all manner of things were kept. But it was primarily for ropes to be stowed when at sea.

I was trying to concentrate on my work, but I couldn't help eyeing the lights of the other ships on that murky January night. Ships of all shapes, sizes, colours and nationalities, being loaded or unloaded with all kinds of goods. Rice, spices, engine parts, cars, trucks, diggers, furniture, foodstuffs. There were the regular British ships: Port Line, Blue Star Line, Shaw Savill, Federal, Steam Navigation, Pacific Steam Navigation Company, Glenn Line, Ben Line. Then there were others from China, Russia, Poland, Germany, Holland, America, South Africa and India. I saw the occasional crew member standing at the bulwark, watching us go by whilst having a smoke. There were all types of unusual-looking people: black, white, tall, thin, oriental, plus the occasional woman, generally these were on the Russian and Scandinavian ships.

Eventually we reached the end of the dock: an area known as the Basin, where it widens out adjacent to the swing bridge. To a series of signals between the tugs and ourselves: toots on our horn and whistles from the tugs, we were turned 90° and pulled stern-first through the cut into King George V dock, and then a further 90° until our bow faced the swing bridge and lock gate, both of which were now open.

The ship slowly eased itself into the sea lock. By this time we were back at our stations, ready to heave our line down to the lock keepers. With mooring ropes attached to hold us fast while in the lock, the tug came in with us and remained made-fast, care being taken with the stern tug lines so as not to foul the propeller.

The lockmaster blew his whistle and our ship began to descend to the level of the tidal waters of the River Thames. During this operation we took up the slack on the shorelines to keep the ship in place within the turbulent water of the lock sluice. Finally the huge lock gates opened. You could almost hear the ship taking a breath and saying to itself "free at last!"

The rumbling engine picked up speed and once again, to the accompaniment of the now-familiar series of toots and whistles, the lead tug moved out ahead of us and took up the strain on the towline. _

All of our shorelines were now let go, and we slowly began to move out of the lock under our own power. The stern tug looked strange as it was drawn out backwards behind us. This, I learned from an old hand, was in case of any problem heading into the river, in which event the stern tug was there to act as an emergency brake.

However we cleared the lock without incident and moved into the mainstream of the River Thames, turning to port and to the east, facing downstream. On a signal from the bridge we let go the tugs' towlines. Both tugs remained with us as we gathered speed, escorting us down the river. We then finished stowing our lines down below, checked nothing was adrift and stood down, all except the watch keepers.

Since we were underway in coastal waters, the watch system came into play. From this point onwards, until we left the English Channel, there would be three men on each watch. Their tasks rotated: on the helm; general bridge work and lookout; and the third (known as the farmer) relieving the other two watches for their breaks. The watches were arranged as follows on a 24-hour basis: 12 to 4 (third officer), 4 to 8 (first officer) and 8 to 12 (second officer). Deck boys and JOSs did not work watches.

By this time it was very dark and cold. I was surprised to see it was nearly 19:00 hours. Three hours had passed since we left F shed on Royal Albert Dock. I had found it all so absorbing it felt like no time at all. As we retired to the mess for our evening meal I heard another crew member saying "three hours overtime".

It was a huge three-course meal that awaited up, with endless mugs of tea. Taking the last mug with me, I couldn't resist going out on deck, finding a sheltered spot and watching the nighttime activity on the river, which was slowly getting wider. We were still being escorted by our tug, which eventually left us at Gravesend. This was the station for tugs whose names began with SUN followed by Roman numerals.

It was a poignant moment for me: at a much younger age I'd made my way on many occasions to that very tug station from Watford, Herts, on Sundays by train – a long journey there and back for a few hours' ship-spotting. It gave me a marvellous feeling of satisfaction to look back now in the opposite direction, from the ship to the shore.

Shortly afterwards I could make out the lights of a little-known establishment which I had some serious issues about. Silently I raised a two-fingered salute to the Pre-Sea Training School, Gravesend, from which I'd managed to escape after just a few days.

I spent the rest of the evening alternating between my cabin, unpacking and wondering how my new home was going to be, and making the other crew members' acquaintance. Chris and John were obviously going to be good friends. Every so often I'd go out on deck to watch the lights of the land getting smaller and smaller as we moved down the Thames estuary, until they became a thin line off our starboard side. We headed due east, then south-east, and eventually south, following the Kent coast towards Dungeness.

As I lay down in my bunk that night I knew sleep would come easily. I was absolutely shattered. Lying in my bunk is always a special time for me, when I think over everything that's happened to me that day, and how it all fits in with my general perception. You can imagine how I felt at this poignant and confirming climax to a great deal of experience that I had gone through. I thought of the things I'd endured the previous six months to reach this point. Thoughts and changing emotions raced around my busy mind from the day I left home, which was also the day the family home was no more. That was one hell of a burnt bridge. Then I thought of trying to live in the hardship of London, after a relatively sheltered life, working toilets in seamen's missions to satisfy my basic needs, whilst avoiding unsavoury advances from some sad men. But I'd also had some brilliant help from good-hearted people. Somehow, in my innocence, something – someone – some incident – would turn up to save me in the nick of time. I remember that I both laughed and cried myself to sleep that night. I was homesick for a home and family that no longer existed. Homesick for the image of home that you'd normally carry inside your mind. But at least I didn't have to worry about having a bed to sleep in or food to eat for the next six months.

I had achieved my aim, fulfilling a dream that had started when I was 13. Finally I was there. Now, what would tomorrow bring?

Tomorrow came sooner than I expected. At one point in the early hours I woke up and noticed everything had gone quiet. The engine had stopped. I quickly threw on some clothes and went up on deck to see what was going on. I looked down the port side of the boat (sailors always refer to ships as "boats" – it's just a thing they do). My eye was drawn to the glare of a cluster-light: a portable extension lamp used mainly in the cargo holds, consisting of a large bold shade with four 200 W bulbs. It had been swung out over the side, illuminating a white-painted wooden rope-ladder lashed to the gunwale rail just aft of the central accommodation. This had been wound down the side of the boat to the waterline. To my amazement, there was a man holding onto the ladder. He was standing in a small craft that looked like a police launch. Surely we couldn't have been stopped for speeding, I told myself, because we only do 15 knots.

The boat had a blue hull with white topsides and what sounded like two powerful, deep-throated engines. It was of a type known as a Nelson, used for all official comings and goings in the sea trade worldwide. I glanced up and noticed we were quite close in: about 2 or 3 miles off what proved to be Dungeness.

Just then one of the cadets appeared. Behind him was a man in an officer's uniform, carrying a brown briefcase. This was the pilot, who had been on board ever since we left our berth the previous afternoon.

His job was to apply his specialist local knowledge to navigating us out of the River Thames and through the myriad treacherous channels and shifting sands, mudbanks, shipwrecks, derelict defence platforms left over from World War II, other ships, flashing buoys and lighthouses indicating hazards of one kind or another, plus handling communications with the tugboats. Most insurance companies insisted on the use of a pilot, and shipowners had to pay for this service.

The "farmer" (the third man on the watch), who was standing by, tied the pilot's briefcase to a heaving line and lowered it to the boatman on the launch below. Then the pilot climbed over the side and made his way down the ladder to the waiting craft. The moment he stepped on board the two powerful engines picked up and the launch took off fast. But not before the pilot had given a wave of acknowledgement to the crew at the top of the ladder, and then another in the direction of the bridge. This was the modern-day salute (ours being a civilian industry).

I stood for a while watching the two men bring the rope ladder back up on deck. Then, realising how cold I was getting, I returned to my cabin. As the engine began vibrating through the ship, a sound which was quickly becoming familiar, I dropped straight off to sleep and resumed my dreams as we picked up speed, heading out back into the English Channel and southwest towards the Atlantic Ocean.

At 07:30 hours I was called for breakfast – just two hours after the incident with the pilot in the night.

A short while after the watch keeper's call at 07:30 hours, I got up and peered out the porthole. It was not quite light yet, and the view was a bit uninteresting, so I had a shower, got dressed in warm clothes and headed out on deck and to midships for breakfast. It was a grey day, but bright enough, with a chilly wind from the north on the starboard beam. The ship was running across a moderate sea with winds of about 4 to 5 on the Beaufort scale. We were making good speed, with a slow shallow roll. This was topped off with the ever-present sound astern of the funnel – dark blue with white HN painted on it, issuing a bit of oily-smelling smoke. The sound of the engine had a strange hiss to it.

I sniffed the air and looked around me. There was no land in sight. I went to the gunwale and stared down at the sea. It was almost brown in the bottoms of the troughs, but the passing, slightly crested waves rising out of it were a dark greeny-blue. They confused my eyes as the ship sliced through them.

Breakfast was a lively affair. The smiling Irish face of George the mess man greeted me with "There you go, boss" as he handed me a big plate of fried breakfast. It was a little before 08:00 hours. The 4 to 8 watchmen were just in from doing their stint, and the 8 to 12 boys had just left to do theirs. There was a deck crew of about 14 on duty, plus the bo's'un and the carpenter.

I sat down at table with Chris, John and the other deck boy, Andy, plus another man. He was tall, slim and fairly quiet, with long hair and a droopy moustache. I reckoned he was about 28 years of age. He was introduced to me as Abby, from Bishop's Stortford.

Another man turned up: a small, mouselike fellow called Ivan. He was Russian, but had worked for the company for about 15 years. Company man.

For the present we were the only day workers, and that would continue to be the case until they reverted to one man to a watch. This would happen when we stopped "rock dodging" and left coastal waters for what was known as "deep sea".

—oOo—

We shared the mess with the two engine room staff. One was a ruddy-faced man with a very broad accent called Geordie. The other, called Brian, was a quiet man of slight build, with dark hair and skin. He spoke little, but when he did his voice had a lazy sound, with lots of W's in it. The pair of them were like Laurel and Hardy, only serious. Nobody envied their job, especially in the tropics.

After breakfast the bo's'un turned us to (i.e. set us to work) at 09:00 hours. Our job for the day was just to tidy up. All the rubbish from the loading activity was simply jettisoned over the side, which surprised me. The various bits of working gear were stowed away or lashed down.

The day went like this: 09:00 hours start; 10:30 to 11:00 smoko; 12:00 to 13:00 dinner; 14:30 to 15:00 smoko; finish at 17:00 hours. There was the option to work from 17:30 to 19:00, which was counted as three hours overtime at time-and-a-half. This was a good deal and most people took advantage of it. At sea, Saturdays and Sundays were compulsory. But at time-and-a-half for Saturday, and double-time for Sunday, this amounted to triple time as you got the pay for a day's leave for every Sunday at sea. But at weekends you didn't get the option to do the evening stint. However there were plenty of other opportunities to earn extra pay: for "stations" when leaving or entering port, for doing watches and for extras such as working during the nighttime hours. You got triple pay for these if you couldn't get eight hours sleep before your next stint on watch. You were also entitled to hot food, known as a "black pan". This was over and above "supper": bread, toast, tea and cold meat salad that was always left in the fridge in case you were hungry during the night.

All this was very helpful, financially, as in 1970 a deck boy earned £24 a month, a JOS earned £36, an EDH (Efficient Deck Hand) earned £55 and an AB £65.

After lunch we had to wash down the ship. Spaced around the bulwarks were fire hydrants. We used these in conjunction with the coiled fire hoses stowed strategically around the boat. At one point I was sent down to the engine room to ask for the hydrants to be turned on. We finished the day cold and wet. As you can imagine, the evening meal was most welcome and we ate heartily.

—oOo—

It was dark by then, so after changing into dry clothes we did our hour-and-a half overtime stint inside, cleaning the washroom in our own accommodation, the bar/recreation room and the showers, none of which had received much attention whilst the boat had been discharging cargo around the coast of Britain from the earlier deep sea voyage. Work of this sort is known as the "home trade" – or "rock dodging". Some of the older seamen – those who have families or who don't fancy long voyages any more – work solely at the home trade for

Just two or three weeks at a time.

We finished at 19:00 hours and most of us spent the evening sorting out our own cabins, settling in for the trip and simply getting to know each other better. This was important as we were going to be sharing our lives for the next six months.

That night, I lay in my bunk looking up at my map of the world, which had spent the last two years on the wall of my bedroom at home. In those days I would gaze at it, wondering about all those exotic places, and dreaming of visiting them. Now here I was, living the dream. For the time being, the excitement of it all chased away the dismal emotions I'd been battling against, faced as I was with a grown-up world, with very few people to help me. Studying the map I realised that sailing south-west down the English Channel, as we had been doing for 24-hours, we must have been somewhere between Weymouth, Cherbourg and the Channel Islands. By the time I woke up, we would be approaching Brest on the north-eastern tip of France, which was adjacent to Lands End. This was the gateway to the Atlantic, at which point we would turn south into the northern part of the Bay of Biscay. This region is renowned among seafarers for its storms, uneasy swells and fog.

Further study of the map showed me Las Palmas, that wonderful-sounding place that had set my head in a spin 48 hours ago when I'd first come aboard. It is centred on Grand Canaria, the largest of a group of islands known as the Canaries. A province of Spain, it is remarkably close to the south-west of Morocco and the Western Sahara, lying a mere 50 miles off the African coast. I knew from the general chat on board that we'd be there in another four days, provided we didn't hit any adverse weather which would slow us up. I remember thinking: four days at 15 knots (16 mph) – God! How could you possibly go any slower? Strange how your concept of time changes as you grow older. At 16 years of age, four days was forever, in my eagerness to experience this elusive place that sounded like paradise.

I woke up to the watchman's shout at the door: "turn to". Consciousness returned to the whining sound of the steering gear below me, and the hum and vibration of the engine itself. The ship didn't seem to be rolling so much, and today was a lot brighter. I was soon up and on deck, ready for some food and whatever else the day might bring.

The weather was a lot warmer, with the wind coming from the south-west. The sky had a scattering of large fluffy clouds with blue sky showing behind them. There was no direct sunlight on the deck, but as I looked around me out to sea I could see occasional rays lighting up the white-crested waves, which were now a deep turquoise. We were meeting the sea head on, so there was very little roll, only a slow gentle pitching motion. So after breakfast that day, I had a marvellous feeling that we were getting somewhere. The English Channel lay astern of us, and ahead the Bay of Biscay beckoned.

It was now day three at sea. Most of it was spent doing the usual washing-down of the decks. We continued to clear rubbish, and stow or dump the various loading paraphernalia.

Something which gave me cause for concern at the time – there were still tons of dunnage – the 14 ft lengths of 4"×2" timber used for shoring up cargo – stacked next to all the holds. We were now told to dump it all in the sea. It took hours, but we had great fun tumbling it over the side. All work on board ship, as I was discovering, turned into friendly competition between the crew. On this occasion it was for the one who could get the greatest number of lengths of timber "over the wall" in one throw, or who managed to to pass a length of timber through a wave before it reached the sea. Schoolboy stuff, but it kept us happy and laughing and passed the time.

There was something tribal about all this: group bonding and rights-of-passage for the younger members. Travelling the world, you get to see many different cultures. Even in remote regions, tribes had this in common: when the men worked together they had special songs for different jobs. You saw this particularly in

Africa, but the Indians did it too. If it wasn't a song they'd chant together, sometimes a single word: the name of the item they happened to be moving, carrying or otherwise operating on. So maybe our play was a manifestation of our own tribal culture in a closed environment, cooped up together as we were in our ship with no escape. It definitely helped to bond us, and anyway it was all great fun.

I realised then that something profound was happening within me. I was starting to learn things about the world and my place within it. I had a lively and enquiring mind: something that had not been recognised during my childhood, nor my time in school. No doubt this was due to circumstances such as the absence of my family at a time when I'd most needed it (I say this without wanting to pass judgement). Now, with childhood behind me, my real education had begun – and I had a thirst to learn which was crying out to be quenched.

I'd been forced to depart from my original plan to reach my goals, and it was only by following my innocent instincts, plus my determination to succeed, which had brought me here this day, to this life. I was going to survive and prosper, and at last gain a sense of self-worth through achievement.

—oOo—

The day continued with the same activities, but the watches were now scaled back to just one man to a watch. With the ship on automatic pilot, it meant that this one man could be on duty on the bridge to assist the officer of the watch, taking the wheel if necessary, acting as general dogsbody: "sugeing down" the bridge, washing the deck and shining brass when he was not running errands. He'd also call the next watchman, as well as calling the rest of the crew to "turn to" in the mornings.

It also meant that there were six more men on daytime work with us, which gave the rest of us the chance to meet them and get to know them better. Up until now we'd done little more than exchange occasional hellos. Since the watchmen were on a

24 hour rota, 4 hours on and 8 off, they'd been sleeping when we were awake.

A good opportunity for getting to know the whole crew better took place that very evening. Our overtime job for the evening (it was still going dark early) was to finish cleaning out the recreation room, plus our aft accommodation. A seafaring tradition was for the whole crew to organise a roster to run the bar for the duration of the voyage. Although it was only a formality, a meeting was called for that evening to arrange it. It was the first time we'd all been gathered together (apart from meals and tea breaks) including the stewards, whose cabins were amidships. However, since ratings shared the bar with us, along with the "donkey men" (the engine room staff), they were included too. So the roster got sorted and we now had a committee to organise events like games, darts, cards, etc. There was also an unofficial library, which consisted mostly of cowboy books. That was something I thought really strange. But it was common on most ships, as I later found out. The books never did anything for me, I must say.

There was however a more comprehensive library run by the British Ship Society, which established them on all ships. It was replenished and kept up-to-date by the society's representatives in all the major ports of the world. It was a very good library and helped me no end in many ways. I now had plenty of time on my hands, so I took to reading a lot.

Our bar was now up and running, and we celebrated by breaking open a case of Tennants Beer. This was the traditional beer to use for the purpose. It had photos of scantily-dressed women on each can and was in bad taste, both literally and metaphorically. But we drank a toast to our bar, which we had unanimously agreed to name the "Copacabana". We now had our bar in-place, and with it an on-board nightlife.

It's worth a mention that the beer sold at the bar was purchased from the ship's bond locker. This was a special locker kept sealed whilst in port to accommodate Customs and Excise regulations. There was only beer to be had: no spirits were available to ordinary crew members. One penny per can was levied on the profits of the bar. This was saved up and used for an occasional free night, which was handy for lower-paid hands such as myself.

It was the end of another day. Before turning in, I took a walk up on the poop deck and enjoyed a nice red sunset. I was feeling a lot warmer now. The weather was generally improving as we headed south, closer to the sun. I could feel the ship settling into a lazy roll between the troughs and crests of the North Atlantic swell. As I went below to bed, I went over my memories of the past and my hopes and fears for the future.

Day Four found us at the southern end of the Bay of Biscay. It was a bright sunny day, a lot warmer than it had been. The sea was surprisingly calm. We were passing the approaches and gates to the Mediterranean (which we couldn't see) with Spain and Portugal on the port side to the east, and Morocco to the southeast.

Our work now changed from cleaning and tidying to the maintenance of all the running gear, as we would not be using our derricks to work cargo until we reached Australia. There was plenty of time to dismantle all the blocks and tackle and their associated ropes and wires for overhaul and parts replacement.

It was hard work. Salted air takes its toll, and it was necessary to keep up a regular maintenance regime for the sake of safety and efficiency. Each derrick needed to be totally checked out. All wires were run off their winch barrels, carefully check for broken strands and crushed parts, fish-oiled and run back on the barrels or else replaced. All working metal blocks had to be taken off shackles and replaced if there were any signs of corrosion.

Corrosion is the second most dangerous threat to life after the sea itself. A given shackle could at any time be part of a rig holding up to 30 tons of cargo, swinging over the heads of dockers or crewmen. Many a good man has been lost due to an overlooked component. Even without having to undertake replacements, a single derrick could easily take a day to check, oil and grease. With 10 of them (plus one large heavy lift derrick located on the after side of the foremast, for use at number two hold) it was clear we were going to be kept busy for a long time. It was hard work and dangerous – and in a running sea difficult and uncomfortable.

After being at sea for a few days you become accustomed to the constant motion, and after a while you begin not to notice it and keep your balance instinctively. Yet every day could be completely different. Interestingly you found yourself adjusting to suit without noticing it. The ship's movements could vary from none at all, on a flat calm sea, to rolling, pitching, or both together – and it could shuttle between these extremes depending on the strength of wind plus the ship's motion relative to the direction of the running sea.

Apart from the obvious physical benefit, I felt there was something about this constant nervous stimulation – the ever-changing extremes – that was healthy and absorbing. It taught me something so profound that it's only in hindsight, years later, that I think I know what it is.

The first day of this much more interesting work passed without significant injury – without finding a broken strand sticking out just waiting to stab a passing hand. There were times you could hardly hold your knife and fork to eat your dinner.

Beyond my friendship with John and Chris, the two JOSs, the crewmen's various characters were beginning to impress themselves on me. My fellow deck boy didn't have a lot to say for himself. His standard answer to every question was "I dinna ken", he was from Peebles. In retrospect he was a nice lad. I might have got to know him better if we'd shared a cabin, as we would have done in the normal run of things.

There was also an AB called Paul, a large, tall, happy, round-faced fellow of about 28 from Colchester. This was something he never let you forget. The way he said it: "yeah I'm from Colchester you know, yeah, Colchester" was almost to sing it, as you might at a football match in support of your home town. But he was okay, organising a lot of tournaments – card, darts, dominoes and crib – that became very focused and absorbing in the friendly competitive spirit that existed onboard. It was all good stuff and would really help us to pass the time voyaging across the oceans in the next few weeks. The tournaments kept our minds lively and I enjoyed them, although I'm not a particularly competitive person.

—oOo—

We had come to the end of another day. As I fell asleep in my bunk that night, I wondered excitedly if our arrival in the Canaries would be as I'd imagined it. My imagination had been aided by the picture the other crew members had metaphorically painted for me in the past few days, some of them having been there before.

Day Five started early. At 5 AM there came a knock on the door from the watchman shouting "Turn to! Stations on the foredeck in 30 minutes." I got straight up and went out on deck. For the first time I felt really warm. As I looked to the east I saw a beautiful fluffy cloudy dawn breaking over the African coast and the Western Sahara. I looked at the West and – my God! – there was a great big lump of land where last night there had just been sea.

Las Palmas and the Canary Islands

As we'd all slept that night, the ship had continued its relentless progress and had finally made landfall at the massive volcano of Grand Canaria, to which we were now quite close in. This was the largest island of the group.

I walked over to the starboard side, heading for the mess to get a cup of tea. I felt a strong fresh southerly wind on my face. There was quite a choppy sea running. Drawn to the bulwark, I saw an amazing sight – the dawn sun rising in the east revealing Las Palmas to our southwest. It was all so exciting. I told myself this was what it was all about: visiting exotic places and experiencing the feeling – this marvellous inner feeling!

After a quick cup of tea I turned to and reported for stations to the fo'c's'le with the rest of the lads together with the first officer.

We brought all mooring ropes up from below and coiled them down on deck ready for use. We then stood in the wind with the sky getting lighter and lighter, waiting for the order to throw a heaving line to the tug that was now moving close in, just ahead of us.

First the heaving line, with its lead-weighted turk's-head, was thrown to straddle the tug. A tug man then made fast the tug's heavy towing line made of rope and wire. We then brought it aboard using the winch.

The line came up through the fair lead, around the barrel of the winch and then onto the bollards. A small length of tethered line was then wrapped around the line, so that it could be brought off the barrel of the winch and tied up on the bollards without losing any of its tension.

When this was done, the chief officer would then signal to the tug by raising his arms crossed above his head that the line had been made fast, and the tug moved forward, taking up the slack, and started to pull us.

The end of the harbour wall was now quite obvious. There was now some concern from the crew at this point over the southerly wind that had been slowly increasing as we had headed west approaching Las Palmas with our engine at dead slow. By now the tug had a tremendous job towing us with a port beam wind, and was heeling dangerously over to starboard.

If we were to stop engine too early, there was a risk of two things happening. Firstly the tug rope might part under the strain and whiplash, inflicting damage on everything and everybody in its path. Wires from a snapped rope have been known to cut through the steel plating of a ship and slice people clean in two. Secondly the tug lay at a critical angle and could turn over to capsize.

But we soon came around the harbour wall and into its lea. It was a huge breakwater, maybe a kilometre long, with ships tied up all along it.

Having recovered our heaving line from the tug's towing line before letting it go, to be recovered by them, we then attached it to one of our mooring ropes. The heaving line would once again be thrown to the waterman, who would catch it and then take our lines down onto the quay to be made fast onto the bollards.

This first line out would be a head line, leading forward. When the captain on the bridge was happy the ship was in position on the quay, he would give the order to make fast. We would now bring that first line onto the winch, and bring it up until it was tight. We'd them put a stopper onto it and then take it off the winch and put it onto a bollard without losing any of its tension.

This would then be repeated with all the remaining ropes that had to be put out, four in all, one more leading forward, one at right-angles to us down onto the quay, and a final one, known as a "spring", leading aft from about a third of the way down the ship.

Having made all lines fast to the breakwater like the other ships, we stood down for breakfast. But not before the deck boy (which was me) had rigged the rat guards on all shorelines. A rat guard was a big galvanised iron funnel cunningly secured around the rope and lashed on outboard down the rope with a large collar. It stopped rodents or stowaways getting aboard by way of the ropes. We all thought this a bit of a joke: why wouldn't they just use the gangway like everybody else?

So here we were, in Las Palmas. It turned out we were only going to be there for 24 hours. We'd only come for "bunkers" (diesel fuel). Las Palmas, it seems, is the nautical equivalent of your local cheap-fuel garage. For that reason it's a very busy port and we had to wait our turn.

It was still only mid-morning, so we had to continue working the day. However we kept hoping, and sure enough by mid-afternoon the bo's'un said " job-and-knock lads." This meant: do something like cleaning out a locker and then finish for the day. So a three-hour job was done in one hour and we were showered, changed into our go-ashore "dungies" and away by 4 PM.

A few of us made our way down the quay, past the police on the gate, and into the town. It was a lovely sunny afternoon and fairly hot. In this very busy city, against a backdrop of low-lying hills, we wandered around, taking in the ambience of the place. Later we found ourselves in a bar – the "Happy Bar" – and had soon made arrangements with the bar owner to swap our cartons of English cigarettes for one-litre bottles of very strong Bacardi rum. This was a regular trade that boat crews had been doing for many years: we'd all previously ordered our cigarettes for this very purpose. It was a convenient arrangement for us because, as already said, only officers were allowed to buy spirits out of the ship's bond.

In those days a carton of 200 cigarettes could be bought on board for 10 shillings (50p), which was cheap. And boy ratings could buy tobacco, even if they couldn't buy beer. It was no secret there was going to be a party on board tonight.

Chris, John and I visited a few bars ashore and had a few beers until we ran out of money. We didn't have much "sub" from the chief steward (an advance on wages) as we'd only been on board five days. We returned to the ship around mid-evening and found our dinners in the hot press, left for us by George ("Good man yourself") and proceeded on to our own bar, the *Copacabana*, to continue the night with our "firewater", as we called it.

So far it had been an interesting visit. Earlier that evening I'd sat in the bar ashore, gazing all around me at the odd-looking people – dark native Hispanic faces – all of them so very different from me. I found myself going over things in my mind, wondering just what else lay ahead to fill me with amazement.

The night continued, people getting very pissed, with drinking competitions which entailed downing half-tumblers of Bacardi. Not having much experience of drink, I presently found myself up on deck with the whole world spinning and whirling round, with no escape. Fighting off being physically sick, I found a coiled-down mooring rope on the poop deck above our accommodation at the very stern of the ship and lay down.

I woke up still on the rope. It was daylight and the sun was shining warmly. I could hear singing. Most if not all the lads were standing by the gunwale holding glasses of drink, looking down on the quayside – and singing. I got to my feet and went over to find out what was going on.

As I've already said, the docks at Las Palmas consisted of one long harbour wall jutting out to sea for about a kilometre. As I looked out seawards along the quay I could see a large passenger liner. It was British and known to us – the *Southern Cross*, a Shaw Savill boat – on its regular round-the-world cruising run via Australia and New Zealand. Although it was still early morning, around 7:30, there was a constant stream of passengers coming ashore. All of them had to come past us, and the lads were in good form, in spite of having been drinking all night without sleep. They were serenading the liner's passengers with songs befitting their age, gender, physique, etc. Someone offered me a "livener", which bleary-eyed I accepted and joined in the singing.

We sang *Two Little Boys* (Rolf Harris) to a family with twin boys who were standing there grinning up at us. Next a group of pensioners came along, so it was *Knees-up Mother Brown*. They stopped and did a knees-up in a line for us, lifting their skirts and really getting into it. It was brilliant, very nostalgic and connected us with home.

Pretty girls were met with songs like *If I said you had a beautiful body would you hold it against me?* (The Eagles). We were laughing and joking and all was well.

Up to that point the whole show had been conducted from the ship. Then somebody noticed that George the Messman had decided to take his very friendly but very drunk Irish conviviality down to the quayside and get among the cruise passengers. In his present state this was probably not a very good idea. But for the moment it was all in good humour.

He was good-naturedly chatting to the passengers until a taxicab came by, one of a regular stream of taxis taking passengers from the liner into town. George decided to stop the taxi, standing in front of it with his arm out straight, showing the palm of his hand, whilst appealing to the passengers for approval of his little act.

The driver however, hard at work and in a hurry, didn't take it well. He leaned on his horn and gestured to George to get out of the way. George, still smiling good-naturedly, turned his back in defiance and sat down on the bonnet, which dented under his weight.

At that point everything changed. I couldn't believe what happened next. The taxi driver, leaving his fare in the back, leapt out of his cab and started shouting in Spanish at George, then suddenly punched him in the head. We watched in shocked silence as they wrestled with each other, trading punches.

Then someone drew our attention to the taxi line next to the liner. The drivers had all got out of their cabs and were running towards the fighting men. Then we turned and looked down the quay in the opposite direction. The police on the dock gate had seen what was going on: they too were running towards the fray.

Somebody – Abby I think – said "Come on, lads, we'd better get George back on board!" So we all ran down the deck, forward to the companionway amidships on the starboard side. The taxi was almost alongside the gangway, so we didn't have far to run.

The driver saw us coming and hurriedly jumped back in his cab. A moment later we were all over it. Two of us grabbed

George, who had been pounding down on the taxi's bonnet, and had now run round to kick the driver's door.

The other taxi drivers and the dock police were nearly upon us. "Quick lads," shouted Abby, "Back on board!" We ran for the gangway, someone giving the taxi a parting kick.

Everything seemed to go into slow motion as we retreated up the gangway, dragging George with us. The police were hard on our heels, their flexible batons swishing and crashing against the chains of the ladder.

We only just made it, but we all got safely back on board. The ship was British territory and nobody, police included, could come aboard without the captain's permission – at least, not without a court order.

What five minutes earlier had been a glorious occasion had now turned sour. On top of it all, exacerbating the fast-deteriorating relations between England and Spain, torrents of abuse were being flung back and forth in Spanish and English.

Nobody could understand a word of what the other was saying, but the body-language was unmistakable. The drivers smacked their clenched fists hard into their palms, then beckoned for us to come back down. The policemen were doing the same, only they were clutching at their wrists, miming handcuffs.

In true British drunken decorum we shook our heads, shouted "fuck off!" and laughed hysterically, giving them the finger, plus a few V-signs.

And it was still only 8 AM.

—oOo—

Eventually those ashore got bored and went back to their work, leaving us laughing over our breakfast. But now we had to try and sober up before turning-to for work. George was back behind the hatch, looking a little worse for wear, though still handing out food with his usual smile and "there you go, boss". But he made sure to add, "thanks for all your help, lads".

We started back to work doing the usual in-port stuff, stowing and making ready for sea. The lifting gear and hatches however didn't need attention as we were only there for bunkers. Sure enough, later in the morning after smoko, huge hoses were brought aboard and screwed into two large deck fittings: the ends of two pipes that led down to the bottom of the ship. For some while the pipes throbbed away, pumping tons of diesel oil from tanks built into the jetty into the huge tanks called bunkers – a name they'd retained from the age of steam, when ships had run on coal not oil. The oil would feed the engine to propel us 24 hours-a-day around the world.

The advent of diesel oil, plus the initiative of some Canaries businessman, must have radically changed the economy of those volcanic islands. You could smell it everywhere whilst it was being pumped aboard. Afterwards the donkey men (the cleaners and oilers in the engine room) had one of their rare opportunities to work on deck, cleaning up the spillage with detergent and cotton waste.

The word went round that we would be sailing after lunch. But we soon found out that this was not to be. The ship had been forbidden to leave port, thanks to the incident with the taxi driver. It took us by surprise, as in our inebriated state we'd dismissed it all as of no account. But the taxi driver had made a formal complaint. He quite rightly wanted compensation for damage sustained by his cab during our "George rescue mission" and we could not depart until the matter been resolved.

Over lunch the chief officer listened to our side of the story, then delegated the bo's'un to be our representative. Whilst we worked a normal day the taxi driver, police, company agent, harbour authorities, someone from the British Consulate – the world and his wife – negotiated with "boss" George. The result was that the captain agreed to pay for the damage to the taxi, George agreed not to prosecute the driver for assault, and the harbour authority agreed to release the ship.

Some time in the early evening we were called to stations. The tugs arrived, we make fast and let go. Aided by the tugs, we headed out around the breakwater jetty, tooted our goodbyes to the tugs and the pilot (seven long blasts for going deep sea) turned south and sailed into the fading light along the coast of West Africa – and that was the end of that. Or so we thought.

The next morning, Day Six, a letter from the captain was posted up stating that money would be deducted from the wages of those crew members over 18 involved in the Great Taxi Assault Of Las Palmas incident. Apart from that, I was surprised at no disciplinary action being taken against any of us. The captain (always referred to as God on board) was someone we rarely saw. But like his chief officer he was a relaxed easy-going sort of person who took most things in his stride, and nothing more was said about the incident. But we felt it a good thing that we hadn't been staying long in port as we'd feared retribution from the taxi drivers, or even the police. Either of them could have set us up for some misdemeanour, beat us up, bust us or even kill us. So we felt we'd got off lightly, although when we'd sobered up we'd had the grace to feel ashamed.

The next day had started as usual with breakfast. The weather had really kicked off by now – with dawn coming early and a roasting hot sun in the morning. It's hard to come to terms with how the weather changes as you move across the planet while at sea for a long time. But it helps bring it home to you that you are in motion and getting somewhere, however featureless the seascape might look.

It was mid-afternoon and I was just reflecting on that very fact when the engine stopped. We spent the rest of the day simply bobbing in the Atlantic. It was a strange and disconcerting feeling. Naturally we, the crew, were the last to know what was going on.

Eventually, at the end of the day, we learnt we had a serious problem with the engine and had stopped them to assess the situation. The upshot was that we needed to return to Las Palmas to get them fixed. Our hearts sank that night when the bo's'un broke the news, with a heavy knowing grin.

The engine started up again with a roar and the usual cloud of smoke, the propeller began to rumble and push us through the sea once more. It was a soul-destroying feeling to go back to where we'd just come from, knowing that we were still looking at 35 days at sea to Oz. It was almost unbearable.

We took it easy and arrived at Las Palmas harbour around dawn. To our surprise, instead of going around the breakwater as before, we headed to a position just off the breakwater, where we dropped anchor.

It was another new experience for me. We were called to stations early and mustered on the foredeck. The windlass, a huge winch centrally located on the fo'c's'le deck, had a barrel on each end that we used to bring in the mooring ropes or tow-ropes. They could also be used independently with each of the huge chains that ran from the anchors hanging either side of the bow. The anchor chains came up through these housings and over the chain locators in the centre of the winch, down through another sender hole and from there down into the chain locker located in the lower bow or forepeak. So to drop anchor you simply put the middle section out of gear, unwind the brake and let her go.

The operator was generally the bo's'un under the direction of the chief officer acting on orders from the captain, who had calculated the amount of chain to be let out. In normal conditions and type of seabed, the rule-of-thumb was sea depth plus two-and-a-half times the length of the ship. The amount of chain actually let out was gauged by brightly-coloured links every 20 fathoms:. These links were large and bold enough to be counted off as the chain ran out. So we had to rig a chain stop from a lug on the deck wrapped around the anchor chain and tied off at the end. This was to prevent the anchor being lost in the event of failure of the brake or gearing. Not to mention the chain leaping up out of its housing in a storm as the bow pounded up and down, or was lifted by waves that engulfed it. Even massive objects like anchors and their chains can't withstand the power of the sea, which can exert a hammer-blow of many tons to the square inch.

We circled about to find the best spot to drop anchor. When the ship was heading into the wind, the captain shouted "let go". The order was repeated by the chief: "let go, lads". The brake was wound out slowly, releasing the band brake which circled the edge of the barrel, and away she went. With a loud roar our port anchor went plunging into the water. The anchor chain rushing out of the chain locker brought up with it a great red puff of rust dust mixed with clay from the sea bottom which had dried onto it from previous use. This billowed up around us, blew downwind in a mighty cloud and settled on number one hatch cover.

When the desired length marker was reached, the brake was applied and the chain came to a stop. You couldn't imagine the noise it made unless you were there.

With the engine now on stop, we waited until the ship settled, with the wind falling astern, until she "came up" onto the anchor. The expression originates from the fact that, as the anchor takes hold of the seabed, you see the chain running ahead from the hawse hole rise up out of the water as it becomes taut.

The weight of the length of chain lying on the sea bed adds to the effectiveness of the anchor's grip. To make absolutely sure of it, the captain rings down to the engine room via the ship's telegraph: "slow astern". The ship moves back until the chain comes up out of the water again. You can then hear and feel the chain and anchor dragging on the bottom until it comes to a stop, which you can also verify with your hand on the chain. It's a unique experience, feeling the energy of 10,000 tons of ship connecting to the seabed.

You can also double-check the ship has actually stopped moving by watching a fixed point on the land for a period.

When the captain was sure the anchor had a firm hold, then it was "stop and finish with engine" – and there was the ship, lying at anchor – "on the hook", as it was termed. Then we commenced the tidying up, washing down the fallen rust, and then stood down for a very welcome breakfast.

So here we were again, back in Las Palmas. Everyone was wondering how long for. It transpired that we needed a new piston – or would do so fairly soon. The plan was to fly out the necessary parts to us, so we could take them with us and do the work at sea when the need arose. We were quite confident our engineers were up to the job. Changing a piston was just as it would be for a car, only the piston was 20 or 30 times bigger.

The anticipated three-to-four days' stay at-anchor ended up being six. It was frustrating to be anchored off a port and be unable to go ashore. During that time we worked at the never-ending task of overhauling the working gear, repairing and replacing parts. The only other work we did was on our lifeboats, which was more stimulating and fun. There were four lifeboats, two on each side, located up on the appropriately named boat deck, just below and aft of the bridge and funnel. Each boat was designed to hold 30 people, and was cradled and normally held in place on two davits by quick-release lashings. When these were released in an emergency, the boat would pivot out on its davits to hang suspended over the sea by wires on a pulley system resembling a drying rack in a Victorian kitchen. The wires went to a winch used to lower the boat to the deck below for people to get on board, and from there it was lowered to the sea. There was also an auxiliary block-and-tackle system in case the winch failed.

We had all been trained to use these boats so we knew the principles involved. We checked them, oiling and greasing all moving parts plus the wires holding them with fish oil.

We did a lot of oiling wires. It wasn't the nicest of jobs. The fish oil was wiped on with rags and worked into the seven cores of the wire. There was a cotton line spliced into the core of each wire, and the idea was that this would soak up the oil and prevent the wire rusting from the inside. Maybe 90% of the work on board ship is rust prevention and removal.

We spent time turning out each boat, lowering it into the water and releasing it, to trundle it around in the small bay outside the harbour proper, testing out its working components.

Some of the engineers were sent out to look at the small auxiliary engines and service them. Since they worked down below in the engine room, this came as a welcome day-out for them. It was fun for us deck hands too, besides reassuring us that everything was in good working order. At any time we might be relying on them for our lives. We also took the opportunity to replenish the water and emergency rations they carried.

Only two of the four lifeboats had engines. The idea was that when used in an emergency, as opposed to occasional use in anchorages, one would tow the other, or go around picking up stragglers in the sea.

In the fine weather we were having, one of the motorised boats was left afloat. It was tied up next to the ship's gangway, which had been wound down against the side of the ship at a 45° angle to just above the waterline. This was for going ashore when the need arose, usually when agents or company personnel visited. For crew use, a jolly boat had been arranged to come out from the shore every evening at 19:00 hours, returning at midnight. This was in case anyone fancied a night out. But so far none of us had earned enough money so early in the trip to be able to do this. It was still only a week since we'd joined the boat. We did go a few times just to have a look round, or for a walk and a change of scene. Initially we'd feared repercussions from the Great Taxi Bloodbath of Las Palmas. But there were no ambushes – no animosity shown towards us – and apparently all was forgotten.

Some nights, with the wind from the east or the south, it was a very bumpy ride there and back in the little jolly boat with its small cabin. I suspect the boatman was secretly hoping it would make us seasick, just so he could tell his friends. You could see it in his face as he looked at us superciliously with a slight smirk. There has always been a bit of seafaring banter and competition between the English and Spanish, going right back to the days of the Armada.

However, we survived. And so the days went by.

At last, on Day Thirteen, the sixth day of our unscheduled return to port, we were ordered to break out one of the two derricks on the forward end of number four hatch in readiness for the arrival of the workboat bringing the engine parts and other stores – fresh milk, bread, beer, and suchlike. Around midmorning a tug-like vessel having a flat working area astern of its bridge with a small crane came alongside on the port side. This was the lea side, away from the wind, handy enough for number four hatch where the derrick we had topped and rigged was able to lift and place the stores on deck near the "flat" (access area) two decks up on the after end of the boat deck, where there was a larger access to the engine room flat. This had a projecting beam with a rolling crane for the engineers' use when moving larger items. The piston in its big crate was covered with a tarpaulin and lashed on deck with bottle screws, ready for when it was going to be needed.

With all hands working, apart from the watchman (retained whilst the ship was at anchor), all was stowed away and lashed. The derrick was dropped and secured and all made ready for sea, with the engine fired up. After lunch, with a wave to the delivery boat as it took off, we turned-to for stations and the order was given to weigh anchor.

We mustered on the fo'c's'le and the procedure was this. The ship reversed and lay on the anchor with the chain pitched ahead, then moved slow-ahead into the wind. As the anchor chain was gradually and noisily winched in, my job was to hose it down whilst others brushed and hooked off the mud and seaweed. Down in the chain locker, others pushed and pulled the chain with long-handled hooks, coiling it as best they could, so as not to kink when next let go at speed. This continued until the chief officer signalled by hand to the bridge that the chain was straight up and down. This meant that the anchor was now sitting on the seabed directly below us. Lifting from here on meant that we were now adrift. Whilst the ship moved slowly ahead to keep steerage, the anchor eventually broke surface and made for the hawsehole where, after a few lowering and hoisting manoeuvres, it finally located itself correctly. We finished off hosing the anchor clean whilst the chain was secured with a chain brake and the winch turned off. We reported to the bridge "anchor up and secure" and the engine picked up speed with that now-familiar wonderful feel and sound of vibration surging through the ship.

At 15:00 hours we at last resumed our voyage south. As we went aft for smoko, I exchanged glances with the others. Like me they had smiles of satisfaction on their faces, tinged with dismay at the thought of at least 35 days at sea en-route to Adelaide.

I stood in my cabin looking at my map of the world. I ran my finger along the route south from the Canary Islands, down the west coast of Africa. We'd sail relatively close to the coast at first, but after we left the big bulge of north west Africa we'd be far out to sea for many days before heading east around the Cape of Good Hope, across the Indian Ocean to the Australias. I figured it was about 10,000 miles. So 35 days meant 12.5 knots on average.

With a service speed of 15 knots it could vary either way, depending on wind, weather, and the sea state at that time of year. At 16 years of age, time goes by very slowly. I couldn't imagine how we would do it. Was it a dream? Would we really get there? What would we do whilst at sea for all that time?

Well, for a start, there's work to do. Weekend overtime is compulsory at sea. Taking everything into account, the overtime would increase my pay by nearly £2 pounds a week.

After work we would shower, change into clean clothes, do our washing, tidy our cabins, and so on. But now that the weather was better, we younger crew members would congregate on the poop deck aft, to chat and watch the sunset which took place to starboard. Curiously enough, this would be roughly the same time every night, the clock change as we sailed compensating for the increased hours of daylight as we moved through time-zones.

These were wonderful moments that I can never forget. Every one of them, every night, in good weather or bad, was completely different and unique to the moment. Sometimes there was a clear bright blue sky with not a cloud in it. The colour would intensify as the bright globe sank lower as the earth turned away from it, the blue darkening to indigo and deeper still, until the tip of the sun fell below the horizon, then returned for a goodnight flash as the last rays reflected off the sea.

Then we'd look up and aft, or north, and find the Northern Star, now becoming visible with the disappearing sun. We would quietly watch as more subtle changes continued in the western sky as night fell. "There it is again!" someone would say, articulating one of those events at sea that are so profound you cannot rationalise your feelings, or even begin to put them into words.

At that time of day many of the crowd (our word for the crew) were present, and we stood in total silence to absorb the experience of those precious moments.

To me it represented an act of perfect communication between us. Each individual with his own thoughts, yet united in a spontaneous and involuntary state of meditation. A purity of mind.

This is the Zen of being at sea.

Another aspect of being at sea that none of us would have imagined as we sat at home, dreaming of our travels to far-off places, was that our imagination now took on a physical and visual form. There we all were, looking, feeling, wondering and learning. We were in the shadow of life.

I began to see in the eyes of some of the older hands a calmness and a knowing. Some years later an acquaintance tried to guess my age, setting it around 10 years younger than I actually was. But someone else disagreed, saying "No, he's older than that – I can see the experience in his eyes." The person who said that was an older man, himself a seafarer.

I was growing up very quickly, beginning to understand why I was there and why I needed to be there. This was where my real education would come from.

—oOo—

After our sun-worshipping ritual we spend the rest of the evening in the bar, in other people's cabins or our own. Most people drink at sea, and some people drink a lot. Probably half the crew of a merchant ship had what you might call a "problem". Though they wouldn't have called it a problem: they liked it that way. Mostly it would turn out to be a problem for other people.

Anyway the bar was very popular.

Besides drinking and exchanging general banter and listening to the stories of other hands with years of experience spent on other ships – stories of ports and women around the world – we played games such as cards and dominoes to while away the time.

A popular card game on our ship was crib – a classical tradition at sea, if not so well-known shoreside. Another game was sevens. This became so popular it seemed to go on everywhere and forever. We found ourselves playing it on all occasions, especially at smoko and dinner breaks. But there were never any tournaments as such. The competitiveness of the players sometimes got very loud, though confined to one game at a time, so that each winner was only a hero for a few moments between games.

Breaks were mostly spent in the mess room, which was not a bad place to spend the evening in, if you were not up for the bar.

But the most popular game by far – and one in which we did have tournaments – was darts. It was to hold our attention for the entire trip, and was taken very seriously by some people. We had singles and doubles teams. I had played the game before, but not much. The difficulty of the game at sea arose out of the constantly changing motion of the boat, although you quickly became adept at compensating for the movement by pitching yourself like a human gimbal. You not only had to judge the movement of the ship as you threw the dart, but allow for the effect of greater or lesser gravity on the missile in flight. On board ship the bow and the stern move the most, the engine room the least. Our bar was at the stern of the ship and it really jumped around. During a storm it was difficult to stay on your feet, especially after a can or two of the unpalatable lager.

It's a curious thing that whilst at sea you soon become accustomed to the constant motion. Thereafter you only notice it when sitting down, in the shower, in bed – or throwing darts!

I'm quite sure that darts taught me a lot of practical physics, plus things about the earth in general.

And not only darts.

On one occasion four of us were out on the deck, John, Chris, myself and the others. We'd just come through a few days of rough weather, the wind had dropped and the sun was out and shining down on us. We were in good form, working up on, and around below, the fo'c's'le head. Although it was good weather, the sea hadn't calmed yet. The storm had been a southerly one, so we were heading straight into the waves and the bow was pitching hard, with a quick movement.

We discovered that if we stood just in front of the hatch coaming of number 1 hold, facing the fo'c's'le head some 10 feet above us, it only needed a little jump at the right moment and we could fly up easily and catch onto the safety rail around the fo'c's'le head. The right moment to do this was just as the bow dropped into the trough from the top of the previous wave.

We thought it was brilliant. I imagine it's very close to the weightlessness you get in space.

We never again found the right conditions to do it, as it depends critically on the ratio between the length of the ship and the distance between wave crests. This was what enabled the bow to plummet down before digging into the base of the next wave and rapidly rising up again.

It was great fun for a while and broke the monotony of the deep sea voyage. We were surprised the bridge didn't send the watchman to tell us to stop, as we were in plain view and it must have looked dangerous. Maybe they enjoyed watching us, and it broke the monotony for them too.

In those first few days after leaving the Canaries, every morning felt a little bit warmer, and with fine weather the days grew hotter. Having got the maintenance of working or running gear out of the way, it was now time to start the painting. Each trip the chief officer and bo's'un note the length of the voyage and work out a schedule to paint and de-rust the whole ship from the prow to the jackstaff.

So one morning we went for paint to the locker of the lamp trimmer (or carpenter) in the mast housing between number 4 and number 5 hatch in the after deck. It is also known as the paint locker.

The lamp trimmer was an older man from Somerset, round, hairy, quiet and cheerful. He was a bit distant in his manner, chuckled a lot and said "alright boy" in his West Country accent. You'd occasionally see him in the bar, but I think he spent most of his off-duty time in his cabin, reading.

On a modern ship he had no lamps to prime, of course. His duties were mainly administering deck and engine-room stores and tools, navigation lights, cargo and soundings. He also did bits of woodwork and rope work, such as replacing splicings on rope and wires. He was happy to teach anyone who was interested in learning.

As it wasn't part of our everyday work, except in an emergency, I used to spend time with him doing just that, and was grateful for the opportunity to advance in those dying skills. You would often see him pottering around with ropes, or doing his regular soundings.

All around the main cargo deck there were pipes running down to the deep ballast tanks and bilges. His job was to "sound them out". He would drop a line with a brass weight down each pipe to check that the water levels didn't vary. This provided assurance to the bridge that the ship was still trim and not taking water.

I must say his habitual calmness gave me a lot of confidence. In those early weeks the slow lumbering rolls of the ship as it climbed the huge Atlantic swells gave me a sense of vulnerability, which I felt especially when I was alone in my cabin at night.

But as time passes you become accustomed to it and your confidence in the ship grows as you work on her. She takes on a life of her own, with her own special character. You are never far away from the beat of her heart, pounding away to a constant rhythm, and when in the neighbourhood of the funnel or up on the boat deck you hear the deep throaty sound of her exhausts.

On the foredeck, where there is no engine sound, just a vibration through your legs, you hear the whistling of the wind plucking her mast stays, and the occasional slam as a wave hits the bow plates flat-on.

You hear the whooshing of the breaking bow wave passing down each side of the hull as you stand staring at the horizon, yearning for a glimpse of the land you know is not there.

Lying in your bunk at night you hear the whine of the hydraulic rams of the steering gear, ever moving side to side in constant correction of the ship's course by signals sent down from the autopilot way up on the bridge.

As I lay in my bunk, mulling over the day, I would ask myself questions like: did I do my job well today? Have I conquered one more fear? What am I doing here? Am I liked by my fellow crew members? And most of all: what will it be like when we reach Oz?

My thoughts would then wander back to home, family and people I had left behind. My mind was a tangle of emotions that were going to take some resolving over the years to come. My heart gave a thump as I thought of my family.

In the early years we were just a normal family. Balmy summer days – outings to the seaside – we were privileged in those days. My father had a removal business, we owned a car, and went out and about at the weekends. Not so many people could do that in our street in Watford in the 50s and 60s.

Normal life prevailed until one day we bought a house situated away from the business, on the outskirts of town. It was in Garston, just outside Watford on the A41 bypass. I was 11 and had just started secondary school. By the time I was 12 it had all gone pear-shaped. Dad lost a big contract and ended up bankrupt.

It then emerged he'd been seeing another woman. Not good. My mum couldn't forgive him, and eventually we had to sell the house and move out to a grim rented house further out at Leavesden.

My brother John was not there much, and my elder brother Peter was in the army. My parents were rarely seen – they were at war now. I can't actually visualise them in that house. I was virtually alone in it, and if it wasn't for my brother Peter's fiancee Angela, who took me under her wing, I don't know what I would have done.

But it was around that time I knew I was going to join the Merchant Navy.

—oOo—

It all started with a strange event when I was 13. My brother John and I took Mum's little grey Austin A35 van out one morning. We left around 4 AM to go and meet an old school friend of John's, who two years earlier had gone to sea. His ship had just returned to Victoria Dock after an 18 month trip round the world. When we arrived we found out it was the *Port Montréal*, of about 8,000 tons.

I was completely bowled over by the docks – the ships – the whole experience. It was so exciting. We met John's friend and brought his personal effects off the ship. There were presents and keepsakes purchased from all over the world. We filled our van up with all these wonders, and after he was paid off we took him home.

On the way he told us of his experiences in Africa, Australia, Singapore… After hearing all about that I decided that this was the life for me.

My father had been hoping I'd join the army like my brother Peter. But aware that I had no prospect of getting any qualification and would be leaving school at 15, he agreed to it and I applied for training.

Just afterwards we moved once more, to another rental house not far from our original home back in the centre of Watford. Finally at 15½ I went off to the Pre-Sea Training School at Gravesend. The very same day that I left home, so did my father. Also my mother, who had been living totally apart from the rest of us in an upstairs room. So I left with my bridges well-and-truly burnt, with no concept or images of home to take with me.

I returned to the here-and-now with a knock on my door: "Turn-to for breakfast" - and found myself in the middle of the Atlantic Ocean, on board the *MV Trebartha*: my home for the present.

That day, painting the ship started in earnest. Armed with chipping hammers, we left the lamp trimmer. The first job went well enough. Painting a ship is mostly a matter of first chipping off all the obviously rusted areas. The tool itself is something like a swatter's hammer: blunt and square at one end and coming to a point at the other.

We started on the bulwarks: the solid metal barriers going all around the main deck to stop you falling overboard. The top (the gunwale) was navy blue outside – the colour of the hull – and white on the inside. It consisted of a series of sections framed by elongated triangles of angle iron (for strength) which reached up to support it. It needed to be strong enough to withstand the enormous force of the waves which swept over it in heavy weather.

Earlier ships had tubular railings, post and rail, which offered less resistance to breaking seas but left the crew, deck cargo, rigging and hatches more exposed to the waves.

This major advance in ship design took place in the 1940s with the revolutionary American "liberty ships" built for the wartime Atlantic convoys. These sections, known to sailors as "fleets", were dotted with a variety of pipes, rig fittings, lugs, fire hydrants, bolts and catches, plus gangway access and suchlike in the sections detachable for access.

The day was spent chipping away at the exposed rust and smashing the blisters of paint lifted by rust growing beneath. It was noisy, boring work; but, as with most things, you find ways of alleviating the boredom. The seven or eight hammers chip-chip-chipping away would fall into syncopated rhythms, and there'd be moments of satisfaction as a big clump of rust fell off, or you got the last little bit out of one of the deeper pits. The more you could get out, the more time it bought for the ship, reducing the rate of corrosion which would eventually kill it.

And so the day passed with banter, jokes and songs, games of sevens in smoko and during lunch breaks – and by five it was done.

After dinner we turned-to for overtime, returning to the paint locker for brushes plus tubs of red oxide paint ("red lead") for the second stage: covering up everything we'd chipped off during the day.

We did the job, but it took its toll of casualties. We retired from the fray at 7 PM with dabs of bright red paint on our clothing as the result of some seriously swashbuckling encounters - sword-fighting with loaded paintbrushes. There's a bit of the buccaneer in all of us.

The following day we were still focusing on the bulwarks. The process was as follows: wash down the work area with detergent, rinse off with fresh water, removing any salt particles still adhering, then apply three undercoats over two coats of red lead, followed by two coats of gloss paint.

Closer to the equator now, the days were getting hotter and hotter, with the result that the paint was drying very quickly. On some days we could manage two coats. But the heat was a growing problem for me, and I found having to work in it utterly exhausting.

One day I was told there were salt tablets available to help with this. I went to the chief steward – who was conspicuously gay and looked at me with shameless lust whenever I had to deal with him – and received a tin of them. The dosage on the tin said four tablets, three times a day. By now it was afternoon, so I thought I'd catch up and take eight.

It was a stupid thing to do. Half an hour later I started to feel very strange and unsteady on my feet, and began salivating profusely. I fell to the deck and nearly passed out. But it passed and everyone had a great laugh about it. I never touched salt tablets again.

However, being fair-skinned, fair-haired and warm-blooded, I've always had to take care in the heat, with sun hat, sun creme and so on.

So the days went by. The weather continued to be good, but it was by no means monotonous. In fact every day was completely different from the last. Some days there'd be big fluffy clouds in a huge sky. It was not like the flat background sky seen in towns back home. There was a strong sense of perspective. The clouds were clear and crisp, and so obviously at different distances and heights. You could imagine yourself up there clambering among them, watching the cloudscape change as they passed in front of the sun. It all reached a crescendo as the day drew to a close. As the sun sank lower in the sky, it produced yet another beautiful display of lights as sunbeams, so intense as to look almost solid, streamed through the crags and gullies of the clouds, lighting up patches on the shimmering sea.

Every night we would all watch this spectacular, ever-changing light show. It really brought it home to me what a truly beautiful and wonderful planet we lived on.

Thirty-five days at sea is a long time. Long enough, after just two weeks, to leave behind the concepts and trappings of the familiar world. Life on board becomes your whole experience: this little floating bit of England, the regime of which is created by the company and executed by the officers, bo's'un and mate. In the main it is a little subculture all of its own. It holds together mainly by the mutual respect that arises instinctively in each one of us. You know everybody and they know you. All are part of the system that keeps the ship running, with every individual, young or old, deckhand or officer, essential to its safety, albeit with greater or lesser responsibility. Perhaps that's why they call the captain God.

But he is a lesser god however. All know that at any time the sea – that great, wonderful, all-powerful force – could rear up and take the ship without even noticing it had done so, and consequently any one of us could be called upon to save another's life. That is our common bond – our Fellowship of Man.

It's about 2,000 miles from Las Palmas to the equator, and we crossed it in seven days. For the first-timers, like me, there was going to be a ceremony. There was a build-up to this event, the older hands saying to us, "Oho, just you wait till we cross the line. Then you're going to know all about it!"

On that fateful day, with the mate taking the role of Neptune as Master of Ceremonies, the first-timers – myself and the other deck boy, two officer cadets and one of the engineering cadets – were grabbed and dragged on deck just aft of the mess, where we were stripped and tied down spreadeagled on our backs, with rope ends on our wrists and ankles. Then, with great glee, everyone proceeded to throw the leftovers from the day's meals in the gash bucket over us, then shaved off all our hair. This was followed by a coat of red oxide paint. As if that wasn't enough, they found some fiery chilli sauce, a leftover from the ship's last trading trip around the coast of Africa, and poured this over our genitals. I spent the next 24 hours trying every way I could to cool them down. The sauce turned out to be so hot that no one on board could stand it on their food, let alone on their balls. But it was all part of the ritual and so to be taken in good part.

I received a certificate to commemorate the occasion, typed by the chief steward and sealed with the ship's seal over an image of the Quaker cut out of a porridge oats box.

Over the next few days I'd see the other victims going about the ship with their shaved heads, walking in an ungainly fashion with their legs apart. There were even exchanges of sympathy with the officer cadets.

Which was as far as we communicated, because as a rule we didn't talk to the officers, or cadets, unless it was a special occasion, or in the line of duty. I must say I found that a bit strange. But after all, we were a little floating piece of England, therefore the class system had to be maintained to preserve the illusion of superiority which comes with having money, education, power and all that bullshit.

Or was it just exaggerated because we were a long way from England? I have always thought that the people who were part of British Raj in India behaved in a way that was more English than the English.

Some of the officers were okay however, getting us the odd bottle of spirits on special occasions. I think they were as embarrassed about it as we were, many of them having working-class backgrounds themselves.

Every Sunday we had steak-and-a-cake, known as a tabnab. it was also Captain's Inspections. He'd come around after breakfast just to check everything was clean and tidy. There were stories of captains wearing white gloves to run their hands over work surfaces or along the tops of doors to discover hidden dirt. This might have been the sort of thing they did in the Royal Navy, but our captain wasn't so pernickety. Nevertheless there was a risk of being fined if your cabin was regularly found to be in an unclean state. In the merchant navy things were relatively lax, but enforcing basic hygiene was obviously essential.

There was no uniform, as such. Officers would wear white boiler suits, likewise the donkey men in the engine room, plus the odd hand, found it necessary to wear them too, as protective clothing. The rest of us would just wear our old clothes for work.

As already said, each passing day had its own peculiar weather pattern. Noteworthy is a region of the Atlantic on the equator known as the doldrums, notorious for its absence of wind: a desperate place to pass through for the windjammers of bygone days. On a tight schedule, or fearful of running short of food or water, they sometimes had to tow the ship by manning the boats and rowing them out to find the wind again.

It was not a problem for us, with our engine.

It was a place of wonder though – of fear even – very hot, sometimes humid and misty, with scarcely any movement of clouds apart from their progress *en-bloc* across the calm sea. Or more accurately, the glassy, mirror-flat sea. We slid through it like a hot knife through butter.

It was a very odd feeling, finding yourself standing on the ship looking out over a spooky seascape with a mirror image of the sky. It could affect the vibration of the crew in a strange way sometimes. There is a syndrome known as *nyrophobia*: the fear of nothingness – of being marooned in a world which is leaving too much to the imagination; of being locked inside oneself.

The one grain of comfort you could take from it all was this: with such a smooth, calm sea the ship would achieve its service speed of 15 knots, so you'd find yourself thinking you might gain time and get to Oz quicker, as you tick another day off the schedule and reassess the ETA. However, it turns out this is all taken into consideration when calculating our ETA, according to the second officer.

Our voyage took us through three sea-areas like this. The first is around 20° north, just south of the Canaries. The Tropic of Cancer. This area is between the Atlantic westerlies and the north-east trade winds. There is another one 20° south between the South Atlantic's southerlies and the south-east trade winds. These two sea-areas are known as the horse latitudes, as in bygone days becoming becalmed there meant there was danger of the ship's rations running out. So horses being exported would be sacrificed to leave more water for the crew, as well as providing fresh meat.

This flat windless sea environment also occurs at the equator, where it's called the doldrums. The word is coined from "dull" and "tantrum" to denote extreme low spirits. The physical mechanism is this: the direct sunshine warms the air which rises up, moves north and south, cools and gently descends on the horse latitudes, reproducing the conditions of the doldrums.

These strange regions are mind-provoking and, for those who are superstitious about such things, terrifying. Legend has it that the spirits of those lost at sea cannot move on due to the stillness.

The mental is so tightly connected to the physical in our world. The real relationship between the two was only now beginning to take shape in my understanding of things – and once again added to my appreciation of everyday experience on a mental, physical and visual level. There was not much discussion of this sort of thing on board our ship, but I had a feeling those around me were all going through the same experience. But their egos would not allow them to explore it freely with each other.

We were pretty much painting every day; the gunwales and decks; the accommodation exterior, midships and aft; the three mast housings located between the hatch coamings, two on the fore deck and one on the aft deck. On top of each were four large electric winches used for lifting or topping the derricks: the cranes for working with cargo in the holds. At some time in the trip they had to be chipped clear of rust, washed down, then red oxide, undercoat and gloss applied.

Saturday nights were always a high point at sea, as it was cinema night. This came as a big surprise to me, to be watching up-to-date films in uncut editions in the middle of nowhere.

They would be shown by the electrician (naturally). In bad weather it would be in the bar, but in good weather the screen would be rigged up on the mast housing, with chairs on number four hatch cover. The projector was mounted up on the after end of the boat deck, next to our spare lashed piston.

This was a great night-out that everyone turned out for, and all for free. So we would sit there drinking our insipid beer, howl with laughter and periodically cheer. Great stuff to take you out of yourself for a while. The officers, of course, had their own private showing in their saloon at the fore part of their accommodation. However the watch keepers would be at one or other of the showings when the timing was right for them.

The films were supplied by the British Sailors' Society. This, like the library, has representatives in most major ports of the world. They simply visited all arriving British ships and swapped the films around from their collection. Being constantly relayed around the planet, many of those films no doubt clocked up several million miles in their working life.

On one occasion while watching a film I had a strange experience. Something caught my eye, and I turned and looked over the starboard side out to sea. It was a very clear starry night, and I saw what I took to be a distress flare. I asked my crew-mates if they'd seen it too, but it seemed I was on my own in this. People even shouted me down for disturbing the film.

So at the next reel-change I went up to the bridge. It was about 10 PM, so I knew it would be the second officer's watch. I told him what I'd seen, out to the west. He noted it down and thanked me.

As a boy rating you didn't find yourself on the bridge much, especially at night. It was a great view up there and a fascinating one: it gave me a feel for what it would be like as a deck officer, the brains of the ship, making sure we were all safe and running properly. I stood on the wing of the bridge for a short while, just to take in the beautiful star field in the sky before returning to the film.

Some days later I spoke to the second officer again about it. He said we did alter course to explore, but I don't think it happened. It might have been nothing but a shooting star, but I felt at the time we ought to have explored a little better. It could have been some poor souls out there, all alone, their lives on the line. Next time it could be any of us.

The ship's log entry could have established the matter either way, but that was something I was not privy to.

The days went by as we travelled further and further south. I knew now that we were not far from the Cape of Good Hope, and I found myself looking out over the port side, forward to the south-east, hoping to catch a glimpse of land.

For the first time in weeks we saw another ship: a German freighter heading north. It took some time for it to pass off over the horizon astern, but I have to say it provided some excitement. But nothing like the excitement of Day 17, when at last we brought the ship around to port, heading for the most southerly tip of Africa and the Indian Ocean.

We were now on an easterly course, with landfall on the port side – the Cape. It was a good distance away, lying low on the horizon. We spent the day at our usual work: painting, chipping rust, stopping and looking up occasionally, convincing ourselves that we could make out the Sleeping Warrior – a famous landmark near Cape Town. If you view this rock formation with an artist's eye, it looks for all the world like a man lying down.

You can't imagine how good it feels to see dry land after a long spell at deep sea, if only for a day.

That was the Atlantic part of the journey done. Now it was 17 days across the Indian Ocean. In parts it is as deep as 3 miles, yet in others only 600 feet, which is shallow in oceanic terms.

As the Cape of Good Hope disappeared out of sight over the curve of the Earth's surface, you could almost hear the bump as we entered the Indian Ocean. It was another 6,000 miles to Adelaide. Still a long time to go yet, but psychologically the whole crew were in great form for those few days of transition, until it was back to the normal routine. Once more I found myself looking out over the ocean from the monkey island above the bridge, knowing that Africa lay astern, Madagascar 1,000 miles to the north, India and Sri Lanka 7,000 miles to the north-east, Malaysia and Australia 7,000 miles to the east, but only 2,000 miles to the Arctic Circle.

With the sun rising off the bow and setting to the stern now, everything looked so different, creating a whole new feel to the ship. Not just visually, but on the psychic level as well.

I know of no explanation from psychology or even astrology to account for it, but I can vouch for its existence. It was an important factor in making the long weeks of our journey tolerable. Yes, we had work and social activities to keep us going, but it was these deep shifts in our ocean environment which kept us stimulated.

The absence of stimulus is something I really noticed in the doldrums, where stillness continued for several days. Imagine what it was like for those sailors trapped in a sailing ship for weeks on end, for example. Spiritless and fearful of the nothingness: the state of *nyrophobia*.

Here we were then, crossing the Indian Ocean. Day following day. We were heavily into painting, which seemed endless. Even on rainy days we would be painting under cover, in the accommodation, especially around the galleys, mess rooms, and store lockers. These areas are in continuous use and need attention to keep them looking clean, both visually and hygienically.

One day I got a rare visit from one of the electricians. Normally we never see these people on the main deck, unless the ship has problems. It turned out he was from Liverpool and he'd heard I was from Watford. Now it happened that Liverpool were playing Watford in the quarter-final of the FA Cup. This didn't mean much to me, as I never quite got football. He offered to bet a case of beer with me on the outcome. I protested that a case of beer was half a week's wages to me, as a deck boy, compared with his salary as an electrician. Eventually we reached a deal on a 5 to 1 basis. This was good for me as all the others offered to chip in for my case in the event Liverpool won. This was quite likely since Watford was in the third division and Liverpool in the first.

To everyone's astonishment Watford beat Liverpool 1-nil, so the electrician had to cough up five cases of beer. I put them behind our bar and we had a couple of free nights. Everyone was happy, even the scouser 'leccy, who eventually came down for a drink or two with us – and he still had a smile on his face. The people of Liverpool are in a league of their own: not much brings them down.

Australia

Days turned into weeks as we slowly made our way to Australia, past little heard-of places such as Prince Edward Isle (Br), Îles Crozet (Fr), Îles Kerguelen (Fr) and Heard Isle (Br). These are parts of either the Prince Edward-Croze Ridge trailing down from Madagascar, or the Mid-Indian Ridge that runs from the Arabian Sea down to Antarctica. We passed them by – these small tips of subterranean mountains just peeking out from the surface of the sea – without seeing them, and without learning what they were like, or even whether anyone lived on them.

At last, on day 32, we were off the south-western tip of Oz and about to cross the Great Australian Bight. This is an infamous stretch of sea renowned for its bad weather, and roiling seas. But our journey across it was not as eventful as I'd been led to expect – at least not on this occasion – and two days later we sighted land. The next morning, a bright one, we found ourselves surrounded by the low-lying sandy hills of the inlet leading to Adelaide. To our great delight we were greeted by a pod of dolphins. About seven or eight of them came swimming up alongside and overtook us. Someone shouted "come on!" and we went up onto the fo'c's'le head to look down on them from the prow.

The dolphins had formed up into a line and were taking it in turns to dash under or over the others. Occasionally they leapt high out of the sea nearly level with us on the deck. It was an amazing sight and made a suitably friendly welcome to Australia.

We went back to work, taking leave of their smiling faces as they brushed their tails against the tip of the bow so gently it seemed as if they were teasing the ship, caressing it, and us. To them we were all part of the life of the sea. It was a sheer delight to watch them. They really must be the nicest creatures on the planet, warming everyone's hearts and bringing hope to the world.

It had been a welcome distraction from our work, the whole day being spent bringing all the mooring ropes and springs ready for the tugs when they came alongside, and for making fast on the dockside. We were also ordered to top all the starboard side derricks in order to swing them outboard, to allow the shoreside cranes to discharge the cargo unimpaired.

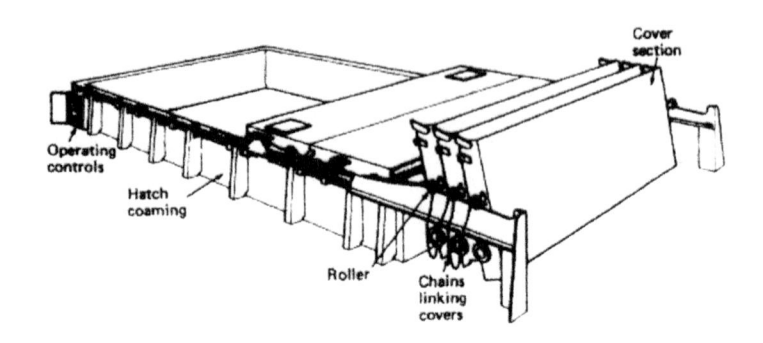

The McGregor hatch cover

We also got ready to open the "tin lids" (McGregor hatches), which meant a lot of work. They consisted of a number of huge steel doors covering each hatch opening. They were in sections, on wheels, and connected by chains. We needed to unscrew and release the hundreds of locking "dogs" – T-shaped bolts – from around and under the edges of the hatch coamings, then jack them up and turn them onto their wheels before rolling them off with a winch and stacking them.

It was a good system, superseding the previous system of sliding beams and short wooden boards, covered with at least two tarpaulins with metal strip battens trapping the canvas behind plugs around the edge of the hatch coaming, secured by wooden wedges hammered in.

The new McGregor hatch covers were not as much work to release, besides being safer at sea, as canvas covers were always vulnerable to heavy weather. You would not want the sea to be entering the hold, especially during a storm, which was when such a thing was most likely to occur.

There was however a curious tale to show that the old canvas covers might have unexpected advantages in extreme circumstances. A ship of the Federal Steam Navigation line (name unknown) left New Zealand en-route for the UK via Cape Town. She did not arrive when she was due, and after some months she was declared lost at sea. Three months later she reappeared *under sail*, heading into Cape Town harbour.

It transpired that at some point after leaving New Zealand her engine had broken down and had proved to be irreparable. However her captain, probably a master mariner who in his younger days had shipped out under sail, managed by using the canvases from this old type of hatch covers, plus the mast derricks, to jury-rig a set of sails to achieve this remarkable feat of seamanship.

—oOo—

So we made Adelaide harbour on the 35th day. We took the tugs' lines, came about with their help and tied up on our starboard side alongside No. 2 Shed.

It was a beautiful day: hot, bright, the sky an intense blue. It was now early March, which is the start of the Australian autumn. The docks were very quiet. There was one other British ship: the Holder Brothers' *Swan River*. Abby, who had sailed on her, called her a "happy ship".

When arriving in port after a long voyage there is an informal tradition of not working out the whole day. It's hard to work with one eye on the job and the other on the shore. Now 35 days is a very long voyage, made even longer by waiting at anchor in Las Palmas for our engine part. It was still only 10:30 AM, so the bo's'un called for a job-and-knock: painting the funnel.

Normally this would take a day and a half. However we had done the preparation over the previous 2 days, so it only needed a wash down and one coat of gloss, which took us two hours. So, showered and dressed in our best go-ashore dungies, we were off down the gangway by one o'clock.

The docks at Adelaide are a fair way from the town. Too far to go, we decided, so we took a walk around the immediate locality, ending up in a well-known watering hole, the Exchange pub, situated between No. 1 and No. 2 Sheds, still within sight of the ship. It was an anti-climax and rather sad of us. But we spent the rest of the afternoon there pleasantly enough, drinking lager that was a vast improvement on the ship's own brew. It came in a jug called a schooner, with a small third-of-a-litre glass for each person.

We returned to the ship for our evening meal and a nap, then back to the pub for more. This wasn't for long, at it turned out, as all the pubs closed at 10 PM on the dot. So we ended the night back in our own bar on the ship, the *Copacabana*, with Abby manning the bar.

Next morning we had to turn to at 7 AM. This was to open the hatches for the dockers to discharge the cargo for Adelaide from different areas within the holds.

Then after breakfast we started painting over the side on the bow, which we were able to do now we were in port.

We worked in twos on so-called stages, with one man above, known as the tender, tending the man on the stage. Basically this was a 12 ft scaffold plank of 10"×2" timber. Two pieces of 4"×4" timber were bolted crossways about 12" in from each end, to keep you safe and served as spacers to keep the plank away from the side of the ship and allow you to sit with your legs through.

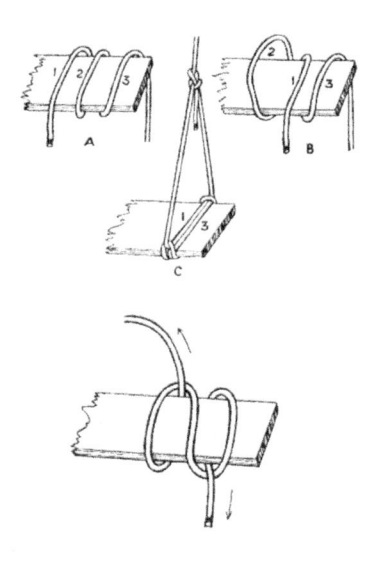

Rigging a stage

Two ropes with metal eyes ("lizards") were made fast on the deck and run over the side 10 ft apart next to your work area (or fleet). The runners – two long lengths of rope – were then tied on each end, taking each of them up through the eyes, back down again and made fast with a series of turns on the end of the plank with a back turn to finish.

This was a simple but effective way to lift or lower both ends of the plank in step.

We collected all the gear we needed and went forward to get started. But when we arrived at the fo'c's'le we were surprised to see two Australian Royal Navy frigates tied up ahead of us at No. 2 Shed.

"Oh my God," said one of the older hands, "we're going to get slaughtered tonight!"

There's always been a certain amount of rivalry between the Royal Navy and the Merchant Navy, they being a bit too smart and disciplined, and we being a bit too scruffy and unruly.

So we spent the day swinging the stages up and down, chipping and red leading. The flare of the bow needed a rope rigging right round the bow from the quarters, which the tender would haul on or let go as needed to enable us to move across the side of the raked-in ship.

At lunchtime we popped over to the Exchange for a schooner or two, then again at the afternoon break. This resulted in us slowly getting more and more drunk. We had great fun amongst ourselves, John, Chris, myself and most of the crew. There was a constant temptation to fall in the harbour simply to cool down. But there was the danger of sharks, so we didn't care to risk it. It worried us when we got down to the waterline and sat on the stage with our legs dangling in the water. But as the day wore on, the more we drank the less we worried.

We knocked off at 5 PM and after dinner we'd recovered enough to take a shower, put on our best Levis to go ashore and headed for the pub.

We found it bulging with hundreds of Aussie matelots. We got ourselves drinks and sat and waited to see what would happen. We started talking to one or two of them, and it turned out they were glad to meet us. Some of them were English and some were sons of families who had emigrated a decade or two earlier.

So it was a brilliant evening. At closing time, 10 PM, the suggestion went round that they should come to our ship to continue drinking in our bar. That night, and the next, was something out of the ordinary. We had literally hundreds of sailors on board, drinking all through the night. The bar now extended to the whole of the crew's accommodation, including most of our cabins, and even the washrooms, bathroom, hallway and spilling out onto the deck.

By day we worked and by night we drank. We couldn't even get into our own cabins to sleep, even though we had to be up early to open the hatches. We had to go and sleep on the *Swan River* a few berths away, returning in the morning by the cold fresh milk shop to work our morning duties. We'd open the hatches, have breakfast and then go around waking up all the Aussie matelots littering every bunk and chair and even covering the floor space. Each morning, after cleaning the bar, I'd walk over to the gangways of their ships with a box of hats, belts, odd shoes and other such things left on board by our visitors, who had departed in a stupor.

—oOo—

There is not much more to be said about Adelaide. We never had a chance to see the city – we'd been too busy drinking.

On the evening of the third day, having discharged all our cargo, we left Adelaide bound for Melbourne. It was about a two day voyage. As usual I was on the foredeck at stations, with commands from the bridge. We made fast to a tug in the usual manner and we came away from the berth. But as we passed the two frigates moored ahead of us we were surprised to see that the outboard side of one of them was teeming with sailors from stem to stern all along the bulwarks. All of a sudden both of the frigates' horns fired up: *wup! – wup! – wup! – wuup!* – the unmistakeable sound of a warship's siren common to all the navies of the world. The crew of the frigate all started shouting and cheering at us. It was an extremely emotional moment. Toilet rolls were thrown to make streamers. It reminded me of scenes at the departure of Atlantic passenger liners leaving on their maiden or blue-ribbon voyages.

Suddenly the bo's'un looked up and said "see that, chief?" The chief officer looked up and cried "fucking hell – get that down as quick as you can!"

I looked up and saw that we had the Australian Royal Navy flag flying from our flagstaff halyard on the mainmast. It's similar to the British Royal Navy flag, additionally bearing the stars of the Southern Cross. It turned out that Abby had managed to get it from a lad on one of the frigates.

It was a great moment and we were all made up with this thank-you from the frigates' crews. They'd really loved us for making their stay in Adelaide a bit more memorable than usual.

The icing on the cake was this: just when we were abeam of them, which is the point at which ships exchange hellos, we saw one continuous line of bums, as they all dropped their trousers and turned and paraded them off the gunwale. Quite a sight.

Strictly speaking, the flying of the Australian flag was a serious abuse of protocol. But in the circumstances it was seen by all ranks as the fun it was meant to be.

I heard later that even the captain had a smile on his face as we left port. He and his officers had no doubt socialised with the officers on the frigates, though probably in a more civilised way than the crews had done.

Everyone had taken it in good part, but I don't think it would have turned out quite like that had the frigates been British.

In the whole of our Adelaide visit there had been only one sour note. There's always that one in a hundred who'll take advantage of hospitality to steal things. Somebody stole a camera and a watch from Chris, lifting it from his drawer in the party cabin. This, like all our cabins, had been open to all-comers to cater for the sheer numbers.

We mentioned this to the visitors, and within hours they'd found the missing watch and camera. The thief was made to give them back and apologise before they took him off for a good beating.

A traditional punishment at sea for theft from a fellow seafarer was to drop a porthole and its deadlight onto the thief's fingers. (A deadlight is the secondary metal cover that would be dogged down in extreme weather conditions to protect the porthole glass: standard fittings on those portholes set into the hull itself.) It was considered due justice to smash the fingers of one hand – a symbolic punishment which not only shamed the thief but served as a warning to others.

Thus Chris was mollified over the incident to some extent, but was disappointed over the loss of the film which had been in the camera. He'd taken lots of photos of everyone on board, so it was a pity to lose that film. But we left the frigate and settled down for a good sleep, and laughed over the story for weeks.

We often drank to the health of those lads on the frigates. We'd made enough profit on the beer we sold, being just (1¢ per can) to have 15 free nights in the bar, which kept us going for the rest of the trip. On each of the three days of our visit we had taken delivery of a pallet of beer to keep up with the demand. I think the ship's bond made a good profit too. All thanks to the lads on the *Swan River* for making our stay so enjoyable.

There followed two days travelling to Melbourne around the Dead Coast, so-called because as you sail along it you can see nothing on the shore. It was a strange feeling – I'd spent all that time at sea looking out for land, and now it was there. We couldn't see it! I'd have been grateful for any sign of life.

We spent most of the next day tidying up after the dockers. The sea was a bit choppy, so we had dropped the derricks back down. Now we had to raise some of them again for Melbourne, our next port of call.

Melbourne is a much larger city than Adelaide. You enter it by sailing inside of Tasmania and into the Bass Straits. Once again you enter it via a large sheltered inlet, through Port Phillip Bay.

We tied up on the east side of the main channel running into the docks. It was a long way from town. Going ashore usually entailed taking a taxi. We had quite a lot of cargo for Melbourne, so we had five days or so to explore the numerous watering holes. One thing about the Aussies: they are a very thirsty lot. Must be the heat.

Fortunately some women turned up. Most of them were known to the British crews who'd been on the Coast many times. They were a group of girls known as ship's molls, who basically party with British seamen whilst they're on the Coast. The usual description of them was that they were easy-going, drank like fishes and went for you like rattlesnakes.

They did however have morals, of a sort. If you ended up getting off with one of the girls, they would only be with you for the duration of your stay. They might even follow you from port to port, up and down the coast. Sometimes they'd stow away on board – a practice known as ring bolting. It was highly illegal and generally not tolerated. But from time to time it happened. So, on arrival, when finding yourself a girl the rule was to get a good one, because amongst themselves they were faithful to one ship at a time.

I recall there was a rather large girl who was keen to relieve me of my cherry (virginity, in shoreside speak). Until that's happened, you are known as a cherry boy. Although she fancied me and was experienced, she was hesitant because she knew I'd probably not want anything to do with her the next day – and she was right.

I can't say it was a particularly earth-moving experience, but that may have been because we were drunk, so it was a bit disappointing for both of us I believe. I felt guilty about it, but the feeling passed off when I saw her looking happy with a guy from the *Scottish Star*, a ship tied up on the other side of the dock across the wide strait of water there – and there were plenty more lovely girls about. So all's well that ends well.

As the days went by, we completed the painting of the bow and stern in stages. For the outboard side (the port side) we used the ship's punt. Punts come in many shapes and sizes, but this was a particularly heavy old thing, more of a raft, with empty 45 gallon oil drums from the engine room for buoyancy tanks. These were held together in a wooden frame, with slats of wood for the deck and a rail along the middle for holding onto. The bo's'un was very fond of it (especially when he was drunk) as he and the lamp trimmer had built it some years before. To paint the lower outboard side of the hull, we would heave it over the gunwale and pull it to and fro along the side of the ship. The stages were used, as I've explained, for the upper sides.

One night we all taxied back to the ship, ratted of course after a night of bar-hopping. There were two girls in our bar – our very own molls – enjoying a free night with us, courtesy of the Oz Royal Navy. At the end of the evening, around 2 AM, another girl and her boyfriend needed to get back to their ship, which was moored on the other side of the channel. It was the Blue Star Line *Scottish Star*. To get to it they were going to have to walk all the way round the dock, a journey of several miles. John had the bright idea of rowing them back across the channel in the ship's precious punt. It was nothing like the distance by land but it was still a long way. But what the hell, we all thought.

So we went out on deck to the bow and pulled the punt around to the bow so we could all get aboard from the dockside. There was Abby, Chris, John and myself, plus our guests: the girl and her boyfriend.

The moment we let go of our vessel and pushed ourselves away from the Bow, a familiar voice rang out. We looked up to see an equally familiar face: the bo's'un, very drunk, yelling profanities in his broad Hull accent. "Where do you think you're going in my fucking punt?" he shouted, whilst throwing planks of wood at us from the fo'c's'le. We shouted back, trying to explain what we were doing: taking our friends back to their ship. But he kept on throwing wood at us, until we were out of range. At that point he agreed to let us continue, so long as we solemnly promised to bring it back. So we did that. "You'd better," was his parting shot, "or I'll have you all!" He was a tough little Yorkshireman – a fair man, but took no nonsense.

As we made ready to paddle, we all started to laugh. The bo's'un had done us a favour by throwing planks of wood at us, because otherwise we'd have had nothing to paddle with except paint rollers and brushes. What a good man! He must have known.

So we set off on our long voyage, but we didn't appear to be making much headway. Somewhere in the middle of the channel we decided to lighten ship by dumping 5 gallon drums of blue paint over the side. As soon as we did so, powerful lights started shining on us from all directions. These turned out to be the headlights of several police cars on the shore, pointing out at us.

We thought this was frightfully decent of them, since it was dark in the middle of the channel, away from the lights of the dockside and ships. So, laughing away, we stopped paddling, formed a chorus line and began singing "Give me the moonlight, give me the girl, and leave the rest to me" – with the appropriate high-kicks of course.

Presently the harbour police turned up in a launch to take us in tow, and threw us a line. Unfortunately, what with the weight of the punt, the power of the ultra-light speed boat and the fact that they'd lashed the rope to the stern of the police launch in a lopsided fashion, we simply went round in circles.

However each circle took us just that bit further until we made landfall just ahead of the *Scottish Star*. Once we'd landed, and after many a thank-you, our passengers took off sharpish into the darkness as the harbour police approached.

The police said "get aboard – we're taking you back to your ship." Rolling around with laughter because we were all very pissed, we explained that we couldn't go back to the ship without the punt because we'd solemnly promised the bo's'un we'd bring it back to him – and if we didn't, our lives would be worth nothing. So with a great show of resignation, the police agreed to tow us back in our punt.

We jumped back aboard the punt and the police launch towed us slowly back to our ship – with us going round in circles as before – where we triumphantly hailed the smiling face of Billy the bo's'un, who was saying "good lads... good lads!"

The chief officer, unflappable as ever, was there talking to the police, whilst the rest of our crew, plus a neighbouring Polish ship, cheered the return of the conquering heroes. We felt really pleased with ourselves.

I recall a policeman saying "do you realise there's a maximum $3,000 fine for dumping rubbish in the dock?" We replied it wasn't rubbish, it was good quality gloss paint. Then a harbour official told us we would have been a serious hazard to shipping if anything had been wanting to enter or leave the Harbour. We saw his point and began to feel somewhat less pleased with ourselves.

Then somebody said "anything to say for the press?" Well, we were all up for that. The next day we had a good laugh as we read in the Melbourne Times a report of our great voyage across Melbourne Harbour. An official spokesman said that no harm had been done, so no action would be taken. We smiled when we read that. We never heard anything more about it, and we congratulated ourselves that we'd got away with it yet again. But all hail to the Melbourne Harbour police for their deep understanding of alcohol and their sporting attitude.

Missed the Boat

On our last day in Melbourne, John got invited back to the flat of the girlies. He was with a beautiful girl called Sandy. Her nickname was Sea Boots, from her father being a British sailor and her mother a ship's moll – what else?

I went along with him, although I knew we were due to sail next morning at 8 AM. There were other girls present, and as usual plenty of drink was consumed, but I don't remember much else about the evening. The upshot was however that we overslept and missed the boat.

I wasn't too worried about it. The boat was due to arrive in Sydney in two days time, and it would be there for about six days. So we had plenty of time to get to Sydney and pick it up again.

We spent the next three days partying. It was like being on holiday – lots of booze, dancing and so on. It was so hot in Oz and what with all the drinking I quite got into the way of it. The Australians love having a good time, and know how to do it.

We were in a suburb of Melbourne known as St Kilda. Finding cold milk for breakfast became a job of mine. Walking down the High Street one morning, looking for the milk, I saw a familiar face. It was a lad I'd been at school with, about three years older than me. He was a memorable sort of guy, being a guitarist. He and a few friends had a band, and you often heard them rehearsing in the physics lab – the teacher was their bass player.

We looked at each other and he recognised me and smiled. He had his wife with him and he introduced us. She was a lovely girl, clutching a tiny baby. He told me they'd got married and emigrated the year before, and were doing very well.

I explained my circumstances, and how my friend John and I were heading for Sydney that same day, or early the next. We left it there and went our ways. But it was amazing to think that 12,000 miles from home you could meet someone you knew in the street, just like that. How likely is that to happen?

At last it was time for us to head off to Sydney. We'd had a great time, though I don't remember much about it. But it had been an education in culture, humour and sex. As we were setting off, Sandy gave us AS$10, since we have no money left. We took a local train out-of-town, found the A31 (nowadays the M31) and soon got a lift. The truck driver wasn't going to Sydney, but in that general direction.

We went through Wandong and Broadford and he dropped us off at Seymour. We had started out late, so it was dark by the time we got there, but we finally got a lift to Albury via Euroa, Violet Town, Benalla and Wangaratta by bribing a driver with some speed we'd been given for the purpose. The truck or rig drivers used it to keep themselves going on long hauls. This particular truck had two tractors on it.

We were dropped on the outskirts of town around 1 AM. Being very tired, and there not being much traffic about, we fell to thinking about finding a haystack or somewhere to kip down for the rest of the night. But before we'd found a place, a police car picked us up and drove us to the other side of town, there being more likelihood there of finding a truck heading out in our direction.

They told us not to sleep in the Bush, and especially not in haystacks – that's where all the snakes went at night. Plus other "beasties": the cop who told us this was Scottish, I recall.

The story we gave was that our ship was in Sydney and we'd had a bit of leave to visit relations in Melbourne. It wasn't really a lie as we definitely "had relations" there. When they dropped us off they wished us well, and we thanked them.

An hour later we were picked up by a mad mechanic in an old 1961 Australian Holden. The man's driving was fast and furious. He told us he was on his way to a broken-down truck which was still sitting just off the A31. Every time we passed a truck, or were passed by one, he would raise his fist and shout "You bastards – getting me out of bed in the middle of the night!"

He complained of feeling tired, so John leaned forward (we were both sitting in the back) and offered him a couple of the speed pills. He took them both, but after a while he shouted back to us "It's no good, I'm going to have to kip for a while."

We screeched to a halt, overshooting the pull-in (Australian lay-by) he was aiming for. It was only when he turned to face us in order to reverse that we realised to our horror that he only had one eye.

Thereupon he promptly backed the car into a ditch. "Okay, lads," he said, "you'll have to give us a push."

The next ten minutes saw us trying to push the car out of the hole, with him keeping up a constant stream of abuse at the passing trucks. "You bastards!" he'd shout. "I'm always helping you – what about me now? Fucking bastards!"

We eventually extracted the car, but not without getting ourselves covered in mud from the spinning wheels. Once inside the pull-in, our driver straightened up the car and settled down in the driving seat to get some sleep, with John and myself trying to do the same in the back. Ten minutes later the speed pills must have kicked in because he suddenly sat up shouting, "Can't sleep with all those bastards driving by!" – and off we went again, our wheels spinning and screeching like a classic car-chase movie.

Around 3 AM he dropped us off at a truck stop, saying he was going to turn off soon to find the broken-down truck and this was our best place for a lift. Then off he screeched in a cloud of dust, and we chuckled to ourselves as we fancied we could hear the strains of "Bastards…!" drifting faintly back to us.

Completely mad!

From there we got a lift in a small truck. It was a most uncomfortable ride: I'd just be nodding off when I'd be jolted awake again as we hit yet another pothole in the road. But the journey was memorable for two notable events.

One was when I awoke at around 5 AM, just before dawn. We were passing through Gundagai, and as we bounced along, I'm sure I had a quick glimpse out of the window of the famous statue of the dog on the tucker box.

The other was the sight of Comet Bennett in the night sky. It was a crystal-clear starry night, with not a scrap of light pollution out there in the bush, which made the comet with its hairy tail gloriously prominent.

We continued driving into the dawn through Yass and Gunning to Goulburn where we stopped for a break and a coffee. Then on through Berrima, Bowral, Bargo and Campbelltown, during which I mainly slept. We were eventually dropped off mid-morning in Liverpool, a suburb of Sydney, from where we took a train to the centre of town with the remains of the A$ $10 we'd been given and made our way to the docks on foot. There we found our ship, the *Trebartha*.

As we approached the ship, Chris, Abby and the rest of the lads were painting its side from the quay with the famous dark blue Hain-Nourse hull colour using 20 ft rollers. When they saw us coming they all started cheering, stopped what they were doing and came over to meet us. Everyone was anxious to hear our story. Happy to be back, I looked up and saw the mate on deck, smiling away. He was a cool customer.

—oOo—

What a great adventure we'd had. If we had not missed the boat I'd have seen nothing of the interior of the country, as we'd have never got past the first bar, let alone driven through the Bush.

We got docked six days' pay for the time we were adrift, plus a fine of one day's pay for the misdemeanour. Since we were both under 18 and had not yet come of age, the company had been obliged to notify our next-of-kin that we'd gone missing ashore. So the captain suggested we write to our parents to reassure them we were all right. I found out later that my mother had got a telegram saying that I was absent without leave in Australia, which had made her very worried. Anyway, all's well that ends well, we thought, and it was good to be back on board ship again.

It was only in retrospect that I came to realise the seriousness of what we done and its possible consequences. A safe ship is a fully crewed ship, and in going AWOL we'd let down our shipmates in the matter of safety, though not a lot had been made of it at the time.

Australia really is a big wild place, matched in size by the hearts of its people. All the while we'd been there they'd been very good to us. And what great thirsty characters they are too!

So it was back to the usual routine of work-sleep-eat-drink. In Sydney the main pub used by sailors is a salubrious establishment called the Montgomery Hotel in Pirmont, an area just outside the docks. We did devote a little time to looking round the city, but most nights after work we spent drinking there.

During our drinking bouts there were a few strange rituals. One of these was that any of us could be called upon to sing: this could happen at any time and in any place in the world. The call was reinforced by a ritual chant summoning you to "sing, sing, or show us your ring". This meant that, in default of a song, you'd have to drop your trousers, bend over and spread the cheeks of your bum, a gesture known as a spreader. The chant would continue with increased gusto as you climbed up onto the table, having announced you were going to spread. If the assembled company were not sufficiently impressed, they'd throw beer at you.

It was all part of the fun, but not a particularly enjoyable pastime. So after I came on board it wasn't long before I made the effort to memorise a song word-perfect. It was *Bonnie and Clyde* by Georgie Fame. Chris had memorised *Let It Be*, and sung it with gushing emotion. John, who couldn't sing a note, was happy to drop his trousers on every occasion as a matter-of-course.

With all our cargo discharged and the hull of the ship now completely painted, we were ready to leave Sydney. With tugs made fast we were led out, then we made our way under our own steam out of Sydney's huge sheltered bay. Which is why Sydney exists at all: 17th-century mariners preferred to stop at the safest anchorage they could find.

We sailed beneath the famous Sydney Harbour Bridge, past the Opera House, still under construction with its sail-like roofs. Fort Denison, formerly a prison island, slipped astern off the starboard side. Then we sailed out into Botany Bay and thence into the Pacific Ocean, heading NNE to Brisbane, roughly 500 miles away: a day and a half sailing for us.

Life on board went on as usual, except that since we were in coastal waters we went back on three-to-a-watch. So the daytime work crew were rather thin in numbers, with random watch-keepers working overtime with us between third watches. I was disappointed about being unable to work watches in those days because I was too young, as I enjoy the unpredictability of it.

We continued up the Dead Coast to Brisbane, the last of our ports for discharging cargo, where we spent a few days.

Since we'd arrived at the weekend, on the Sunday the local Seamen's Mission organised a horse riding trip for us.

About seven of us went along. A minibus picked us up and we drove out of town for an hour or so, arriving at a farm which had a herd of horses. The people there chose the horses for us: they weren't mere ponies – they were big: 16 to 17 hands high. Mine was white, and seemed at first to be nice and easy to handle.

We wandered through a flattish land dotted with widely-spaced eucalyptus trees and saw a variety of animals: koalas, 'roos as well as birds and other small creatures. I found it nerve-racking, especially when our guide decided it was time for a gallop. Like everyone else's, my horse took off like a rocket and, just when I thought I was back in charge, another white horse galloped up alongside. This was evidently my horse's rival, because it turned to look at the newcomer and promptly went into top gear. It was as much as I could do to hang on, let alone control this beautiful animal. Eventually we stopped. I looked around me and it seemed everyone had had the same experience, dodging in and out of the trees and, more worryingly, some strange round 7 ft high mounds of earth. I thought to myself – God! – the moles are big around here. They were of course termite nests. You wouldn't want to be falling into one of those!

During our journey we stopped and ate meat, beans and salad like real cowboys – or linesmen or buckaroos, as they are known in Oz. We had a good day and all agreed it made a pleasant change from the usual booze and partying.

Now, with the boat void of cargo, nobody knew what was going to happen next. Many ships of the other traditional companies, the Federal Steam Navigation, Port and Star boats, had their regular ports of call. Generally these would either head back down the coast, or across to New Zealand or to Tasmania, to pick up cargo for the UK or Europe. Hain-Nourse was more of a tramping company, which meant they tried to pick up cargo for the ship as it went from port to port. So now we could be sent anywhere worth sending us, economically speaking. We were hoping for New Zealand of course, which was famous for a good time, or at least for a run back down the coast. In this we were to be disappointed. We were to pick up a full load of cane sugar and thus heading straight back to UK via Panama.

Brisbane being a seemingly conservative town, it had been a quiet run ashore. We'd only had a small amount of cargo for there, so we soon set sail for Port Townsville further up the coast.

A strange and unexpected thing happened in Brisbane though. Our friend John, whom I'd been adrift with in Melbourne, went missing and we sailed without him. Nobody knew what had become of him. He may have got bogged down with some woman as before – he did have an eye for them (and they for him). We were hoping he might turn up again at Townsville as before, but he didn't. My theory was that he'd gone back to Sandy in Melbourne.

We left Brisbane, heading north up the coast towards the Coral Sea into the Great Barrier Reef, famous for its marine life. It was only 500 miles or so to Townsville, but bad weather and tricky navigation turned that into two nights at sea.

It was a three day voyage, with plenty of work to do. Since we were a cargo ship, having discharged all our cargo we were in ballast. With all the holds empty, the ship was comparatively light and rode high in the water, offering a lot of hull and superstructure to the force of the wind. This made life difficult for the helmsman, especially in close quarters, i.e. close inshore, or entering or leaving a port or its approaches along an estuary or river.

The situation was improved by filling the deep tanks in the hull, the ballast tanks, with seawater, which is what is literally meant by being "in ballast". This settled the ship down to a certain extent and improved its handling.

In the aftermath of discharging cargo in four separate ports, the holds were a complete mess. So over the next three days, in a moderate sea, we lifted cargo nets full of dunnage and other rubbish up out of the holds, dumping it over the side as usual. It saddened me: some of the stuff still looked useful, especially the dunnage. But the rest was just that: rubbish. Wood and paper, broken cases, fag-ends and packets, beer cans and wine bottles, rotting food… it looked as if the dockers who'd been working down there had spent the time partying.

After clearing out the rubbish we swept out each of the five holds. These had two "tween" decks, some partitioned into smaller chambers, plus a much larger one, the space at the bottom being called the lower ceiling ("ceiling" being the nautical term for the floor of a hold). This arrangement made it easier to load smaller, lighter, or more valuable goods into the tweens, to secure them better, or for unloading at different ports. Some were refrigerated for perishables, whilst Larger, heavier goods were loaded into the lower. Most internal designs are customised to suit the ship's general usage, some customised especially for ships that make regular trips to given countries.

We started at the top and swept our way downwards. After that we washed and scrubbed the holds with water plus teepol, a common industrial detergent at the time. Finally the holes were fumigated to get rid of bacteria and vermin. All this needed to be done for our cargo of sugar.

We also needed to cement over the drains in the ceiling, which led to the bilges for pumping out. Because we were loading bulk sugar, the drains needed to be plugged over to stop the sugar going down them, crystallising in the pipes and blocking the bilge pump. It was a lot of extra work for us to do down in the holds. In bad weather it was far from comfortable and made me nauseous at times. It was also a bit spooky. Each lower hold, when empty, was a vast open space lit by clusters of lights which swung to-and-fro with the motion of the ship, creating an unfamiliar lighting effect.

Even the cadets and the chief officer had to work down in the holds to get the job done in time. In those three days we all earned 60 hours overtime, even though it had only been over a weekend. Overtime would double after a certain time in any 24-hour period, and triple if you were not going to get eight hours sleep before your next spell of duty.

After it was finished, the chief officer had us in his cabin for a celebratory drink, and to thank us for the extra effort. Ever a good man, who had everybody's respect on board.

We eventually arrived in Cleveland Bay on a bright sunny day, passing Magnetic Island to our starboard side and tying up adjacent to the sugar silos in Port Townsville. Sugar was obviously a major part of the local economy here: you could see the sugar canes growing on the hills above the town.

—oOo—

We were only going to be there for 24 hours, since loading bulk sugar is much faster than conventional cargo. Morale in consequence was very low. Most of the crew were sad because they'd been looking forward to a trip back down the coast, especially those who had met nice girls. Now they'd have to leave them behind prematurely.

We opened up the hatches and topped the derricks for one last time in Australia, and once the sugar was loaded we closed the hatches again, stowed everything away and made ready to head out over the Pacific to Panama. But first we set off along the coast to a little-known place called Marilan, just a few hours sailing away. It had to be entered through a narrow opening in the rocks, leading into a small bay.

The dock consisted of just one sugar silo. We only stopped there a few hours to top up with another 400 tons, to complete the full 5,000 ton load of raw brown sugar. We jokingly told ourselves it was all destined for the Wimpy Bars. In the late 60s these were the first American-style burger bars in the UK, famous for their coffee and the brown sugar they gave you to put in it.

The 6,000 mile journey to Panama was due to take us around three weeks. Though a long time, it seemed relatively short compared to the six weeks voyage we'd had from the UK. We sailed on the tide (with still no sign of John), heading out into the Pacific Ocean in an easterly direction, crossing the Great Barrier Reef in broad sunshine and entering the Coral Sea.

The first two days were spent doing the usual tidying up. There was plenty to do after a month on the East Coast discharging cargo. All the derricks, hatches and running gear had to be sorted out as usual. After all that activity, the running gear had to be checked for damage and replaced where necessary, and the winches and their wires had to be lashed or stowed away for the long voyage.

At sea for a long period, you could never be sure of the weather. One day it might be sunny and barmy, then the clouds would start coming together, the atmospheric pressure drop, and you'd watch the weather systems coming and going. Sometimes when you were painting out on deck you could see a rainstorm coming a long way off, and have plenty of time to get under cover just before the rain started.

Although visiting places on the other side of the world sounds very exciting. We really did Any conventional sight seeing, most of our evenings were spent out drinking and chasing those ubiquitous women for some instant gratification.

I was grateful for the molls of Oz, who serviced the Merchant Navy with a much-welcomed and much-needed accommodation. They made it feel as if you had a genuine relationship for the short time you were there. Some of them must have felt the same way – not a few of the girls actually came to the UK looking for the men they'd fallen in with. Sometimes they were successful. But most of these follow-up relationships failed, as they were meeting again under different circumstances, in a Pommy culture and environment completely different from what they were used to.

Roaming the seas on this beautiful planet is a completely fulfilling experience. It never lets you down, unless you lack the necessary humility when confronting it. Its profundity continued to challenge, bewilder and gratify me – the last of these in a far better way than any short-lived physical or emotional relationship with a woman ever could.

So here we were again, letting deep sea life purify us once more. This time we were in the Pacific Ocean – the largest, with some of the deepest parts of all. It also had a different look and feel to it. It wasn't the Atlantic, nor the Indian Ocean: it had its own signature, its own special character: an energy all its own. I wonder if this special character is really the result of its appearance, or an energy welling up out of my expectations or concepts based on things I'd heard or imagined. about it since early childhood. But anyway – there it was, in all its glory.

The days went by and we got back in the routine of games of sevens, food – that's something that takes up a lot of time. You really are what you eat. The skill of the cooks, plus the company's budget, determined the quality of the food. But, good or bad, there was always plenty of it on this ship, and no one had any reason to be hungry. Sunday was steak day, and also tabnab day (the Arab word "tabnab" for a cake or pastry comes from their association with the Seamen's Mission, whereas fruitcake in any shape or form was always known as plum duff).

Sailing on – and painting on – after work, overtime and dinner, we would congregate on the stern for our ritual of yarning away the day's end. The sun was now setting directly over Oz, and at those times my thoughts strayed back there. But mainly my attention was directed towards the future, and the stories I was hearing about the Panama Canal.

Saving your leftovers from the gash bucket (the slops) for the mules used in the locks to pull the ships in and out – that was a favourite joke to play on first-timers. Another was to get the innocent lad to nip down to the engine room and tell the chief engineer to pump 50,000 gallons into the port ballast tanks as we had a starboard list!

—oOo—

Once they tried to kid me the youngest on-board had to read a passage from the Bible at Sunday service (that never happened). But the best joke of all, I thought, was to send the victim to the stern of the ship to wait for the mail helicopter.

Abby once asked me: "how would you get a 10-ton shackle from number one hold forward to number five aft?" I came up with a cunning plan to rig various derricks at each of the holds and operate a lifting and letting-go procedure. "That's plausible," he said, "but I'd simply pick it up, put it in my pocket and walk it there." (A 10-ton shackle is one capable of supporting 10 tons: it is quite small.)

Clever, but embarrassing for me.

Light Recognition is the topic of recognising what is meant by a given configuration of lights displayed by a ship or a shore base at night. The lights used are generally white, red, green and amber. The second officer once asked me: "what would one red light over three white mean?" I thought for a while and said "I haven't a clue." At which he said, to general laughter, "It's a whore house on the fourth floor!"

The weather continued variable. At times I felt we were like a small leaf or a piece of wood on a pond, sometimes floating peacefully when the sea was gentle, sometimes thrown about in confusion by its massive energy and fighting to stay on-course.

In this ever-changing seascape, my mind would go back to the days when I was a child, trying to decide what I wanted to be when I grew up and trying to imagine what it would be like. The reality of life On the *Trebartha*, now far exceeded any expectations I had then, by any stretch of the imagination.

Our bar still had plenty of cash in hand – profits on sales to the Royal Australian Navy – enabling us to have the occasional free night. One of these was to mark the crossing of the International Date Line (IDL).

Basically the IDL lies 180° east of the Greenwich meridian, i.e. halfway round the world from the UK. It does however bend in places to avoid populated islands, such as New Zealand, some South Sea islands such as Wallis, Tonga and Fiji, and (at the Arctic, and Antarctic Circles) some (but not all) of the Aleutian Islands lying between Russia (to the East) and Alaska (to the West).

It's eerie to think that on two neighbouring islands lying either side of the International Date Line it's a different day. This bizarre fact was a matter of great significance to us seafarers, because it affected our pay. As we crossed the IDL on this occasion, we quite literally sailed into yesterday.

On this voyage we had been sailing in a easterly direction around the world. In the time it took us to get to the IDL, we advanced the clock by an hour proportionately as we sailed across each time zone border, 12 in all. Then, crossing the IDL, we notionally set the clock back 24 hours, which strangely gave us two Mondays.

We then continued eastwards on the rest of our voyage back to the UK, still advancing the clock by an hour for each time zone, 12 in all, which got us back to Greenwich Mean Time on the right day by the time we reached London.

If crossing the IDL in a westerly direction however, this is completely reversed. Crossing the IDL you advance the clock by 24 hours, effectively sailing into tomorrow.

Interestingly, most ships cross the IDL on a weekday, either way. This is to avoid any complications with wages during the cruise, where you might gain or lose a calendar day at this point. As you are being paid time-and-a-half on Saturday, or double-time on Sunday, it matters if either of these days gets shortened or skipped, or you get an extra one.

In case your head's beginning to ache from all this logic, here's a true story. The passenger steamer SS Warrimoo was knifing through the waters of the mid-Pacific on its way from Vancouver to Australia. The navigator had just finished working out a star fix and brought Captain John D. S. Phillips the result. The Warrimoo's position was LAT 0° 31' N and LONG 179 30' W. The date was 31 December 1899.

"Know what this means?" First Mate Payton broke in. "We're only a few miles from the intersection of the equator and the International Date Line."

Captain Phillips was prankish enough to take full advantage of the opportunity for achieving the navigational freak of the century. He changed course slightly so as to bear directly down on his mark. Then he adjusted the engine speed – the calm weather and clear night working in his favour. At midnight the SS Warrimoo lay on the equator at precisely the point where it crosses the International Date Line. This bizarre position had the following consequences:

The ship's bow was in the Southern Hemisphere, where it was the middle of summer. The stern was in the Northern Hemisphere, where it was the middle of winter.

The date in the aft part of the ship was 31 December 1899. In the forward part it was 1 January 1900.

Therefore the ship was not only in two different days, two different months, two different years and two different seasons… but in two different centuries – all at the same time!

I must say I'm finding it extremely difficult to explain, and possibly it's even more difficult to understand. Think about it. Good luck!

—oOo—

The weather was generally good in the Pacific. No extremes of anything. Consequently one day was much like another. Then one morning I woke up and there was something different. In my blurry half-awake state it took me a while to work out what it was. Then it struck me.

The engine had gone silent.

We'd stopped in the middle of the Pacific, literally thousands of miles from anywhere. At breakfast we found out that the engine problem identified off Las Palmas had now got so bad we had to do something about it. We had the parts; the long-range forecast showed we were in a virtually static high; so now was a good time to replace the piston.

This was no small undertaking. We were to be stopped for four or five days. When I first heard this I thought this was a joke. With still another ten days to go to get to Panama, the prospect of a further five days not making any headway seemed a living hell.

We never saw the engineers so much as we did in those few days. I'd never seen their white overalls so dirty either. So, with a lot of activity on their part, the days went by. The piston went from off the boat deck and was taken down below. That was engaging to watch.

—oOo—

One day, whilst we were adrift, Abby and I were working together, painting the canvases (little covers protecting various bits of equipment throughout the ship) with "Gunue", a special waterproof green paint. This included the covers of the lifeboats, four of which were located on either side of the boat deck, one deck below the bridge.

Whilst doing this we came across an old sounder – a barrel of fine strong wire with a weighted end. We thought it would be interesting to see if we could find the bottom. Having cleared it with the officer of the watch, we broke it out and put the end over the side and paid it out. It had obviously not been used for some time. Its total length was unknown, but we never found bottom.

The third officer said we were in one of the deepest parts of the ocean. It made me feel even more out on a limb, so far from land as we were. Though, as Abby pointed out, looked at in another way, we were only 7 miles from land!

I liked Abby – he was a cool customer.

We checked the line, brought it in, oiled and painted it. Then with gearing overhauled, we replaced the cover and painted that too. It was a welcome distraction in those difficult days, as everybody was frustrated with the delay.

At that time we also had the job of painting the main mast. This was something I was not looking forward to, as I was never good with heights. But I knew that somehow I'd have to find the courage to do it. A man that couldn't do everything expected of him is next to useless at sea, and gets no respect from the rest of the crew.

You had to climb an 80 ft vertical metal ladder, rust coming away in your hands, carrying a lizard rope strop, plus your running line and bo's'un's chair. There was a rope near the top known as a *dummy gantling* which led up and through a pulley at the very top of the topmast, underneath a sort of cap called the button.

You climbed to a platform below the topmast, bent on your lizard with its metal eye on one end, fed the end of your runner through the pulley, replacing the dummy gantling, pulled your lizard up and through, replacing the dummy gantling with your lizard.

You then made fast the end of your lizard onto your bo's'un's chair, which is a piece of wood rigged with spliced rope culminating in a special knot. The knot enabled you to sit in the chair, pull yourself up to the top and then let yourself down bit by bit, following the usual procedure of chipping, washing and painting in each descent down the mast.

It's surprising how easy it is to hold yourself in this position by lightly gripping and holding the two ropes together. It works brilliantly with the old type of fibre rope. It's still a highly dangerous procedure, but it really teaches you confidence in yourself, and enables you to understand the saying that one hand is for the ship and one is for yourself.

It goes without saying that there was only room for one person on the topmast. It was scary at first, but after a while I got used to it and took it in my stride. Everything was done with sisal rope or manila – no safety harnesses or safety ropes. But we did it, and made a good job of it too.

I might add that lots of fun was to be had swinging in the rigging and having sword-fights with paintbrushes.

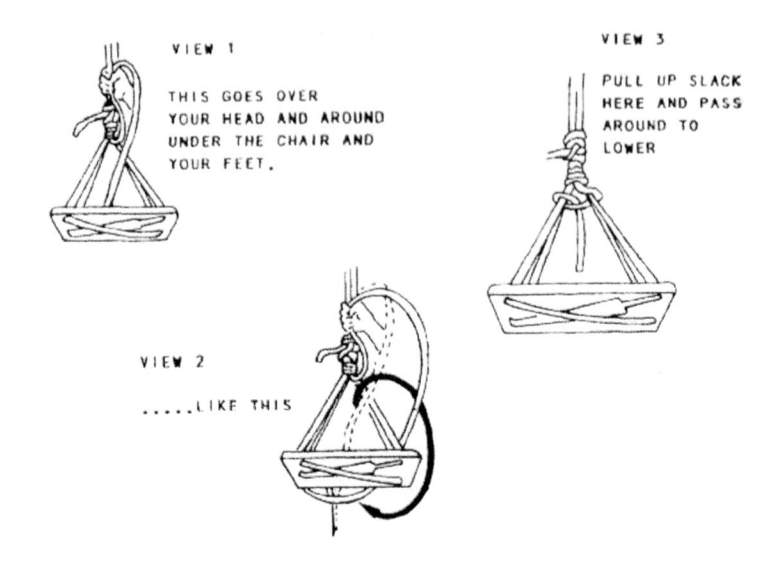

VIEW 1

THIS GOES OVER YOUR HEAD AND AROUND UNDER THE CHAIR AND YOUR FEET.

VIEW 3

PULL UP SLACK HERE AND PASS AROUND TO LOWER

VIEW 2

.....LIKE THIS

A Boatswain's Chair

At last there came the day we were rewarded for our patience with the rumbling and shuddering of the engine firing up. After a few plumes of black smoke as it backfired it was running again, and we started moving once more. You never saw so many happy faces.

Apart from our feeling of relief from the boredom, there was a sense of release from an ever-present danger on a lifeless ship drifting in the ocean. If the weather had turned bad during that period, we would have been in a very dangerous situation without the ability to turn our bow into the wind.

This was brought home to us on one of the days we were stopped. The wind got up a bit, and all that day the ship had the sea on the beam, making us roll slowly from side to side. We fretted about our cargo of bulk sugar. If it was to move over to one side, this would result in a list. All that could be done to correct it, i.e. to trim the ship, would be with water ballast, though the scope to do this was limited to about a 10%. It was a strange, worrying day. All went well for us however and we survived.

That evening, heading on our way, I went up to the monkey island above the bridge and looked out ahead – and smiled into the wind. Homeward bound!

Hats off to the engineers. A job like that – replacing a piston – was something normally done in dry dock, along with other major jobs. But they foresaw the problem getting worse, got the part and did it. Good men!

—oOo—

The weather stayed calm for the rest of our journey to Panama, without seeing them we passed the Marquesas Islands and the Galapagos north-east of Polynesia, and a line of undersea mountains – the Line Islands. This was very deep sea. The Pacific is the deepest ocean, 7 miles at some points. Yet probably on our run into Panama, the last 3,000 miles would only have been from two miles to 600 ft deep. But there were some very deep trenches. The Maimones, running offshore from mid-America, the Guatemala and the Peru-Chile trenches to the south, are some three miles deep.

The day came at last when we caught sight of land. After 25 days it looked pretty good. In a flat calm sea we anchored off Bilboa and Panama City to wait our turn in the queue for the first set of locks. I was surprised to find that the canal ran north-south, as I naturally expected it to run east-west.

As we sat at anchor, we congregated on the stern as usual. It was the most incredible classical evening. The glassy sea was flat and calm, the air hot and humid, the sky graduating from a pale powder lime to orange around a deep red sun surrounded by haze.

There was an abundance of birdlife. The most striking sight was a flock of herons, 40 or 50 of them, strung out in a line.

The lead bird occasionally stepped up or down, following the thermals. This gave rise to a bizarre visual effect, like waterfalls in the sky, as the whole line of birds bobbed up and down, seemingly flowing over invisible obstacles.

There were also cormorants diving in the water, swimming down to catch a fish, coming back up to the surface, shaking themselves and then taking off with their catch. With such a calm sea it must have been easy for them to see their prey.

We all sat in silence, just taking it all in. It was a good time to relish the beauty of our planet, a pure way to enrich our lives, and an opportunity simply to marvel at it all.

That night I could hardly sleep, what with the humid heat, plus my excitement at the prospect of heading through this wonderful engineering feat famous throughout the world. I dream of many things that night: epics born of inspiration, romance, excitement and wonder.

The Panama Canal

I was woken early by the watchman calling "Stations! Turn to!" The anchor was being lifted, and as usual it was my job to wash off the mud and seaweed with the hose. As the capstan churned and clunked, followed by vibration from the engine and smoke from the funnel, we began our slow approaches to Panama and into the canal.

We were moving slowly enough for the pilot boat to draw alongside and let our pilot come on board. He was dressed in whites and carried the now-familiar black bag containing all his charts and reference materials.

With the land closing in on us, I began to make out cars, buses, lorries and people going about their daily lives. It was a strange sight for me. After spending so long at sea, I was forgetting how most of the world's people spend their days, never travelling far from their homes. You can see why I was finding it hard to understand when you consider where I'd just come from. This was also the first country I'd arrived at which could be described as exotic and tropical. It was very exciting.

The bridge came up on us and we passed under it. There was a town and an industrial area off our port side, and to the northwest there were docks, shipyards, and passenger terminals with large liners tied up alongside, for their passengers to go ashore and sample the delights of Panama City.

The channel now reduced very quickly, and we slowed as we made our approach to the first lock. We "went to stations". As we entered the lock we threw down our heaving lines, each being made fast onto a wire eye coming from a little diesel train known as a mule. It was at this point I'm sure that the catering boy, who (urged on by the older crew members) had been saving up the contents of the gash bucket all that previous day for the mules, had a moment of revelation.

We then heaved up these wires leading through the fairleads in the bulwark on the bow and from the winches, and slipped them over the bollards. We had eight of the mules assigned to us, running along a little train line. As we moved forward into a lock of unimaginable size these now took complete control of the ship, being themselves commanded by the pilot, who remained on the bridge throughout the two stages of locking.

Unnoticed by us at that point, a team of six Panamanians had come on board via the pilot ladder. They wore overalls and hard hats and carried large plywood sheets. These were to make a makeshift shelter for the duration of their time aboard. With three moving forward and three aft, they relieved us and took over our stations, remaining on board for the duration of our 80 mile transit of the canal.

By then it was midday, so we went off to have our lunch. Afterwards most of us hung around on deck, taking in all the amazing sights on offer. For by now we were surrounded by equatorial jungle.

We came out of the first set of locks and very soon entered the second set, leaving the mules to retract their wires and go back down their railway track to collect the next ship, there being a continuous stream of vessels entering and leaving the canal the whole time.

We picked up the wires from the mules that were going to see us through the next set of locks, a task that was now performed for us by the shoreside crew. Exiting these locks, we returned to work for the afternoon as we continued north along a cut through thick jungle. It was bursting with life and interspersed with factories and villages – a whole range of activities going on, everyone trying to take advantage of the canal to scratch a living.

For some time we continued up the cut until it opened out and we entered a large lake. It was late afternoon now and we dropped anchor for the night, the canal not being navigable during the hours of darkness.

We didn't have the lake to ourselves. We shared it with many other ships, from all over the world, making the passage north or south.

That night was different from anything I'd ever experienced, and altogether surreal. It was hot and humid, and filled with the sounds of all sorts of jungle birds and animals, which blended with the lights and the generator noise from nearby ships. As usual we sat on the stern, bemused by the contrast between the open ocean to which we had grown accustomed, and the equatorial jungle we were surrounded by now. Yet here we were, still on the same 10,000 ton ship.

It was a hot night's sleep, as the air-conditioning never worked all that well, though it was something I only noticed in extreme conditions.

Next morning we upped the anchor and set off again. There was quite a lot of work to do in cleaning, washing and stowing the anchor, thanks to the mud it dredged up.

We made our way across the series of inland lakes which form this particular stretch of the Panama Canal. As we went about our usual morning's work – painting! – I kept one eye on the beautiful jungle view, looking out for the elusive alligators I knew to be there.

I fancied I saw one on the distant shoreline, but it could just as easily have been a floating log set in motion by the wash from a passing ship. There was a constant flow of these: cargo boats, tugs, dredgers and passenger liners, plus all sorts of smaller vessels such as the fishing boats of local people, going about their daily lives.

Later that morning the bo's'un told me to report to the bridge. I was doing my steering ticket (certificate), towards which I had to do 18 hours on the helm, four of which had to be under pilotage. I had been up to the bridge in deep sea on occasions, where the officer of the watch would knock off the autopilot and I would just follow the compass course. Easy enough in fine weather, but hard work in rough or heavy seas. The experience also varied from ship to ship, and as ever no two days was the sea state ever the same.

When I arrived on the bridge, it was crowded. Both the deck cadets were there, all three of the deck officers and the captain. Plus of course the pilot, an American (a North American, the Panamanians would say). He was slouching by the starboard door which led out to the wing of the bridge.

I relieved the watchman on the helm. He formally reported to me that we were currently under pilotage and "steady as she goes" – which meant that we were not following a course. I formally confirmed that I understood what he'd said, repeating the words "steady as she goes".

So there I was, with my hand on the wheel. It was a superb feeling. I could see all around me, which gave me a different perspective on the whole experience of being on board a ship. When I turned the wheel and the whole ship turned as a result, it gave me an immense feeling of power. It also made me feel like a real seaman, this being hugely important to a 16 year old, eager to prove himself.

Looking ahead I could see we were about to enter a narrow channel cut through solid stone to form light-coloured cliffs. These reared up on both sides to such a height that they dwarfed the ship. There was no sign of jungle any more, and it all looked spectacular.

I stood at the helm, nervously awaiting my first command. Would I be able to perform properly? These were seriously close quarters, with no margin for error.

Issuing and acknowledging commands on the bridge follow a strict etiquette. The pilot tells the captain the required change of course, the captain tells the officer of the watch, who in turn gives the command to the helmsman. The last-named acknowledges that he has heard the command, and once again when he has completed the action. For example:

PILOT: Port 10.
CAPTAIN: Port 10, number one.
FIRST OFFICER: Port 10, sir. Port 10, helmsman.
HELMSMAN: Port 10.
PILOT (after a pause): Midships.
CAPTAIN: Midships, number one.
FIRST OFFICER: Midships, helmsman.
HELMSMAN: Midships.
HELMSMAN (again, on completion): Midships.

This little ceremony varied from ship to ship, depending on its type, its size, and the character of its captain. But apparently things were different in the Canal. The pilots prefer to give instructions direct to the helmsman: *me!* As I was to learn, to my consternation.

After going over in my mind what to expect, the pilot emitted a deep-throated groan, "Ahh!" Then he continued in a broad Dixie drawl, "Just come left a bit, helmsman."

My mind went into turmoil. I thought to myself: he's supposed to give degrees port or starboard. "Left a bit" – what's that meant to be? Now what do I do?

I glanced up at the chief officer and he was smiling. He winked at me and gestured towards the port side with his head. I moved the wheel slightly to port and saw the head of the ship moving over.

"Okay helmsman," said the pilot, "Midships."

"Midships", I acknowledged, and brought the wheel back to the central position. But before I could report completion of the manoeuvre he said, "Okay, hold it there."

"Okay", I said – and everyone on the bridge smiled.

I soon got used to the pilot's style of giving me directions as if I was driving a car, and we continued sailing on through the cut. Not many changes in course were needed to negotiate this narrow channel because it was straight. Also there was no oncoming traffic, as ships would convoy. This avoided any risk of collision, aggravated by the magnetism of a closely-passing ship which can be strong enough to exert an appreciable pull or push.

Presently I noticed a huge plaque carved into the rock, and as it drifted past us I got a good look at it. It commemorated the fact that many men's lives had been lost in the building of the Canal. They died from a variety of different causes, but mostly from malaria, since the channel had been excavated through swamps and virgin jungle. Many also died as the result of accidents with explosives removing rock, and through land slippages. It made me realise just how cheap life was in those days, in certain places, and to certain people.

And still is.

At last my two hours at the wheel came to an end. The time had passed very quickly. The ship was just coming out of the cut as I left the bridge, and the pilot thanked me. I felt good, plus a bit wiser after my experience.

Later I learned some more about the Panama Canal. The plaque I'd seen earlier stated that the canal was 80 miles long, and that one person had died (women as well as men) for every foot of progress in its building.

Another thing I learned: whilst he's on board the pilot takes charge of the ship and has total responsibility for it – much to our captain's dismay. That's why the pilot is able to call the tune.

I also learned that taking a vessel through the Canal was charged by the ton. At least it was back then in 1971. For our 10,000 ton ship it had amounted to around US$35,000. To me that sounded like a lot of money. Yet it must have been cheaper than incurring the additional running costs plus overheads of sailing round Cape Horn. Or going back to England the way we'd come, via the Cape of Good Hope.

I returned to the main deck in time for dinner.

—oOo—

As we were approaching the final set of locks, which was just before we turned to for work, somebody spotted another British merchant ship coming the other way. We all rushed to the port side, to be greeted by the dazzling sight of the *Auckland Star*, a ship of the Blue Star Line, on its way to Australia and New Zealand.

The Blue Star ships were famous for being very smart, fast and modern, with good food and plenty of pomp and ceremony. They were cargo liners, so this one probably had a few first-class passengers on board, which we fancied we could see up on the bridge.

When she was abeam of us (the time for exchanging waving signals), someone said "let's give them a spreader". So we all dropped our trousers and hung our bare bums over the bulwarks. There were about eight of us in line, and as I looked back over my shoulder at the other ship, lo and behold! – the other ship had returned our salute in kind. There was a small line of bare bums along their main deck too.

Why we sailors can't wave nicely like the officers I don't know. But it put smiles on our faces.

Officers wave when all boats pass each other. They come out on deck only when the ships are abeam. The gesture comprises one hand briefly raised.

We had more in common with the crew of the *Auckland Star* than might first appear. Both our shipping companies ran out of the Royal Docks in London. Different docks are associated with different trade routes, and the Royal Docks are synonymous with the Australasian and New Zealand runs. Consequently our crew and theirs would have been on the same pool, members of which were known as the KG5 Cowboys. So we had a reputation to live up to – as party animals, for whom anything goes.

The "pool" was a mariners' labour exchange run by the British Shipping Federation, to which all the shipping companies were affiliated, and which they supported financially. We, the crew, were all members. This enabled us to find a job when returning to work at the end of our paid leave.

In the absence of jobs, i.e. ships needing crew, the Federation would also pay us a nominal amount for food and accommodation handy for the docks. The most reasonable places to stay were either the Missions to Seamen in Silver Town or central London, run by the Church of England, or the more comfortable (and correspondingly more expensive) Catholic counterpart, the *Stella Maris* hostel in Stratford, known as the Apostleship of the Sea. Staying locally you could go each day to the pool in the KG5, check the noticeboards and pick a ship from the choices posted there daily. All the British docks had pool offices in those days.

—oOo—

Approaching Cristóbal we picked up more mules and entered the eastern sea lock. On leaving it, we left our shoreside Panamanian crews who had been camped out on the fo'c's'le and the poop to handle all the shore and tug lines. It had felt a bit odd to be letting someone else do our usual stations work. But we had our job back now, and after letting go farewell to the mules, slowly eased our way out of the lock, out into a large bay fenced-in by a huge sea wall, where we tied up for a few hours for bunkers and provisions at the port of Cristóbal, the eastern gateway to the canal. Conspicuous among the victuals we loaded were cases and cases of Tennants Beer. The amount of the stuff we drank was phenomenal. It was after all being sold to us in a shop on board, along with soft drinks and chocolate.

That afternoon we were all on the outboard side of the ship having our smoko when we noticed an old wooden sailing boat with it's hull painted green

We waved and they waved back. A lot of hairy people gave us a smile and the peace sign. This was in 1970, when the peace and hippie movements were still gaining ground in America, and the UK was beginning to catch up.

The boat was probably on its way west, back through the canal. We have no idea what they were doing but It got me thinking how life at sea for me must be far, far different from how it was for them, bobbing along in a small boat on vast oceans of dimensions which are unimaginable until you've actually crossed them. To say nothing of their sheer power and fickleness.

Roaming the world in our large cargo boat, we were accustomed to humbling other people in our travels. But the Greenpeace crew humbled us with their courage and the righteousness of their cause. There is a kindred spirit between seafarers, whatever their country, class or creed, or the sizes of their respective vessels. I did however have the opportunity to sail some lovely boats later on in life.

Some time later we were back at our stations, there having been no time to go ashore. We picked up our tug, letting it go when we were clear of the harbour wall. Then we headed out on our away again, through the long breakwater across the bay, back to the fresh air of the sea. We picked up speed in a north-easterly direction, sailing into a dark rainy sky – the tail end of a huge storm – which we now had to contend with. We were due to cross the Caribbean Sea back into the Atlantic Ocean, the Sargasso Sea and, thanks to the Gulf stream, we'd be home in three weeks or so.

What a great experience that had been, coming through such a marvel of engineering. It had saved the shipping company a vast amount of time and money spent coming round the infamous Cape Horn. This, among other unpleasant things, would have added 4 to 6 weeks to the voyage.

I thought of the huge cost in human life of building the canal, and wondered if you could set against that the saving in sailors' lives, or portions of their lives spent at risk on the longer route into the Southern Ocean in the future.

5,609 lives were officially lost in its building, 4,500 of which were West Indies workers and 350 white Americans. Out of the 56,307 workers, 11,873 were Europeans, 31,071 from the West Indies and 11,000 from the United States. Furthermore it's believed that approximately 22,000 people died on the failed French attempt in 1880. We can only wonder.

I wonder, too, how the cost in human life gets balanced against the economic benefits of major projects today, compared with the early 1900s, when the canal was built. Things are not so very different I imagine, just subtler.

We were now on the last leg of our homeward voyage. It was the first week of May. We headed out across the Caribbean Sea towards the Greater Antilles, then to the south of Jamaica on the left hand side, and towards the Windward Channel between Haiti to the south and Cuba to the north. We stayed inside of the Turks and Caicos Islands and the Inaqua Islands. We were then heading up through the Bahamas and into the Atlantic and the Sargasso Sea, then making use of the, up to 1.5 -knot NE current of the widening Gulf Stream in the North Atlantic for getting back to England.

Incidentally, the Gulf Stream averages about 4 knots. Reaching 9 knots at times, running northwards- immediately off Eastern seaboard.

The day after leaving Cristóbal the clouds began to gather and the sea to pick up. That was the last bit of painting we would get done for a few days, as we chased the tail of the hurricane.

We strung man-lines about the ship, especially on the foredeck. There were storm lines strung down the lee side of the boat, the starboard side, about a yard out from the hatch coamings, from the fo'c's'le head ladders, running down the deck past each of the hatches. They were interrupted by the two mast housings lying between them at the base of the masts.

We knew the weather would worsen considerably in the next day or two, so the lines would enable us to go forward if necessary, giving us something to hold onto in the more exposed areas of the deck.

Sure enough the weather did worsen. I went to sleep that night as usual in the after end accommodation, my cabin jumping about. At times it would quite suddenly start pitching and rolling.

By the next morning we were really going for it. There was a lot of noise, mostly the howling of the wind at gale force, and I could hardly see out of my porthole for waves and spray.

After a slightly hazardous journey from the after accommodation to midships for breakfast.

We turned to and were put on painting in the steering and galley flats – the entrances to both! It became really difficult to move around the ship: she was pitching and rolling so much. At the height of the storm we were scarcely making 4-5 knots.

I went as usual to my private retreat, the monkey island above the bridge. There is a repeater gyro up there, plus engine telegraphs, with access to all the signalling and flag communications. From there I had a great view right down to the foredeck as I stood there holding on tight, facing into strong gale force winds as they howled and whistled through the superstructure.

The ship would rise up onto the crest of a roller, then go over it, pivoting for a spell, and then the bow would plunge into the following trough. At this point you would feel the ship lurch, almost coming to a stop, then the bow would slowly rise up again for the next wave. There was a deep throbbing vibrating sound as she laboured through the sea. Every third roller was a little bigger, with every seventh bigger still.

As the ship plunged into a trough, the whole bow section would be engulfed by the sea. You could feel the ship vibrate and hear a high-pitched whine as the screws came clear of the water at times whirling free. Then gradually the bow would emerge, pushing and shoving its way up through the water, finally emerging with a large breaking green wave rolling and thundering down the foredeck. This would break over the mast housing between 1 and 2 hatches and between 2 and 3, then hit the forward part of the accommodation, rising up nearly to where I stood above the bridge, before dropping back down to cascade, green and white, over the side and out through the scuppers.

This continued relentlessly for 24 hours, with driving rain and strong gusts of wind whistling through the stays like the strains of an intimidating song.

After a while a pattern emerged and I could predict the onset of the larger rollers as the ship corkscrewed its way through the murk. It was a most exhilarating experience to have been through, and a useful one too.

By the second day the storm had eased slightly – or else I had grown accustomed to it – when one of the lashings on a derrick on number 1 hatch came loose. We were sent forward to make it fast and to check the lockers to make sure none of their contents had taken any damage from the violent pitching of the previous day.

The sea was still running wild and waves were still being shipped, but if you timed it right you could move along supported by the man ropes whilst a large wave was running away, and get to the next mast housing or duck behind a hatch coaming. Once you had the rhythm it was easy. Besides which, there was always somebody watching your back, and the officer on the bridge could be relied on to give you a blast of the horn if anything out of the ordinary lay ahead.

Sailors say that every seventh wave is bigger, and every hundredth wave is bigger still, but the thousandth wave is truly enormous. But you could never really predict it. At any time something could happen to surprise you. You had to be fully on your guard, both for yourself and for the others around. But one thing you could rely on was that every man on board would put their lives on the line for you, just as you would for them. It's a very special relationship that teaches you important things, developing character and strength of mind and heart.

   I once read an account of a Royal Navy frigate, heading across the Atlantic, which was off the coast of West Africa one night. Bad weather was forecast, so the whole ship was rigged for it, with all watertight doors closed and all hatches dogged-down – as indeed we were. All of a sudden the frigate plunged into a huge hole that was moving across the surface of the sea. For a spell it was entirely underwater in a vertical position moving downwards, when at last it stopped and bobbed back up to the surface.

   It was lucky that it was a frigate, fast, light, and water tight with plenty of air trapped inside. Had that been us in our fully-laden ship, heavy and low in the water, we would just have carried on down: never to be heard of again and nobody having any knowledge of what had happened to us.

   At sea you are always vulnerable, whether you are in a rowing boat or a supertanker. You never presume anything, always crossing an ocean with humility and respect, asking its permission each day for safe passage. A true seafarer knows this is all part of the Law of the Sea, which sets us apart from other people. You cannot really come to appreciate this without putting yourself at the mercy of an extreme environment, which allows you to understand the Zen of Life, and how fragile the latter is.

   Eventually the wind continued to drop, the sea became calmer and things began to get back to normal as the storm and ourselves parted company and went our separate ways.

   We now had to tackle two of the nastiest jobs on this part of the trip, namely fish-oiling the mast stays and chipping rust off the decks prior to repainting.

Oiling the stays involved wrapping yourself up in old cloths or hessian to protect yourself from the clinging foul-smelling oil, climbing to the very top of each mast, attaching your bo's'un's chair by shackle to one of the stays at the top, bringing the runner attached to your chair through a block or lizard above you, and dropping the surplus rope down to your tender, who would turn it up on the nearest winch barrel.

Next you'd bring up your bucket full of fish oil on a heaving line. You'd then sit in your bo's'un's chair, having tied your bucket to it, let the runner take the weight, then slide slowly down each stay on the shackle, with your tender down on the deck lowering you via the winch. As you slid down you would work the oil with rags into the wire, getting it to permeate right down to the rope at its core. This stopped the wire rusting from the inside out.

It was an important job to do, lessening the possibility of the wire failing and parting one day when you least expected it, there being nothing to see on the surface. But it was a horrible job. The oil stank really badly and it got everywhere, its smell hanging around on you for days afterwards.

The job was parcelled out among the deck crew of ten men, but as there were about 28 stays throughout the ship it was clear I'd be shimmying up those stays on more than one occasion.

The other nasty job was using the shipping hammers to chip rust off the decks. These machines looked like big heavy vacuum cleaners having a flexible cable with a rotating inner core. This held a cylindrical head with a reinforced snake pipe coming out of it with a series of rotating clusters of small sharp bits of metal. It was a noisy lethal thing that was hard to control and showered bits of rusty paint over the user and anyone else standing nearby. Shifting maybe 30 layers of paint, it took days to go over the whole deck. At the end of each day's work you'd spend your overtime painting the area you'd done with red lead, to be covered eventually by several coats of red or green deck paint. Like oiling the stays it was a horrible job which nobody liked – and the unpleasantness didn't end when the job was done. For days afterwards you'd be extracting bits of rusty paintwork from your ears, nostrils, crack, and every other bodily orifice.

The days passed by as we sailed along in the Gulf Stream. Presently we entered the Sargasso Sea. This is a very strange region of the ocean, covered in clumps of seagrass in varying numbers and sizes. Seagrass is a light-coloured floating seaweed, moving in a wide circle around the Sargasso Sea: the only sea without a shore.

Bounded on all sides by ocean currents, the seagrass circles in a trap formed by the Gulf Stream to the west and north, the Atlantic ridge on its east side and the Caribbean to the South. It is roughly 2,000 miles long by 1,200 miles wide. It's not all seagrass: 40% to 70% of it is clear water of a very deep blue,clean with 200 foot visibility in clear weather. Once upon a time it was thought to be full of trapped or wrecked haunted ships, but this was probably due to it being in the unlucky doldrums, aka the horse latitudes.

The Sargasso Sea is well known as the breeding ground of the freshwater eels of the world – and young loggerhead turtles from the east coast of America arrive on the Gulf Stream, brought by their mothers to hide and feed in the floating seagrass until they mature.

The Sargasso Sea nowadays has large amounts of non-biodegradable plastic waste trapped in it , like the part of the Pacific Ocean known as the Great Pacific Garbage Patch (a mysterious place which has also been the setting for many a haunting tale).

It seems that after many years of rubbish all along the American seaboard being disposed of by simply dumping it in the sea, there is a vast amount of plastic floating permanently in the seagrass. Enough, some think, to make it worthwhile recovering and recycling. The same goes for the North Pacific Gyre, another circulating current which traps non-biodegradable waste. There's a man who sails in those waters who has recently made a business case for doing just that. So should we look upon these natural traps as an environmental nightmare – or a natural store for a valuable resource?

It took us three or four days to pass through the Sargasso Sea, following the Gulf Stream and benefiting from its 1 knot current to get us home. One knot doesn't sound much, but over 14 days it's worth an extra 350 miles, or 24 hours saved in terms of time and money.

With only a short while to go before getting to England, the mood on board was good, and with all the excitement it would generate to tell about the exotic places we'd visited, home was looking sweet. But as I lay awake at night in my lonely bed I would often wonder where "home" actually was. I didn't know where my dad had gone. I had visit my mum at the flat with her new man Rod (so at least I knew she was okay). One brother, Pete, was in the army, but I didn't know where my other brother John was. So what I'd be doing during my leave I'd just have to wait and see. I believe the main problem was that there was no family home for me to think of and return to. I needed to feel a part of home, having a right to be there when I returned. However if you're going to see your family in different new environments, then you're just a visitor.

Perhaps this was my home now – on board ship. Perhaps this was my destiny. Did everything that had happened to me serve the purpose of giving me this sense of freedom at last, after feeling I'd been imprisoned for most of my life, first at home, then at school, neither of them giving my enquiring mind the scope to develop my full potential?

These days it seems to me that education is much more progressive, more person-centred, offering alternative ways to learn based on your special abilities or lack of them. Many disorders like dyslexia, autism, hyperactivity and attention deficit, are now being identified in time to take corrective action. There are free schools, special schools or facilities for home education to help children to learn for whom conventional education would have been useless.

I had many questions for myself that I needed to find answers for.

Journeying on, the heat was as intense as ever, Yet there was a sense of freshness as we moved north-eastward into the northern parts of the North Western Atlantic Basin. I did not know the exact course we were taking at the time, we must have been at the latitude of New York, which was roughly 1,500 to 2,000 miles north-west of us at one point. Perhaps closer to us at another the south-eastern tip of Newfoundland Island, level with the USA-Canada border.

It was then mid-May, so when we arrived back in the UK it would be the start of summer there. Wherever I ended up, it promised to be a pleasant leave – weather-wise at least.

Having finished chipping the decks we now had to cover them with the usual multiple layers of paint. Most ships' decks were painted red, as was ours. However the upper decks, notably the boat decks, were laid with wood planks set in bitumen caulking. The wood was usually of a hard variety – ash or white mahogany – but teak was preferred. It was regularly scrubbing these decks that I was introduced to "holy stoning". This procedure used a lump of sandstone, the shape and size of a large brick, secured to the end of a 12 foot broomstick with a bolted metal strap so it could be replaced when it was worn down. You'd wet down an area of the deck and sprinkle it with detergent and sand, then push and pull the stone with the handle. This literally sanded down the deck whilst washing it. Afterwards you'd rinse it off with the deck hose.

The hoses were intended as fire appliances, but were generally used for washing down the ship, which was done most mornings at sea. They delivered salt water pumped up from the engine room.

There was also a fresh water system for drinking, cooking and washing up with, as well as cleaning the decks and bulkheads prior to painting. The water was desalinated seawater, processed through carbon filters and stored in tanks. There was also a system supplying chilled drinking water throughout the ship. It was fresh drinking water, brought aboard and kept in separate tanks.

So the days went by, up at 8 o'clock for a 9 o'clock start, peering out of the porthole to watch the ever-changing weather. Increasingly there was wind and rain as we headed into the

North Atlantic on the warm waters of the Gulf stream. The flying fish reappeared, breaking surface and gliding away from our bow wave, which was fun to watch in our breaks.

As well as the monkey island I was in the habit of visiting the fo'c's'le head and staring down at our bow wave slicing its way through the sea. I was reminded of the dolphins swimming just in front of our prow as we entered the port of Adelaide. They always seemed to be rubbing their tail flukes on a special point on the bow. This was the very point at which the unsuspecting sea began to part, gently at first, then forcefully, as 10,000 tons of steel and sugar drove through. The effect was most noticeable when the sea was calm and smooth, but not at all when there was a large sea running. At those times, far from the water allowing us to part it gently, huge walls of water would roll towards us like so many upraised hands declaring "No! You shall not pass!"

There were times when the resisting hands achieved exactly that. If the storm was strong enough, the force of wind and waves would stop the ship in its track. Then all we could do was stand our ground and keep her head pointing into the oncoming waves. Thanks to our powerful engine we could manage that on most occasions.

Sometimes the ship would move backwards with the whole mass of the sea around it, surging through the water at full speed ahead, but making absolutely no progress.

One can imagine the difficulties faced by the square-riggers of old in such conditions. All they could do then was to "heave to", which meant setting the sails as best they could to keep the ship's head facing into the wind as she was slowly forced backwards, and slightly sideways. It was an extremely hazardous situation for a sailing ship, especially in coastal waters, where they had the tide, the shore, shallow waters and other ships to contend with.

In those long periods spent at sea, there was less to worry about during an actual storm than in the fear of one occurring in the days that lay ahead.

Every day was occupied with working, and every day would be different. There would be large skies with different cloud formations, and the sea and the daylight had different colours and a different look about them. The day would be enlivened by banter and games. There'd be a drink in the evening – and of course there was no shortage of books to read. I always had a book on the go, to read before I went to sleep: a sleep filled with dreams inspired by the events of the day, or by wondering about, and premonitions of, what lay ahead.

Inspiration was everywhere. At 16 years of age I didn't really notice it at the time. Retrospection is a wonderful thing.

However the profundity of those days definitely left its mark on me. It gave me an intuitive education, a confidence, and a feeling of presence on the earth that is still with me. It has opened many doors in the past, and still does to this day.

By now we had crossed the North Eastern Atlantic basin, and were into St George's Channel, heading for the southern tip of Ireland before entering the Irish Sea. Closing St David's Head, off the Pembrokeshire coast, was the occasion of another seafaring tradition. This was the last night at sea, the night we needed to finish up the beer in the bar and say our farewells to each other, as pay-off day was always a bit frantic, everyone doing their last-minute packing and aiming to get home as soon as possible. It was also the time to throw away everything you didn't want to carry back home. Such as your work clothes, by now ragged and covered in paint. Anyone hesitant about getting rid of it, or some other article we'd all seen too much of, would be taunted into throwing it "over the wall" into the tide, or the "ogin".

Next morning, heavy-headed from all the beer we'd drunk, we turned-to early. I had a little radio record-player I'd bought cheaply in Las Palmas, which had done good service in the party cabin. Although reception was poor I managed to pick up BBC Radio One. I recall hearing on the Tony Blackburn Show the first-time broadcast of a new entry into the charts: *Sugar Sugar* by The Archers. Brand-new in the UK at that time, yet we'd heard it to death on the Australian coast. Similarly with *Yellow River*, *Ruby*, and *The Wild Side Of Life*.

I had tuned-in to the BBC because I was desperate to hear news of what had been happening in England in the five months we'd been away. We had set out in January and it was now late may.

We came around Anglesey past Holyhead and entered Liverpool Bay and the approaches to the Mersey – and pay-off. We were all very excited and looking forward to 20 days leave. Sadly however this was not to be. At least, not just yet.

—oOo—

After a morning of pretending to work whilst constantly looking over the water towards Liverpool as we edged closer, trying to make out structures we knew, or even people, we went to stations at lunchtime only to drop anchor in the Bay along with another 20 or so other ships. This might have been a normal occurrence, as quite often there would be a queue to enter the larger docks, for a berth, or simply to wait for the tide. All the larger docks were very busy in those days: containerisation was only just starting to appear, and handling of cargoes dockside was still very labour-intensive.

But after dropping anchor, the chief officer told us on the foredeck there was a tug strike on. It was uncertain when we'd be able to go in. Even after they'd resolved the issue at stake it would still take a few days to clear the backlog of ships: both those waiting to get in and those waiting to get out.

It was a strange time for everybody in the industry. The unions could see a lot of change coming with the new technology. Increased mechanisation would threaten many of their members' jobs, and the unions themselves would battle for survival. Against all this the greatest weapon was to strike, sending the message that cost-saving measures were going to require their cooperation. This hit companies badly in the pocket: it cost on average about £3,000 per day just to keep a ship in a UK port. So delays like this were very expensive for the company.

Meanwhile all we could do was wait and see what happened.

—oOo—

This of course was a devastating blow to all of us, and we had to settle back down to painting. We spent most of our time touching up parts we had painted much earlier in the trip, where the rust was showing signs of coming back, or the surface was getting dulled from the constant exposure to salt spray. We concentrated on the areas around the ladder to the Accommodation, midships. This was where visitors would board the ship – company men. It would give them a good impression when first coming aboard.

A major disappointment for me was missing my father's wedding. I'd received a telegram telling me it was happening in three days time. I had no idea who he was marrying! I had hoped to make it, but it was not to be.

I did however manage to send off a telegram to him. It read: "Greetings and congratulations from the Irish Sea. Weather forecast: close, becoming hot and sticky later". Years later I heard that when it was read out at the reception my father commented "What's he doing, going on about the weather?" He had a poor sense of humour.

As it happened, the marriage was short-lived, so I suppose it was no great shame to have missed it.

After a week we were at last able to watch tugs escorting piloted vessels in and out of the port, clearing the backlog of ships at anchor.

The ships that had finally begun moving again were of all types and sizes, and from many different nations. Some were in the middle of delivering cargo from all over the world to ports in the UK and Europe. A few, like us, were British ships back home after long voyages, their crews looking forward to going home to family and friends with presents to give and stories to tell of far-off exotic places – some, even censored hard to believe.

At last it was our turn. Early one beautiful day the rumble of the engine vibrated through the ship, and a plume of smoke from the funnel headed downwind. We brought the pilot aboard from a typical Nelson launch with its throaty twin Gardner engines.

We turned-to for stations and headed into the Mersey from the Bay, taking the lines from two tugs before turning sharply into the huge lock for admission to the dock. The whole operation took about two hours. We were accompanied by the tugs manoeuvring through the numerous cuts, passing many other ships on the way. Finally we let go of the tugs and tied up alongside the sugar silos, where our cargo of cane sugar would be unloaded.

In those days Britain only had three months supply of imported food commodities. So we were just one small part of an essential supply chain.

Now our job was done. All our derricks had already been topped, and our very last job was to swing them outboard so the shoreside cranes could gain access to the hatches. At the same time, The Tin Lids were being pulled open for immediate unloading to commence.

The knock-on effects from the tug strike was surprising, as the dockers had been idle after dealing with all the ships to-hand, as had the transport trucks delivering and collecting goods, plus a backlog of barges waiting to head up the Manchester Ship Canal, or the Leeds-Liverpool. It affected the income of many families, and thus the whole economy at grass-roots level. The repercussions of the strike were immense: it contributed to the Tory party wanting to destroy the unions, who still held tightly to their traditional ways, many of them dwindling and obsolete. The world changes – and in the end people have to change with it.

We had arrived in dock and finished work early, but since we were not paid off until 2 PM we went ashore for a drink. Coincidentally we were there with the *Trewidden*, another Hain-Nourse ship, one I'd been associated with before. Sure enough, in the nearest pub to our berth was the bo's'un of that ship, a man I knew called Sparrow.

He was a really small, tough little fellow who drank like a fish. But it was good to see him again, as it made me feel part of things, reminding me of the long road I'd come and the chain of circumstances that brought me to this point. It represented a sort of closure.

Although this had been my first deep sea voyage as a deck boy, I had actually been to sea briefly before on the *Trewidden*.

After that welcome pint of decent beer we said farewell to Sparrow, as it was now time to return aboard for pay-off and then head off home.

Home? Where was that now?

I returned to my cabin for the next-to-last time, to find a baggage pass from the Black Gang (the Customs and Excise men). One of my two extra packets of 20 Dunhill cigarettes over the 200 limit was gone, leaving me just 20 extra, so they'd gone 50-50 with me. Fair enough.

The Black Gang had come aboard at the sea lock to search the ship, check the paperwork and leave baggage passes for us to exit the dock with. This was all quite normal. Not quite so normal was the police coming aboard at the same time, arresting one of the two catering boys and taking him away with them.

We heard later that he had allegedly hit someone on the head with a hammer during an affray. It was a sad ending to the trip for him. A Scouser, he seemed a nice enough lad, although he kept to himself and never spent much time with us.

But there again – the catering staff led a different life to us. Their work was a compulsory seven days a week, both at sea and in port. We, on the other hand, could go ashore and explore at the weekends.

That's why I transferred to the deck department when I got the chance, though due to circumstances I had started in catering. I changed to the deck department in spite of the fact that catering was where the money was – they always earned and saved far more money than us deckies.

Leaving my cabin, I went up to the officers' saloon with the others to sign off and get our discharge books. Mine was duly stamped with two "Very-Goods" for ability and conduct. This was the system that served as a reference for my next ship.

I also collected my money – or what remained of it after deductions such as tax, national insurance, fines, money paid-in directly to my bank (known as an allotment), my shop and bond bill, and of course various sums of cash to spend while ashore in the ports we'd visited.

It worked out like this:
Gross pay   £115 4s 0d
Overtime: 64 hours at 1/9   £64 13s 9d
Total £200 3s 9d
...

The end result was: £18 2s 3d in cash, plus £72 paid-in to my bank. That didn't give me much cash-in-hand, but they also gave me a train pass to get back to the port at which I'd signed on, namely London.

We all recovered our hidden contraband just before leaving. I'd put mine in a fire extinguisher outside my cabin. The only other person whose hiding place I can recall was Chris, who'd hid his on the after-deck, folded up in the Red Ensign, which was brought down and folded at foot when not at sea.

Having got our pay and signed off, with our cigarettes now in our bags, all that was left was to say our goodbyes, order a taxi and head for the station.

As we left the dock, the taxi driver slipped the policeman on the gate two pound notes in amongst our baggage passes from customs. It represented ten shillings each from us four passengers. This was the drill to avoid getting searched on leaving the dock.

I learned later that this little tradition would triple or quadruple the average policeman's income, which made manning the dock gate a much sought-after job. Across the country, £2 from each of an estimated six taxis per ship's crew would soon mount up, making a sizeable contribution to the black economy. And that wasn't the only thing to seep through the porous gates of our ports.

I heard of one case where a solid bronze ship's propeller went missing one night from a London dry dock. It would have needed a large crane and a low-loader to shift. They must have come into the dock through the main gate, loaded up the propeller and left again the same way. And – would you believe it – nobody saw a thing.

We cheerfully waved goodbye to the *Trebartha*, took the London train from Liverpool Lime Street, spent four hours of the journey drinking, and finally went our separate ways. Chris headed for Paddington en-route for Devon. Abby went to Liverpool Street for Colchester, and I headed for Euston to get to Watford.

Travelling with us was the second cook, a middle-aged Jamaican who had left his homeland during WW2 to settle in England. Whilst getting here he had been torpedoed twice, and rescued twice. For all that, he decided to make a career of the sea, trained as a chef – and that was what he'd been doing ever since.

On the train he had got into a card game and lost his entire pay-off money. So he was heading straight back to the KG5 pool to get another job. I couldn't believe it at the time, but he had no home, spent all his spells of leave in seamen's missions, plus partying in London in the Soho area. That was his life. I felt extremely sad for him. I've never forgotten him and I wish I could remember his name.

—oOo—

I arrived back in Watford, not sure where to go myself. By then it was early evening. I had my mum's phone number and called her from the station. She and her partner Rod were still in their rented flat in Bushey, near Watford. So that's where I went.

It was only a one-bedroomed flat in a large semi-detached corner house, so they made up a bed for me in the living room. To my surprise, when I arrived they were all pleased to see me, which made it a sort of a homecoming after all.

We spent a long time chatting, me telling them about the voyage and hearing all the local news, such as dad getting married the previous Saturday whilst I was anchored off Liverpool. He was still in his new wife's council house, her two youngish step children living not so far away. My other brother, Pete, was back from the BAOR in Germany and living in army married quarters in Colchester with his wife Angie and their first child Karen.

On the whole it was a difficult time I spent with them. The events of the recent past had sundered us and we were no longer a family. I feel that once a family has had its heart torn out with the breakdown of the parents' relationship, it means there's little point in reminiscing about the past, reaffirming the connection with each other and enjoying the nostalgia of old memories. The end game overwhelms all else. It gave me no confidence in my own future, especially as regards relationships, marriage and building a family.

Maybe it was different for my brothers. They had moved into adulthood and were able to understand the situation better and learn from it, applying it to their own marriages. I, however, did not – and it plagued me in all the failed relationships I was yet to experience. Consequently my leave was a lukewarm one, as I had seen the family and looked at my home town from a new and very different perspective.

However I did try to look up a few old school friends and managed to visited two of them. But I found it difficult to connect with them, being unable to relate to their lives. They seemed mundane and lacking in vision from my new perspective, which now was quite literally worldwide. With my mind on my next voyage of adventure, I actually hesitated to tell them about my fantastic new life, afraid they'd feel I was belittling theirs.

There was one exception though, a lad who'd been a good friend of mine in my last few years at school. I didn't see him at home, but I spoke to his mother and discovered that, like me, he'd joined the merchant navy soon after I left their house, where I had stayed for a short while before leaving. I was delighted with this news, which I'd never even suspected, and said I hoped to meet up with him again in my travels. He was an unusual person: he suffered from epilepsy, his father too had left home, and when ashore my friend now lived with his mother.

—oOo—

At last my leave came to an end and I happily said my goodbyes again, and returned to the East End of London, where I registered with the KG5 pool, and scanned the large board each day for the jobs that were going.

The London pool was a mixed bag of seamen. The ships sailing out of the Royal Docks went mainly to Australasia, South America and Africa. Our nickname was the "KG5 Cowboys" – and we were proud of it. Most of the destinations were good runs ashore, especially Oz and Kiwi. Party-party and good women.

So, having signed-on in order to receive money from the pool while waiting for a job to come up, I checked into the *Flying Angel* Seamen's Mission at Silver Town, a short bus ride away cheap accommodation run by the Church of England. I had a connection with the *Flying Angel*, before, as I had resided there prior to going deep sea, working for my keep at one point.

So it was nice meeting up with the staff again, especially Jeff the proprietor. It gave me the opportunity to thank him for being so good to me when I was at my most vulnerable.

So here I was, back in London. I met up again with Chris and a few others– it was good to see them all again after our three weeks' leave. I didn't have much to say about my time at home – or perhaps I should say my spell back in Watford. But Chris had lots to say about being back in Devon. It sounded like he had done a lot of partying. However he was happy to be back in London, and excited to think where our next voyage could be taking us.

It was around Midsummer's Day, 22nd June, so our spirits were high. Most days would commence with heading down to the KG5 pool to see what jobs were on offer. I thought it would be good for us to get a job on the same ship, as we got on so well. This did make finding a job a bit more difficult. But we still had money, so we were not in any great hurry. Besides, things were changing for me in a very profound way.

I'd grown up a great deal in the past six months. Many of us had started to experiment with smoking hash, and I found it to be a much more interesting alternative to our continual drinking. After visiting the KG5 pool we'd head out for some lunch in the pub, or back to the Mission, where there was a jukebox, snooker table, table-tennis and TV.

We'd also go to the cinema in East Ham. This was mainly in the afternoons, as our evenings were taken up with having dinner, smoking a bit of hash, having a few drinks, getting more stoned, having some more drinks – and then out to the local pubs which had live bands, or taking a taxi up to the West End and hanging out there all night.

One or two of the other lads from the *Trebartha* were back in town too, including Abby, and we'd also made some new friends. So Chris and I had managed to gather quite a group around us, of all sorts, from all over the country. Cooks and other catering staff, donkey men (engine cleaners) as well as deckies like ourselves.

MV Pacific Stronghold

MV Pacific Stronghold

This carefree life went on for about two weeks. However we were all running out of money, so on 8th August we took jobs: Chris as SOS and myself as a deck boy, on a little ship called the *Pacific Stronghold*, owned by Furness Withy & Co. Ltd.

This was just a temporary job for us, doing the "home trade" – or "rock dodging", as old hands used to call it. The ship was built in 1958, 9,439 tons gross, refrigerated cargo just for hatches, and was in London discharging cargo from her last deep sea voyage from the West Coast of America. It had been a mixed cargo of peas, beans, cheese and other foodstuff.

We were only aboard her for eight days after joining her on 8 July. The next day we took her out of London's KG5 dock. We negotiated our way out of the docks, through the swing bridge and headed out through the sea lock at the top of the tide around 1400 hours. After releasing the tugs we used the ebb tide to bring us down the Thames and out into the estuary, after leaving the pilot at Gravesend. Once clear of the shifting sandbanks we headed north, continuing up the coast past the approaches to Harwich and Felixstowe.

I was amazed at how much traffic there was. It was a nightmare for navigation, especially for the lookouts on the watch. I was still a boy rating, so I didn't do watches and was supposed to keep to day work. However, with so much traffic, I had to wait until late that evening to do my practice helm for my ticket.

I recall standing at the helm for an hour that night, following a compass course, obeying occasional manoeuvring commands to avoid other ships, or according to marked navigation changes-of-course timed from the sail plan, which had been pre-drafted by either the second officer. the navigation officer.

I was on the third watch with the captain on the bridge. Occasionally I would look over to the port side, where I could see the lights of the coast. Sometimes I could make out car headlights moving along when closer inshore.

In contrast, ahead and to starboard (out to sea) I saw a mass of ships' lights: white, green and red, plus flashing lights from the navigation channel and wreck buoys, and bright flashing lights from lighthouses or lightships. These temporarily lit up the sea around us as one of the synchronised signature beams passed over us.

There were regular reports of new lights from the lookout as they appeared on the horizon. Given this information, someone – the third officer or one of the two officer cadets – would find it as a contact on the radar and plot its movement. This gave the watch officer a clear picture of the sea around us, and a prediction of where all the other contacts were going or not.

All this was necessary to enable us to navigate safely through a minefield of traffic, in what was at that time the busiest stretch of water in the world. Hopefully, if all the other ships were doing the same thing, we would be able to pass through safely.

It felt really good to be back at sea again. It was very exciting and I had that incredible feeling of control and confidence again. Once I could see and feel 9,000 tons of ship move as I steered, knowing it needed all our wits and concentration to navigate through the apparent chaos.

I eventually got to sleep that night after getting used to the motion again. At 4 AM we were all turned-to and came out on deck to a lovely summer dawn. We were passing Spurn Head: a long finger of land protruding from the north shore of the Humber Estuary which sheltered the pilot station.

It was a beautiful morning. I remember looking down at the familiar churning waters as we passed through the channel where this large fast river empties into the North Sea, adjacent to Grimsby on the southern shore.

Within an hour, after a big mug of tea, we were called to stations. I was on the fo'c's'le head crowd again. We took the lines of the tugs and moved through the lock, settling in our berth in the Alexandra Dock under the direction of our Spurn pilot. We made fast and were done by 8 AM, when we went to breakfast.

There was a very strange deckhand on board from Hull, whom we nicknamed Batman. This was mainly because he wore a cape when not working, and seem to be flying about back-and-forth from the ship all night.

He was what I would come to know as a "speed freak". He introduced us to the wonders of Benzedrine ("speed") and Dexedrine ("dexies"). I thought they were marvels: they gave me a great sense of euphoria – everything and everybody was just wonderful. So our stay in Hull consisted of working by day and quite literally speeding around town all night. It made you very thirsty, so naturally it needed to be washed down with pints of beer, topped off with the occasional joint of hash.

Our work on board mostly consisted of cleaning up the holds after the shoreside dockers had finished discharging the cargo from them. It was bizarre work: there were all sorts of mess to remove. I remember it being great fun though.

In reality we were all still hung-over each day after the drugs we'd taken, having had little or no sleep. We spent most of the work time down in the hold playing around, throwing large lumps of discarded cheese at each other and taking off the broad Yorkshire accents of the dockers. How we managed to survive I don't know, but we had a good time on that ship.

With the job all done we found ourselves paid-off and, given our usual train pass, back to London to find another ship. Life readjusted to relative normality, but without the "speed". Batman must have gone back to his cave. He was seriously into the stuff: whereas we might take 10 pills, he would down 30 or 40. It was highly addictive – and he was addicted.

We never saw him again.

After we were paid off, the *Pacific Stronghold* was sold off to a Greek company and renamed *Aegis Honor*. Then she was sold on to another company in 1972 and renamed *Famagusta*. Eventually, sadly, in 1974 she was broken up in Whampoa, Singapore.

As for us, we were back in the Seamen's Mission, having signed on again at the pool. What were we going to do next? In the meantime it was back to the old routine: down to the pool in the morning looking for jobs and hanging out for the rest of the day.

—oOo—

We had got back to London on 17 July. One afternoon we were sitting in the Mission drinking a few pints of beer when, out of the blue, in through the door walks John. Well, after a lot of hooting, big hellos and cuddles, we settled down and he told us his story.

It turned out that after jumping ship at Brisbane he got a job for a week or so driving a truck around a large quarry. Then with the money he made he went off back to Melbourne to try and catch up with Sandy again. Unfortunately when he got there she was with somebody else and she told him she was only interested in permanent relationships anyway. So John turned himself in to the authorities, was deported and came back on a passenger liner as a DBS, that is: a Distressed British Seaman, not so far behind us. So we were now back to normal again with our small group, intending to ship out together once more. He was a bit crazy, John, but we had missed him.

MV Douro

MV Douro

We soon found a ship to fit the bill and could accommodate us all as she was looking for a full crew. However she was in Rotterdam. So we got packed up and, having been given plane tickets, we flew out from Gatwick. We arrived at the ship and signed ships' articles on 23 July 1970.

She was the *MV Douro*, an old fridge ship owned by the Royal Mail Line since 1969. She was built in 1946, around 10,785 grt, twin-screwed and flat-bottomed. She had six hatches, one with seven "tween decks", all with giant refrigerators.

Formerly known as the *Hornby Grange*, she was then owned by Holder Brothers and employed specially to take general cargo down to the South American East Coast, returning with Fray Bentos beef from Buenos Aires in Argentina. It was usually a quick trip of about 2½ months, the ships being known as the "BA Flyers". Though not in the case of the *Douro*. She was too old to "fly", doing around 14 knots, unlike the newer Blue Star boats that now made 21 knots.

She was the proverbial Sight For Sore Eyes as we arrived at her berth, nestling in amongst the vast sea harbour that is Rotterdam. Older in design, very square-looking, with a bow that went straight-up-and-down, wooden decks and white railings which exposed the deck to the sea, unlike the solid bulwarks found on newer ships.

The three of us went aboard. John and Chris, as SOSs, shared a cabin. I was buddied-up with a lad from London – the less said about him the better. The accommodation was small and dingy. However it was midships on the main deck, making it handy not having to go aft each night.

She was also what was loosely termed a cargo liner. As I discovered, this meant she could accommodate 12 first-class passengers, in accommodation which was surprisingly salubrious compared to ours, or judged by how the ship looked on the outside.

She also had a small swimming pool aft of the passenger saloon on the boat deck, and a huge crew of about 70 souls. This was mainly due to additional engineers to service the fridges and her very big old engine. Apart from a normal engineering crew there were four fridge engineers as well as donkey men, plus additional catering staff to look after them. Most modern ships had a far smaller crew – the *Trebartha* only having about 35.

The *Douro* was not a bad old girl. But she lived up to the reputation of twin-screwed ships, that they were very difficult to steer due to cavitation. She also had a flat bottom like a barge, which meant she would roll badly at sea, especially in heavy weather.

Her flat bottom was because she had been purpose-built to withstand grounding in the tidal meat berths at Dock Sue in Buenos Aires. She was in Rotterdam for repairs. Now these were completed, we would be leaving and heading for London to load general cargo for a string of destinations, including Rio de Janeiro, Montevideo on the River Plate, and Buenos Aires.

We let go of our holding berth on the tide. I was on the "after deck crowd". It took a little time to work out how the winches functioned and where the various mooring lines were coiled down.

There were generally three stern lines: large polypropylene ropes which went down and out astern of us, plus two shorelines directly adjacent to the quay. Then there was the spring: this would normally be a mixture of rope and wire leading forward onto the quay from the quarterdeck to midships.

With three tugs in attendance, we headed out into the main stream, the Calandka Canal. Then, coming west, we entered the Nievee Waterweg, going out past the Hook of Holland into the North Sea.

It was a wonder how things all worked in this very busy port cluttered with ships, barges, tugs and small waterman craft hustling and bustling around. It must have been a very stressful time for the officers and the helmsman, whilst we, the rest of the crew, just watched this city of ships go by.

We eventually let go the tugs and headed out into the North Sea, briefly pausing to drop the pilot. We continued out in a south-westerly direction, heading for the Thames estuary and the London docks. It was an uneventful trip that took us a day and night.

We came upriver on the tide, taking on the pilot at Gravesend. We were shadowed by the sun tugs until, approaching Greenwich, we took their lines. We went through the sea loch and manoeuvred through the KG5 dock, through the cut, into the basin, then through the swing bridge into the Albert Dock, continuing on up to nearly the last berth by the now familiar F shed. This was next to the meat berth at G shed, synonymous with the Argentinian meat trade It normally took about 2 to 3 hours to perform this manoeuvre.

We passed all the other British company ships: Blue Star, Bank Line, Castle, Federal, Port Line, Shaw Savill, and other boats from our own Royal Mail line, but of the Furness Withy Group.

Like all the ships from the aforementioned companies, the *Douro* was a regular here. She was quite a lady, and there is a story attached to her birth. She was commissioned by Holder Bros specifically for the Argentine beef trade (Fray Bentos) and was launched at Hebburn, Tyneside, in 1946. At that time she was the largest fridge ship afloat.

Earlier in the century, with the brisk meat trade with Argentina, Holder Bros had commissioned their own fridge ship in 1890 – the steamer *Hornby Grange*. The name was used again when the present ship was built by Hebburn shipbuilders Hawthorn Leslie, which subsequently became Swan Hunter. She was delivered in December 1946.

Later in the 1960s, most of the shipping companies operating the world trade were combined into the Furness Group, especially those involved in the now declining Argentinian meat trade. In 1968 the *Hornby Grange* was sold to the Royal Mail Lines owned by Furness and renamed the *Douro*. It was the last few years of her trading life and she was eventually dismantled in Spain in 1972.

Now she was in London, loading for South America, so we had a few days in the capital, Chris, John and myself. We visited our usual haunts: the Missions. The Bridge House in Canning Town was a good spot for live bands, all knocking out rock covers of current chart numbers. We always managed to find a bit of dope, and sometimes some speed. Quite often, after a night of sneaking joints and drinking light bitter after an evening listening to a cover of the likes of *All Right Now* (Free), we would grab a cab and head up to the West End in search of more action, plus the elusive "acid" everybody was talking about but we hadn't tried yet. We knew it was very strong and not to be messed with. However we had no idea just how powerful it was, and what a profound effect it would have on our lives, both present and future.

For the present, alcohol was our main tipple, and smoking joints was a peripheral activity. However we were meeting more and more people who were well into it all. We were all growing our hair, and creating our own subculture: "hippy sailors" – yes!

Soon enough however, whatever we did the night before, we were always back on board the *Douro*, ready for breakfast and turning-to for work. That meant working among the chaos of assorted cargoes being loaded by the dockers into the various holds.

There would be a very clear loading plan, calculated by the company's supercargoes and the chief officer. All-and-sundry of cargo would be brought on board, stowed safely and shored up by the carpenters, complete with their hammers and bundles of 4"×2" dunnage used for that purpose.

We spent most of our time tidying up, plus loading ship's stores: the vast amounts which were going to be needed for an anticipated 2 to 3 month voyage. Also, as each hold was completed, we shored up all its derricks, perhaps stowing them by dropping them down into the crutches – the usual procedure for deep sea voyages.

Interestingly you could always recognise an American ship at sea, as the derricks would always be topped. This was because the crew were awarded a bonus every time they had to top them. Therefore the companies tended to leave them topped, only lowering them in anticipation of very heavy weather.

We had a great deal of energy in those days. We'd work hard all day, then play hard all night – at least most of the time. Sometimes we would get the first underground train in the morning back from the West End to Stratford, take the 69 bus to Silvertown and the docks and drop in for a pint at 5 AM in the Connaught, a pub found at the swing bridge between the KG5 and Victoria Docks, close to F shed. The pub had a 24-hour licence and opened at 4 AM for the dockers on the night shift, as they worked unsociable hours on an alternating 24-hour system. As this was their "evening" it enabled them to have a drink after work.

The day came when the Blue Peter flew from the flagstaff on the foremast, traditionally raised 24-hours prior to sailing. We finished off battening down the hatches. These were of the old type (unlike the McGregor), having sliding beams and hatch boards, all with several large heavy canvases secured by wooden-wedged steel batons.

"Station, lads," the old bo's'un called fore and aft. This time I was still on the after crowd (at the stern) with the second officer. We made fast to the two tugs standing by. The now-familiar SUN tugs, based at Wapping, have been working on the river since 1883. The original company also had lighters plus some ships. At their peak they had nine tugs and 150 barges, some of which were involved in the Dunkirk evacuation. In 1969 they came under the ownership of Ships Towage Ltd.

Most times, when leaving or arriving on the Thames, you'd see SUN tugs on the pier at Gravesend, which was generally where you would be joined or left by the tugs and pilots. Now with the tugs made fast, and with the usual tooting of horns used for communication (the ship and tugs also talking to each other via radio or intercoms carrying orders from the pilot and captain on the bridge) we received their order to Single up, then let go all lines, and depart.

It was now the end of July. Aiming to catch the ebb tide we made our way down the Albert dock, through the swing bridge, into the basin, then east into the lock at the bottom of the KG5. There was quite a lot of work for us to do in the lock as we still had to put out a temporary shoreline whilst in it. It was a bit tricky as the tugs would also come into the lock with us.

We moved out of the lock and headed downstream as usual, just below the North Woolwich Ferry, and the hive of wharves including the Tate & Lyle sugar refinery that I'd worked at for a few weeks the previous year whilst living in the Seamen's Mission.

The amount of time the tugs assisted us would vary from ship to ship, weather conditions, pilot confidence, insurance and other economic considerations. Companies would be charged by the hour, or according to tonnage as in the Panama canal.

We left the tugs at Gravesend along with the pilot and gave the seven long blast on the horn which denoted heading out to deep sea. Then off we went, heading south-east into the hazardous Thames estuary, then around the Kent coast and into the bottleneck of the Dover Straits, "ferry dodging" in the fading light.

It was the usual procedure on turning to the next morning. As the watchman hosed down the decks – a morning ritual performed every day at sea – we day-workers started to get things sorted out. Because we were still on three-man watches, we were shorthanded on deck. We had to check that everything was stowed or lashed down securely, and to clear the deck of all rubbish along with the surplus piles of dunnage.

The sheer waste of throwing all this wood over the wall never ceased to amaze me. In my more recent experience of small sailing craft, it was a dangerous practice to. Hitting a large piece of wood could easily hole the hull, break a prop or destroy a fishing net. I wonder where it all ends up? Washed ashore, no doubt, On the coast of France, Britain, the Isles of Scilly, the Channel Isles or even Ireland, there are probably buildings or even works of art made from some of it.

Eventually we got everything stowed away. By then we were heading into the Bay of Biscay out of close quarters, so the ship went back to one man on a watch. This put the rest of the crew back on day work, so now with ample hands we settled into 16 more days of sea, heading south-westerly across the Atlantic towards our first port of call: Santos, Brazil, on the central coast of South America in the South Atlantic.

Quite often I would find myself standing on the stern, or on the monkey island, just watching the sky and the cloud formations. Or on the bow, watching the ship move ahead, taking deep breaths of air and being happy simply for its freshness. After a few months of messing around "rock dodging", it was great to be back deep sea again, blowing away the cobwebs and the stale emotions of the occasional trip home.

Having turned 17, I was maturing, gaining confidence in myself and making some good sound friends. I was learning about companionship and how to get along with others, forming a deeper understanding of my obligations as a crew member. It felt that now with all the new experience I was having, plus the mind-altering drugs I had been introduced to, were revealing other ways of looking at the world, at politics and social behaviour. My own past experience, plus the values handed down to me by my elders, were being reassessed.

Meanwhile, to be back at sea, looking out into this pure earth of ours, gave me an inexplicable feeling. Years later I've come to the conclusion it's a feeling of presence: being present on the earth, and becoming aware of it, confirming my very existence. There was also something about the *Douro* itself: it had a completely different feeling to my previous ships.

I woke up one morning in the Bay of Biscay to find we were sailing along the large swell, which made us roll badly. My cabin was on the port side amidships – where all the accommodation was. Below the main deck, I could see out of my porthole that we were heeled over so far at times I was quite worried.

One moment I would be staring at the sea surface close up, being nearly tipped out of my bunk, the next moment I would be squashed against the bulkhead staring up at the sky. The ship would labour slowly from one extreme to the other. It was most alarming.

This was due to her being flat-bottomed. She was basically a large refrigerated barge: a unique ship, apart from a slightly larger similar counterpart, the *Duquesa* (Furness-Holder Argentine Lines). The *Douro* was famously hard work to steer, with Her T2 engines had a very particular sound of their own, like no other ship I sailed on. When cruising at service speed (i.e. the economic rpm of the engines, giving 14 knots) she sounded much like the background track of Led Zeppelin's *Whole Lot of Love* strangely.

Two other interesting aspects of the ship deserve mention. Firstly, she had a small swimming pool on the passenger boat deck for the use of officers and passengers – plus us crew members at certain times. This was marvellous on very hot days.

Secondly she had a snooker table – an unlikely thing to find on a ship, for obvious reasons. But instead of balls it had pucks, like big draughts pieces, and was made of smooth plywood painted green. Otherwise it was just like a normal table, with cues and pockets. It was superb, and we had tournaments among ourselves and against the fridge engineers. It was surprising how skilled you could get at it, relatively speaking. It proved to be a very popular way of passing the time, in addition to darts, cards, reading and drinking. And pleasingly, until it ran out, a little Lebanese and Moroccan dope.

I have to say that most crew members didn't drink during work time or watches, though I was certain one or two of the older hands sometimes sneaked a quick one. Some of them, after years at sea, were virtually alcoholics – it's hard to see how they could have avoided it. But as soon as it got so bad that they'd start missing a watch, or a turn-to, they'd be disciplined or with the way things were going thrown out.

When at sea it's dangerous not to have all your wits about you, especially in heavy weather, when anything could happen. As well as the danger to the ship, your obligations to other crew members would be compromised. You need to be able to have complete confidence in your crew mates, and them in you. Any doubts about that have to be sorted out quickly.

My friends and I were careful not to drink or get stoned on duty. There was one occasion on the *Douro* when we missed two hours at the end of a day shift in port, but apart from that we never misbehaved on any of the ships we were on. You just know instinctively what's acceptable and what isn't. The captain and the officers know this, regardless of what we might get up to in our own time or ashore. They have to be sure that in an emergency – something never far away whilst at sea – you can be relied upon to play your part.

Daily life at sea is pretty repetitive. Most jobs get scheduled to be done at some time during the voyage: overhauling the running gear, wires, winches, ropes, boats, safety gear and so forth, in addition to the endless painting and fighting rust. Short two-month trips were famous for overtime, since it was impossible to do all the work needing to be done inside normal hours. But not the longer ones, as the work was spread out over a six-month period.

But there were opportunities for extra overtime cleaning out the refrigerated hold whilst general cargo was being discharged at ports on the South American coast, in order to be in ballast on arrival at Buenos Aires.

In those days the once-vibrant trade that had been going on for the past 80 years along the east coast of South America was winding down. To maintain commercial viability on this trade route, ships had to take whatever cargo they could get.

Only a few years earlier there had been many refrigerated cargo liners, plus three large Royal Mail Line passenger ships: *Amazon*, *Andes* and *Akaroa*, along with the Blue Star fridge boats known as the "BA Flyers". Now however most of the fridge boats had been transferred to the Australian and New Zealand lamb trade.

Yet even that was slowly coming to an end. Little did we know it, but the pool (the federation) and the traditional companies would soon all be gone. We were close to the demise of the British Merchant Navy, as it was known.

So we settled into our new routine. Chris and John were by now senior ordinary seamen (SOS). I was still a deck boy and sharing a cabin with a fellow from Stratford, London, a tall lad who acquired the name "bonehead" – I'm not sure why. We didn't get on very well. I spent most of my off-duty with John and Chris, so it wasn't a problem. Anyway, with all the overtime to be had there wasn't much downtime, and I would return to my cabin, read my book and sleep.

I always slept well at sea. I was always full on, non-stop, what with working all day, and in the evenings playing games and drinking. But sometimes it could be difficult getting to sleep in heavy seas, or if the weather was very hot. I seem to recall that the air-conditioning was good on the *Douro*. After all, she was a fridge ship, besides being equipped to carry up to 12 first-class passengers.

She was a large ship, but with such a large crew our accommodation midships was a bit dark and cramped. "bed my sleep as the noise the engines made. It was their fluctuation as they struggled to push her huge hull through vast waves.

I could feel it as I lay on my bunk. The ship would lurch, stopping sometimes. Then finally the power of the twin propellers would punch the ship through and over the waves. Most nights however, the tiredness would win over.

I'd arrange the pillows to support me to suit the motion of the waves. Most cabins had their bunks fore and aft, with a daybed arranged athwartships. So if we were sailing along the swell, or on the sea's quarter just into the wind, the ship would tend to roll.

So quite often I would climb down from my bunk onto the daybed, as I found it more comfortable going forwards and backwards instead of side to side. This was not only difficult to counter, but could be somewhat nauseating. This is of course through design, with most ships' cabins having a daybed arrangement like this.

Dreams always came in abundance, extremely vivid, clear, and full of content. The sea is such an inspiration and, without the trappings of life ashore such as motorcars, rent, utility bills, tv, shopping and so forth, instead of complicated left-brain-inspired dreams you are free to dream outwardly, involving your emotions and the people in your life.

About 12 days into our voyage I had a flying dream which I've never been able to get out of my mind. At the time we were entering the South Atlantic and were probably off the most easterly point of Brazil. I dreamt I was standing on deck, looking ahead in the direction of Rio de Janeiro. I took off from the ship and flew around, looking down at it. After circling the ship, I could see land straight ahead from my vantage point high above the ocean and I made for it. Soon I was flying over this great city, over the Sugarloaf Mountain and the enormous statue of Christ the Redeemer. I flew above the city for a while, swooping down low over the beach and its cafes, with their parasols emblazoned with the clasic Martini Bianco insignia.

After a while I felt tired, feeling the urge to get back to the ship, so I headed back east out to sea. I saw a small speck floating on the water which grew larger as I approached it, and there she was: the *Douro*. As I circled around her I suddenly realised that I had a problem: howe was I going to land on the ship? I was high up and travelling very fast. I made my approach and swooped down, aiming for a space on the forward boat deck, clear of the derricks, winches and other clutter. But it was no good – I was too high and going too fast – so I aborted my landing.

I came around again on a second approach. I was lower this time, but still going too fast. Reluctantly I aborted the landing once again. By now I was feeling exhausted and rather anxious. Whatever happened I had to land this time around. I was slower and lower – not ideal, but I had to go for it. I brought myself down onto the wooden deck, aft on the starboard side, crash-landed – and woke up.

I was so looking forward to reaching Rio after so many days at sea, and with four days still to go, May have Been the inspiration for the dream. With my inspired imagination, after watching the albatross which followed us day after day astern of the ship, only disappearing three times a day to stop and pick up the "gash": the waste food from our galley and mess rooms that was routinely dumped over the wall after breakfast, dinner and teatime.

As for my unlucky landing, this was probably a release of my inner anxiety, along with the concept that it was always said to be bad luck to have an albatross land on the ship. The substance behind this superstition was perhaps that the bird had landed because of extreme weather ahead, or because it was ill (poisoned by the ship's food, maybe).

Whatever the case, I understand they mostly had to be killed because it would be unable to take off from the ship. Whenever they land on the sea (a rare event), they need a peaking wave to help them take off again, and on land they choose a home island with long flat areas so they can run along before take-off.

As for killing one, it was probably the only thing to do with it. Feeding unnaturally on the discharge from the ship, it would be overweight. At the best of times they are large, heavy birds, with a wingspan of up to 18 feet, which makes them difficult to deal with, or even downright dangerous as they peck all around them and flap their huge wings in fright as they try to escape.

However it was a fantastic dream, and somehow it enriched my life. At the time it felt totally realistic, and I was so surprised to wake up.

The remaining days went by with us working our routine: cleaning, scrubbing, chipping, oiling, greasing and painting – as ever. Soon enough we found ourselves at Rio de Janeiro: the best-known seaport in South America – as we had general cargo to be delivered there. We entered this exciting city from the Atlantic at the eastern end of a huge deep-sea inlet known as Guanabara Bay.

Rio de Janeiro lies on the east side of the approaches. It is truly a spectacular sight, especially after 18 days at sea. A large sprawling city, it is dominated by its huge statue of Christ the Redeemer on Corcovado Mountain, plus the Sugarloaf Mountain, which stands by itself on a peninsula jutting out into the Bay with the Amazonian (forest covered) mountains in the background. The city nestles into the jungle-covered lower slopes. Groups of houses, both large and small, are sprinkled around, thinning out as they climb the mountain side.

At the narrowest point of the approaches we passed the low-lying airport on the seashore. Turning west, we found our berth in a very long line of ships strung out along the water's edge, well past the berths of the passenger liners closer to the town.

It was now well into August and the weather was extremely hot. We were due to be there for just a few days, so with hundreds of shoreside dockers on board we just did small jobs here and there. We worked during the day and went ashore at night. The red-light district was situated conveniently near the docks, so that's where we spent our two nights ashore, generally getting drunk in a variety of bars and cantinas.

These all looked very Hispanic. Brazil had started off as a Portuguese colony in 1500, gaining its independence from Portugal on 7 September 1822. As a result the architecture is very Portuguese, especially the older buildings. The capital of Brazil is now Brasília, but prior to that it had been Rio.

Cultural exchanges between us and the natives took place on the hot evenings. But it was on a personal level with the local girls, who gave out signals that left us in no doubt of their intentions, or the line of work they were in: sometimes quite blatantly revealing their bits and pointing saying "this very good!" They were extremely friendly and we found them very gratifying, they being most inventive in their sexual techniques whilst acting in a friendly, loving and affectionate way.

Somebody told me at the time that Santos was even worse. I remember wondering how much worse it could be, until we got there some days later. Everywhere in the mean impoverished areas of this city, sex was in abundance and very cheap.

Soon enough the tugs were there and off we went again, heading out to the east, then turning south, clearing the Point and the small jungled islands. We followed the coast down, watching the last remaining Rio landmarks disappear astern, with an occasional peninsula displaying white sandy beaches with coconut palms.

Santos was 200 or so miles south of Rio, so it only took us 12 to 14 hours to reach it. Next morning we entered a large semicircular bay, with the River Santos at the northern end, following a line of ships on our port side for what seemed like forever, the river getting narrower and narrower. We eventually tied up at what must have been the very last berth.

I recall a small ferry crossing over the river towards what looked like proper jungle, or at least where the jungle started. For the two evenings we were there I saw this little boat trundling back-and-forth, watching it carry all different kinds of people and animals, plus carts carrying bags, and thinking maybe I could travel over there with just a few clothes and set off into the jungle, just to see what it was like. But I was so caught up in the romance of the sea that it wasn't going to happen. At least, not yet awhile.

Santos nightlife lived up to its shocking reputation. It was absolutely outrageous. Hundreds of women approached you for sex. There was so much poverty in those parts that anything was fair game. Women would stop you in the street and pull their clothing up or down to show you their naked bits, quoting you a price. In those days you could go out, get a meal, get drunk, buy a pair of jeans and have sex for around £2. Good value – but very dodgy, as sexually-transmitted diseases were rife.

Boy! Did we have some wild times there. The main drag was just like a cowboy town. It actually had saloons with swinging harp-shaped lattice doors and sawdust on the floor. The jukeboxes were very loud and every bar had a small shiny brass or class dance floor with flashing lights. This was mainly for the women to dance on by themselves, displaying what was on offer. Wearing very short skirts you could see everything in the reflection, which revealed highly provocative knickers – or nothing at all, which was usual. I don't think they had invented pole-dancing back then.

I got drunk and it all became a blur. I don't remember much of it, so I must have had a good time.

In all this debauchery there was one small piece of morality however. If you did choose a girl, you stayed with her for the duration of your stay. You didn't have to pay her anything, but you did pay for all her food and drink. So the thing was to be selective and find yourself a good one. There was somebody for everybody.

Mostly people just sang, danced and laughed – it was all there was to do. You would never be in port long enough to conduct any kind of courtship.

However some older seamen did fall in love with women from all walks of life, and many of the women would turn up in England and get married to their sailors like the Australian girls did. But even fewer of such marriages survived, I'm told. The most successful love-matches were when the man jumped ship and stayed in the country to settle down. I sometimes wonder where all those people are these days? Probably a lot of the girls are dead by now. Some may have ended up in Europe or North America – anyway, a better place (hopefully).

Occasionally you would arrive in a bar and it would all be quiet. From time to time the police would round up the women (just like cattle), do health checks, bust the gangs, send illegal immigrants back home and lock up the traffickers and pimps. It was all such madness, with numerous tales of abuse and corruption. I was 17 at the time, and naive. All of us were young and to us it was all just good fun. One simply had to follow along and presume it was all normal.

The older crew members always looked after the boy ratings. The toughest people in the world, they took very good care of us and were generous towards us in all sorts of ways.

With all that experience under our belts, we set sail after three days and headed south for our last stop before Buenos Aires: Montevideo, the capital of Uruguay.

It was in Montevideo, during the Second World War, that the British Navy trapped the German pocket battleship, the *Graf Spee*, which ended with it being scuttled by its captain in the River Plate.

Montevideo was around 1,000 miles away to the south, where it was supposed to be a little cooler. It took us three days to get there.

The journey got much more interesting, following the Brazilian coastline southwards. It was a little distracting when working however, as it was tempting to stop and watch the coast go by, with its white sandy beaches forming a fringe to jungle-covered hills. Villagers were scattered here and there on the hillside, plus cultivated fields in clearings.

After three days we entered Montevideo Bay in great excitement, and found our berth close to the centre of town. We were still in the estuary of the River Plate, which was constantly very muddy, the mud being brought down from inland by the many fast-flowing tributaries.

The town lies on the northern side of the estuary, which is the national boundary. Uruguay is only a very small country, lying between Brazil to the north and Argentina to the south-west. Yet its culture was completely different from either country.

It was very Catholic, and seemingly very puritanical for this day and age. This was in complete contrast to Brazil. It was originally settled by the Spanish but later taken over by the Portuguese. The cars on the roads were conspicuous for being old US and British models from the 1930s, 40s and 50s.

There was no in-your-face red-light district that we could find. Indeed we were warned not to get too familiar with the local women as this would cause offence and you'd find yourself facing jealous husbands or be in trouble with the police.

They had a law there known as "technical rape", I was told at the time, which could get you arrested if someone saw you ogling a woman or undressing them with your eyes. So we all had to be very careful, in stark contrast to the debauchery of Rio and Santos. Quite honestly it came as a breath of fresh air. Being relatively inexperienced and still rather shy of women, I didn't feel it as such a restriction on my activities as it was, no doubt, for other members of the crew.

For all that, the people were very friendly towards us. It didn't strike me at the time, but our ship would have been a familiar sight in the harbour, having been visiting the town for years, 4-5 times a year, not only as the *Douro*, but under its previous name, *Hornby Grange*. The only thing that would have changed for the townsfolk would have been the colour of the funnel, from the large H for Holder Brothers to the bland buff-colour of Royal Mail Lines. She was one of two slightly old-fashioned ships that docked there, which made her distinctive.

We were only in for a day or so, and runs ashore were short. I remember it all being very clean and tidy, with no obvious signs of deprivation. Which struck me as strange, considering the unfashionable dress of the inhabitants and all those old cars, still in perfect condition. It gave me a feeling of being transported back 30 years in time.

It was odd but I liked it, as I'd had a rather older stuck-in-the-past concept of what the world looked like. My image of the planet had come from photos, books, films, and TV – all of which just give you snippets of any given destination. Most would have reflected the historical past, and the snippets had been cold, impersonal images.

I must say that wherever I visited in the world, there was always a small feeling of disappointment with modernisation, even in the most exotic and romantic places. This arose out of the modernisation I saw, but also from my preconceptions. In practice: nothing ever lives up to our imagination.

So we left Montevideo with the usual routine of letting-go shorelines, making-fast tugs and so forth, and headed out into the Rio de la Plata for Buenos Aires. This was only a six-hour,

80 mile sail. We left Montevideo's deep water port, at low water, catching the flood tide to reach Buenos Aires at high water. This was necessary as we would be on a drying berth adjacent to the Fray Bentos meat processing plant.

We came to BA late afternoon, with the city on our port side, that is, to the south. It was a strange sight, with a red muddy river moving around the headland. We entered the River Matanza, passed the tanker berth and entered Dock Sue to find our berth.

Coming alongside it, we positioned our BA fenders over the side with her now tops derricks. These being large cylindrical lumps of composite wood, around 8' x 6', covered in rubber. They were stowed on the decks of all the BA meat boats precisely to protect the side of the ship from buffering up against the quay here, which was not too well-maintained. They also kept the ship fended out sufficiently far that, as she took the ground at low water, the ship would sit flat on the bottom. Otherwise she would have listed downwards towards the river, making loading very difficult as well as putting unusual stresses on the hull. This was why the *Douro* had been custom-built with her flat bottom.

This was a dirty filthy place, surrounded by oil refineries. There was a permanent scum of oil and petrol on the surface, and it stank – especially at low water. It was doubly disgusting because all the waste-water from the meat-packing plants, laden with blood, was also discharged into the same dock.

Although the dock was tidal, it was situated in an inlet that came to a blind end. So there was no through movement of water: the tide would come in and go out without flushing away any of the oil and offal. Indeed it generally brought up all the other spillage from berths lower down to add to the problem. It really was a disgusting place, known to all seafarers as the Arsehole of the World (or at least one of them). And we were loading meat – the famous Fray Bentos beef!

I should mention at this point that during our voyage from London we had spent time down in the holds cleaning out the sections that held no cargo for other ports. The *Douro* had six holds, the one in the centre, the largest, had seven tween decks (or storeys, in shoreside terms). Each of these tweens were refrigerated, four sections to each level: fore, aft, port and starboard. Each of these sections had to be swept, all wooden rubbish removed, then scrubbed out, rinsed and finally fumigated against vermin: rats, flies and other insects.

After the first port at which we discharged cargo, all this activity intensified, as the short distances between ports gave us little time to prepare for loading a full cargo of meat for our home journey from BA. This was of course our main function, representing the major part of the economics of this particular trade route.

We had to work every hour there was to make sure the whole ship was as clean as a whistle to receive this precious cargo. We all earned a lot of money with overtime on this ship: it would be the ship of choice of many seamen working out of the Royal Docks. Most voyages were only 10 weeks – short trips with lots of money to be earned.

We did do all the work that needed to be done, and all the fridges were cleaned and made ready to receive their cargo. In no time at all the ship was awash with small Hispanic-looking workers. We had topped all the derricks whilst crossing the River Plate. As ever, all of them had been let go and swung outboard, so the shoreside cranes could be used unhindered to swing in large cargo nets containing sides of beef over the deck, and down into the holds for the dockers to receive and hang on meat hooks in the various fridges. The crane drivers could not see the dockers, so every hold had a man standing at the hatch coaming directing the crane driver with hand-movements. It was a kind of universal tick-tack code, used throughout the world's ports with only slight cultural variations.

We we would rarely take part in any of the cargo handling in larger ports. The only exception to this rule was likely to arise when we were anchored offshore, and barges were alongside. Then it would be our job to work the derricks.

There was also a gantry with a conveyor system. This was for boxes of meat products, organs such as kidneys, hearts, tongues and who-knows what else. They appeared to be steaming as they came aboard, and I guess they were being frozen down on board, just like the sides of beef.

The factory was vast, and in a large area next to it and upstream from us was a shanty town, with a company canteen at its centre, where all the migrant workers lived. This was a very squalid place.

In between them and us were long lines of trucks bringing in live animals. A continuous stream of cows were herded in at one end of the factory and at the other end spat out in bits directly onto our ship, fresh and warm. This continued for five days or so until we had our full cargo complement of approximately 6,500 tons. This was the meat that would go into the familiar Fray Bentos steak and kidney pie in a shallow tin, that persists to this day.

I had heard tales about the run ashore. It was a very dangerous place in the 1970s: poverty stricken, with an almost fascist government. Going ashore here was dodgy.

Some of the older hands were so casual about it that it warranted a pep-talk from the chief officer. He advised us to go ashore only in groups of six, and to take great care. At no time were we to leave cabin doors or portholes unlocked.

We took heed of this, and whenever we went ashore we'd go in groups, armed with makeshift weapons such as short lengths of timber, iron bars and chains. There was a bridge we had to cross to find the city, and the only way to get to it led through the shanty town. We'd hide our weapons under the bridge and collect them on the way back.

Once over the bridge we were still a long way from the BA city centre and had to take taxis there and back. However the taxis would not enter the docks after 11 PM, so when returning to the ship we would be dropped off at the gates, leaving us to walk the rest of the way through the shanty town.

In those days you were not even safe in the city centre. Every other person seem to be wearing a military uniform of one kind or another. There were five different kinds of police, or so it seemed. The ordinary civilian police, a type of Carabinieri, traditionally on horseback, with their nets and *bolas* (three balls on strips of leather for throwing), plus the army, navy, and airforce police.

In the absence of enough ships or planes, many of these forces were used as police, all roaming around town in small packs, armed to the teeth with automatic rifles plus grenades hanging off their bodies. We were continually stopped by such groups, who would ask you for cigarettes with broad smiles on their faces and the barrel of a gun pointed at our stomachs. It felt like armed robbery and was very scary.

We didn't spend much time ashore there for that reason. If out on the town and drunk, we would have been very vulnerable. Even doing our daily work on the ship we weren't safe. One day I found someone trying to climb in a porthole. When he saw me he quickly retreated.

There was a famous story about a 2nd deck officer on one of the ships that went missing in BA. They thought he must have jumped ship for some unknown reason, and a replacement was sent out. It wasn't until they were discharging cargo in London that the dockers, to their horror, found the missing 2nd officer. He was on a hook in amongst the sides of beef. How or why this happened nobody ever found out.

However when you were loading or unloading there would possibly be cargo in the holds destined for other ports. The dockers down there would easily be able to steal it if it took their fancy. So in such situations there would be a crew member stationed down in the hold to act as a deterrent. It's quite possible that the unfortunate 2nd officer was on watch down there and tried to stop some pilfering, the perpetrators, in abject poverty and living under an unforgiving legal system, resorting to desperate measures. I could well imagine dockers doing this to protect their jobs and their liberty – especially in the BA of those days.

After five days we eased our way down the length of Dock Sue, came around to starboard and out into the River Plate once more. By next morning we were heading east along it, passing by Montevideo off the port beam, out of the River Plate estuary and back into the South Atlantic. Then we followed the Brazilian coastline northwards. We were due to call into Santos and Rio again for two brief days to pick up some general cargo for home.

We spent an uneventful night in the red-light district of Rio, doing the same old routine: drinking and dancing. But during the day we were working, doing little jobs here and there.

On the last day before leaving Rio, as we broke for afternoon smoko, I grabbed a mug of tea and found John, Chris and a few others in their cabin. There were also two Brazilian lads there – dockers I think. They had some grass they wanted to sell us, and passed around a pre-rolled spliff for us to try before buying. So we all had a puff at this beast of a thing.

After a few minutes I found it really difficult maintaining a normal train of thought. As reality evaporated I suddenly felt a bit frightened.

Then I heard the familiar gravelly yet high-pitched voice of our old bo's'un. He was about 70 years of age and used to be on the "A" boats in their heyday, the passenger ships *Amazon*, *Arianza*, and *Aragon* before they were sold to Shaw Savill and re-named *Akaroa*, *Arawa*, and *Aranda*. The bo's'un was a good man, fair and easy-going. He shouted "turn-to, lads", so most of us got up and headed out of the cabin, leaving John and Chris to do the deal.

I vaguely remember the bo's'un saying he had a job for me to do at the gangway. It was on the main deck, port side, alongside the quay. The bo's'un met me halfway. He looked very strange to me – the extremely strong grass I had just sampled was taking away my recollection and I started to hallucinate. He was explaining something about rigging a net to be draped under the gangway, preventing anybody or anything falling in the water between the ship and the quayside. But I simply could not quite work it out.

He was speaking and pointing, but his words sounded like a tape-recording that was slowing to stop. Realising I was not in a fit state to do anything useful, I managed to say something vaguely understandable – "okay, I'll go and sort some gear out with the lamp trimmer" – and hurried off as fast as I could.

I needed to get to my cabin before I passed out. It was a very long journey, I can tell you. It was like a bad dream: the faster I tried to go, the slower the progress I seem to be making. My entire consciousness was focused on the objective of simply getting to my bunk.

Fortunately I made it, I lay back and plunged into a psychedelic dreamland. It was very beautiful and I eventually relaxed enough to enjoy it. But the experience was so intense. Eventually I fell into a sort of sleep, dreaming profusely.

After some time I awoke to the sensation that my tongue was the size of my head, and was scraping away at the inside of my skull. I slowly woke up some more and realised the sensation was my tongue licking the inside of my extremely dry mouth.

Then came a knock on my cabin door. It was the bo's'un again, saying "Are you turning-to, lad?"

I could only reply "Sorry Bo's, I'm not feeling well."

There was a pause, then I heard him turn away, muttering "nor am I, son, nor am I."

I remembered there was an iced-water fountain at the far end of the companionway which all the cabins led off. Waiting until the bo's'un was well gone, I got up, crept to it and drank deeply. It was wonderful. I don't think I'd ever tasted anything so gorgeous.

By now I had more-or-less come to my senses, so I began looking around. I remember thinking: God – did all the other lads in that cabin manage to work after that?

I went over to the port side cabins, where I heard music. Was I still in a confused state? I followed the sound, recognising it as one of the few albums we had at the time: probably Led Zeppelin. I knocked on the cabin door and opened it.

There they all were, lying all over the place, laughing. None of them had managed to return to work ether. So I went in and joined them.

Fortunately the bo's'un didn't report us. He knew we were all good lads and worked hard normally, also it was near the end of the day and we would be turning to station shortly anyway.

Later we let go of the tugs after they'd moved us off the quay. Heading out of the bay, we set course for London and our 18 days return voyage.

We spent the rest of that day dropping the last of the derricks, throwing all the rubbish over the side, stowing all the ropes and rigging and battening down for the voyage, in readiness for anything that the sea might throw at us on on route.

We sailed northwards on our way home, heading to the equator once again, as we did so the weather became much hotter. We were back in the tropics for a week or so, with the temperature soaring. Those were balmy, humid hot days, working on deck, trying not to burn. Our ship had provision for up to 12 first-class passengers, for their benefit, the main and upper decks were laid with teak. In the high temperatures this had to be hosed down regularly, sometimes twice a day. There for this was an appropriate time for holy-stoning them, as we did on the *Trebartha*, only ten times more, along some repairs to the caulking in the joints of the deck to prevent lifting.

Five days from home the weather grew colder. Sunshine, blue skies and green seas gave way to more cloud cover, darker skies, more rain and shorter days. But autumn in England was not too bad.

We arrived back in London on Sunday, 27 September 1970 at G shed, the meat berth in the Albert – but not before winding our way up through the docks. It's always an interesting time, observing what ships are in, and whether you know anybody on board you might meet later ashore.

We were paid off at lunchtime. We had smoked quite a lot of the grass we got in Rio, but there was still some left. So it had to be hidden from the "Black Gang" (Customs). This was standard practice with many inventive ways being employed to hide this stuff, along with our cigarettes – there was still a duty-free limit of 200 per person. The grass was stashed behind some pipes in one of the cabins. Unfortunately it was stashed so well we never found it again, so we had to abandon it. There wasn't much of it anyway.

I was paid off with £14 0s 4d, plus £40 paid into the bank. Being Sunday, there was little public transport, so we all decided to check into the Seamen's Mission, for one night at least, and see who else was around. Of course we had a celebratory evening, drinking at the mission in Canning Town, and managed to find some hash. So we clubbed-in and bought an ounce, which cost us £8 back then, and very nice it was too.

We relaxed for a day or so, turning-on and drinking vast amounts of light and bitter. Somebody told us of the whereabouts of some. "acid" – LSD. We'd heard about this extremely potent drug that took you away on a mental trip with multi-coloured hallucinations. This sounded interesting, if a little scary.

Anyway we decided to try some, and I bought half a tab of something called "California Sunshine". Each It looked more like a little crumb of bread than anything. We had a few pints and then took our "acid". It took some time to work, but after an hour or so things began to change.

There was quite a large gang of us in the bar, relaxing on easy chairs in several large circles. It was all very strange to start with, like being in a fish tank. With only the people who were participating being familiar to me – everybody else seemed strangely distant or detached in some way.

I will never forget how stark red were the lips of Father McGuinness, who ran the mission. After that my memory of things are sketchy. I recall walking from the mission down Canning Town High Street and getting into a taxi – there were five or six of us, I think. Certainly there were Chris, John, Digby (I think), plus some others. After that I can only remember colours – lots of them – plus isolated snapshots of London's West End, slot machines, cafes, West End roads with the reflected lights looking like stars in the night sky, sometimes turning into aerial views of the cityscape, building looking soft, spongy, and almost cartoon like. Constant abstract hallucinations occur as your mind struggles to find a tangible answer for what you were looking at, through the varying states of high, fluctuating as this chemical makes its way around your body. Detached from reality, all your concepts leave you in a kind of pure state, It was both a magical and intense experience. I think there must have been some people there looking after us that night as it was not possible to operate normally.

I finally came down, as we all did, around 5-6 AM, just walking around town, slowly becoming aware of who – and what – I was again. It was an extremely profound experience, watching the central concepts of my life falling back into place, revealing my recall gradually returning, moment by moment.

It taught me a very important lesson, right there and then, although I really only understood it properly in retrospect, years later. It was this: you are in adult life whatever influenced you as a child. Many concepts and values are brought about by your environment, social status, those you love, your education, what climatic ore political part of the world you were born into – these all have a very strong bearing on what you perceive as relevant to you and Will have undoubtably a bearing on what happens to you in your life, with those values affecting decisions you make for yourself. But if you can manage to take away all your judgement or concepts, yet remain conscious, you are in the immediacy, with no point of reference to allow you to take clear decisions on anything. Hence the hallucinations: because you have no recall to confirm your understanding of what you are seeing.

Although I didn't know it then, I would subsequently strive to take a second look at my existing values and structures, redefining them as necessary, Whilst taking great care over what values I would take on board in the future.

The experience changed my life profoundly and (eventually) very much for the better. But not truly until the eradication of the drug itself had been Substituted with meditation techniques. As I believe It to be a slower, more natural or gentle approach that amounted to the Same end

However at that time it was a dangerous thing to do and you needed strength of mind to deal with it. It's not for everyone: I consider myself to have been on the borderline here, and on subsequent occasions when taking larger doses of this strange substance, I was sometimes prey to extreme fears whilst fighting to retain some control of my mind.

So beware – and be aware.

We walked some more, then as reality hit us we found we were cold and tired. Still slightly bewildered, we took the District Line back from the centre of London to the East End, then quietly back on the number 69 bus from Plaistow station to the Mission, where we had a most bizarre breakfast. Then Falling back to one of our rooms, whilst listening to some quiet music, we had a few joints and slept away the rest of the day, only to wake up, eat again, head for the bar for a round of light and bitter – and start all over again.

It's amazing how we could just go on like this, with little or no sleep at all on many occasions. We could even work all day and go out all night, taking any quantity of stimulants of one kind or another, always laced with alcohol. That in a strange way kept us balanced, by keeping us a bit earthed.

When taking psychoactive substances it helps to be in a good space to begin with, keeping it all light-hearted, with no sense of anything being serious. Sadly the profundity, integrity and euphoria induced by these substances can draw you in to become solitary and inward looking if you're not careful.

This however depends on your character. If you are well-balanced and basically okay with the world, you can keep things light and maintain control. But if you are coming from a depressive, or an angry place, then it could happiness you experience is a far better place than your normal one, even though you know it is only induced by the drug. I believe this can make dependency more likely

For our part, in those days we could do any amount of drugs and drink without losing a single day's work, with the exception of a few hours on that one afternoon in santos. But we were fine as we all knew new we would unfailingly be away and back to sea with the life we all loved. By its very nature it always gave us the greater "high".

Nine weeks on the *Douro* gave us nine days' leave before we'd be obliged to report back to the pool and sign on as available for another ship.

There followed an unremarkable yet levelling period of leave at home for a week, staying with my mum and partner Rod and visiting brother John and Linda, plus my dad, who was in a new relationship – I'll say no more.

Sadly, with all the things that had happened in the last few years, the family had become distant. Only in retrospect can I see the full effect it had had on me. It meant that only a fragmented sense of family existed now for me. Nothing now could bring back those home fires and evenings round the table that would have drawn me home during my leave between-ships to recapture those nostalgic days for a while. Besides, with the new social culture and the almost institutional life I was leading, I had found a new family at sea. Its allure beckoned me back from home, not to mention the drink and the drugs. As I matured I was beginning to enjoy my new life. Consequently I was very happy to return to the East End of London, book into the Seamen's Mission and meet up again with The lads, and our ever-widening circle of sailor friends.

By it's very nature, the relationship between shipmates would normally only a temporary one. It generally comes to an end after most voyages – for that reason sailors used to refer to other ship mates as "Board of Trade acquaintances". But we now found ourselves in the forefront of an amalgamation of the European and American drug cultures with its far-reaching influences: we were a new breed of "hippy sailors". All the same, we managed to as usual keep our work and play separate: we played hard but we worked hard, and understood the importance of doing our duty and keeping our obligation to safety whilst doing our jobs.

Little did we know, when we signed on at the pool, that we wouldn't be around in the East End of London for a lot longer than we'd anticipated. Again there weren't any jobs to be had, just like it was before we took the *Douro* jobs, when the dockers had been on strike until the end of The previous July, which had

had a serious knock-on effect on the scheduling of voyages. It made things a bit more difficult that we all wanted jobs on the same ship so that a few of us could ship out together.

For the next few weeks we settled back into our normal shoreside life: partying all night, sleeping away most of the morning, drinking, smoking dope and periodically dropping acid, speed (amphetamines) and occasionally downers (barbiturates), although we mainly used these to get some sleep.

One interesting development was that relationships began to develop between our group and the hostesses that were bussed-in from the nursing college in Victoria. The trainee nurses were mainly Irish girls – all Catholics, I guess. To understand this set-up you have to remember we were staying at a Catholic mission: the *Stella Maris* in Canning Town, where procuring good Catholic girls for the seaman residents, to dance with us on the occasional evening, this was standard practice, as it was at most of the missions.

There was a large function hall to one side of the huge bar lounge for this purpose. Once a week (sometimes twice), 20 or so young girls would turn up on the bus, and gradually one or two of them started to "turn on" discreetly with us. It turned out that a lot of them were already at it anyway. Therefore In a very short space of time the majority of them were at least smoking dope, eventually some of us started meeting up with them in town or their lodgings to take it all a little further.

I was taking a back seat in all this. When it came to girls I was not all that courageous – indeed I'm a very shy person in that respect. I went to an all-boys school and had no sisters, so women were a bit like aliens to me. In a lot of ways I was insecure and naive. I guess I rather lived in the shadow of others in our group, who were much more forthcoming.

I did see a lovely girl whose name was Bridget a couple of times, but lost touch when subsequently after shipping out again I was too embarrassed to write to her, with my writing skills being what they were. Shyness with women has never really left me, which has been the source of a great deal of frustration throughout my life, both emotionally and sexually. Also I probably missed opportunities that could have a mounted to something more permanent and full filling, Who knows.

There came a day we went to the pool in the KG5 Dock as usual to sign in and check the jobs – and there was the *Douro* again, looking for a full crew. So we all took jobs on her. I can't quite remember who exactly was on that voyage, but certainly John, Chris and myself. I was promoted from deck boy to JOS (junior ordinary seaman) as by now I had acquired the necessary sea time. This doubled my pay to £44 7s 6d a month, and my overtime went up from 1s 9d to a massive 6s 7d per hour.

Back aboard MV Douro

We'd left the *Douro* 23 days earlier at the end of September. During that time she'd discharged her cargo of beef at G shed in the Albert Dock, had signed on a home-trade crew and gone up to Hull, then across to a few ports on the continent. As we had done prior to the first deep sea trip on her. Then she'd returned to the Albert Dock F shed. Now, having finished loading general cargo, she was once more bound for the east coast of South America.

20 October 1970 was the day we all signed on. Winter was really starting to draw in, with temperatures dropping. After a day or two preparing the ship, along with a few last "sleepless" (stoned) nights ashore, we were once again called to stations. We let go, made fast the tugs, moved out from our berth down the Albert Dock, through the cut at the bottom, through the sea lock into the river, and downstream into the Thames estuary. Then we turned southwest through the busy Straits of Dover, St George's Channel, into the Bay of Biscay. Rio bound once more.

To be honest, I don't think it was a moment too soon for any of us. We'd had a brilliant time, but now it was time to get some fresh air into our lungs and heads, do some work and earn some money. There would be 18 days at sea to prepare once again for the delights of Santos, Rio, Montevideo and Buenos Aires.

I remember watching the sunset on our first night at sea and getting the first good night's sleep I'd had for over three weeks. For the first few days I thought we would all be showing withdrawal symptoms. But instead we had some beer, a bit of blow and a lot of laughter together, reminiscing on our previous exploits. With plenty of work plus good food – a large healthy breakfast plus two full three-course meals a day – we were soon back up to strength, physically and mentally.

It was good to be back on the *Douro*, too. When I first saw her she looked like a rusty old tub – very odd-looking. But this was because she had been custom-built for the BA meat run, in 1948 which demanded a flat bottom. The only thing that made her look old-fashioned was her straight bow and cruiser stern. Most ships built after the war and into the 1950s were more flared at the bow and had more rounded features, which made them look prettier.

The *Douro* was on the cusp, having replaced the *Baronesa*, built in 1918. They probably used the same plans as the *Beacon Grange*, built in 1938, which was torpedoed and sunk by the U522 in 1941. Both cargo vessels had been built in Hebburn, Tyneside.

Ships are living beings in so many ways. My image of the *Douro* was affected by our own concepts and expectations gained from previous ships, plus our own personal likes and dislikes. But she was a good old tub, along with her now even older bo's'un, who was very accepting of us and a very relaxed person all-round.

I like to think that whatever we did, or looked like, with our long hair and wild habits, he knew we would never let him down. And the work went smoothly because we already knew the ship.

In retrospect I believe he knew he would be retiring soon enough, as the writing was on the wall for the *Douro*. She went for dismantling to San Juan de Neva, near Bilbao in northern Spain, in June 1972, less than a year and a half after we were on her.

Some years later I had a van that was built in 1972 (she was a good van – affectionately known as Larry (Larry the Van), and I wondered at the time if there was some way that steel from my old ships could have possibly been recycled into it. Reckon I took some comfort in that thought, not being beyond the realms of possibility.

—oOo—

It was back out then across the Bay of Biscay, heading initially south-west for Santos. We commenced by overhauling all the running gear again before starting on the stripping and painting.

It was such a beautiful experience being at sea once more. Yes, it was cold, wet and miserable in UK waters in October, but our excitement compensated for that. A few days sailing south and the weather improved quickly, apart for the occasional rare storm. Four or five days at average off 15 knots, which is 1,500 to 1,800 miles, brings you into springlike weather as you pass between the Canaries and the north-west coast of Africa.

Although John and Chris were now SOSs, they had taken the deck boys' cabin again and we had it as the party room as before. It was a good big space and served us well. It also meant I got to take a single berth again, which I always preferred.

We were all a bit bored just sitting in it. One night, sipping our cans of beer, we suddenly remembered the little bit of Brazilian grass we'd hidden in the cabin on our last trip, and subsequently, previously given up for lost. Our eyes lit up and there were big smiles all round as we set about searching down behind the air-conditioning pipes. We had to take some bits off the bulkhead as it had slid down behind the cladding. but eventually we found it again. Eureka!

Immediately a large spliff was built and passed around. The next thing we knew, we were all off our faces. Wow! – what seriously powerful stuff. We had all forgotten just how strong. Coming on top of a few beers it got us completely spaced out, listening to one of our growing collection of albums: *Deep Purple* (Led Zeppelin), Stones, Beatles – on a really good Panasonic portable stereo player we now had, given to us as a present by a friend, an Irish fellow: a steward called Tony Mullens.

It was just brilliant finding our grass again, and using it sparingly it lasted us until the South American coast. It was a curious turn of events: we never expected to do another trip on the *Douro*, and until that point we'd all totally forgotten about it.

—oOo—

The profundity of being at sea is nearly impossible to put into words. It is decidedly romantic, and you can understand why. It is such a good inspiration – even poetic – as it totally exposes the beauty of the planet. Every day was new, fresh and different as we made our way across the Atlantic, with my senses heightened and feeling more self-realised with the use of herbs that at the time appeared to open up your minds, enabling you to see and expand on subjects in a much deeper, intellectual, or more creative way than you may have considered before.

I spent many hours wondering at the glory of such intense natural phenomena, wishing with all my heart that the people I knew shoreside and at home, could be there seeing it and sharing the experience with me. As a result I embraced every new day with excitement, wonder and intuitive knowledge that would remain with me forever.

So after three weeks at sea, with varying weather conditions, alternating between bad weather days with pitching seas, to perfect balmy hot days.

We finally arrived at Santos in mid-November, ready once more for the surreal and contrasting delights of the South American dockside culture, with its strange yet unmistakable commercialism.

The strip in the red-light district of Santos in particular was still just one long series of bars, clubs and houses crammed full of women and men, from very young to very old, all there to sell you pleasure. I was young and naive, and was given a good time by some half-decent girls. But subsequently I found out that every sort of appetite you could possibly imagine was being catered for.

I was however hormone- and pheromone- driven at the time, and felt the need to take part in the accepted way. But I did manage to keep it all reasonably down-to-earth.

Poverty is a very compelling affliction, forcing people to endure what they might not choose for themselves. Few of the people there would ever experience what we'd consider a normal life. At the time I took it at its face value and enjoyed it, but mine was the naivety of youth.

Since then I have adopted and promoted the attitude that this world must be changed to make it possible for every living soul on the planet to live a normal life, eat enough, enjoy good health and have a family, without having to prostitute themselves, to do so.

In retrospect, on a moral level, was I exploiting them? Possibly. However they needed the money to simply survive at that time. Therefore in the absence of any alternative we were in a strange way, helping them. I have no clear answer to this – it's just the way it was.

Surely any philosophy of life worth following awards every individual the right to experience normal life, and the stronger have an obligation to support the weaker in achieving this. I'm told there's a Jewish saying that if everybody were to save just one other person, then everybody in the world would be saved.

—oOo—

For the next three days we discharged cargo in Santos, then once more south to Montevideo, and Buenos Aires, working all hours to clean out the fridge decks as they were emptied, getting them ready for loading beef in BA's Dock Sue the same as our previous trip.

After we had completed loading, we left the abattoir in Dock Sue one evening, assisted by tugs, made our way out of the docks and into the river. Unusually the tugs stayed with with us, and to my surprise we turned up and into the centre of the city, tying up on a quiet berth in the posh end of town near where the passenger ships normally docked. We hadn't a clue what was going on, and there was a lot of speculation.

At about 9 or 10 that evening a large convoy of military trucks arrived at the quayside, along with a considerable number of civilian workers and an escort of many soldiers and police. They then proceeded to load what we later learned was tons of silver bullion into the mast house lockers between number three hold and the forward part of the officers' accommodation. This location was no doubt chosen because it was easily seen from the bridge. And even making it easy to recover in the event of the ship sinking. Having done that, they welded the heavy dogged metal doors closed.

Next morning we were all summoned to the officers' saloon where we were told to sign the Official Secrets Act. To this day I still wonder what it was all about. Had we not been made to sign the Act, I think we would have simply taken it to be a valuable commercial cargo, nothing more.

The Act made it governmental. But who knows?

Some years later, I discovered our chief steward got two years in prison because for years he had been bringing tons of pornography back to England on the *Douro* under an alias name.

I can't recall him now, but there were some memorable characters on board. There was an interesting man/woman, the captain's steward (or "tiger", as they were known). She/he had a regular gig spot as a drag-artist in a BA nightclub. I remember that outward bound she would spend hrs making a new dress for this gig using thousands of sequins. She was probably in her 50s and was known as. Somewhat surprisingly: Gilda the Gash.

There was another character called Clancy from London, Jewish I think. An AB in his late 40s, he'd been at sea all his life. "Pickled" would be a good description of him, as he drank steadily and talked endlessly. But he was okay.

There was also an old AB from Northern Ireland, angry and volatile. He drank too, and when really drunk you just had to keep out of his way. He had a cabin next to Clancy, and one evening in port he got seriously drunk and gave Clancy a really bad beating. I think he was trying to get to sleep, and Clancy (sozzled) wouldn't stop talking.

It was such a serious beating that it left him bedridden for days, but it certainly quietened him down. However the incident created a bad atmosphere and the Irishman was disliked for it. He knew it, so he went on the defensive, becoming increasingly aggressive with each and everyone. For a time he terrorised the mess, trying to rule over us all.

This went on for a week or so, when he was stopped in his tracks by a Scottish AB: a very quiet, level-headed man. I can picture him, but I can't recall his name. Alec I think.

We were all eating lunch when the angry Irishman came in, half-drunk, cursing away as usual. The Scotsman calmly put down his knife and fork, got to his feet, went over to the man – and proceeded in a relatively calm and controlled way to beat the shit out of him.

Having pummelled him to the floor, he said evenly, "If you don't shut up and behave yourself from now on, I'll do it again." Then he hauled the man out of the mess and threw him in his cabin, came back, sat down and continued his lunch.

It did the trick. The Irishman never again gave any grief to any of us. The respect we'd already begun to develop for this quiet Scotsman increased enormously.

We headed out of the BA docks that night, back into the huge, muddy River Plate, passed Montevideo again and went on to Rio. Our stay there was a memorable one for me, even though it only lasted 24 hours. We were only there to collect some cargo for Lisbon, Portugal, and to pick up two British DBSs (distressed British seamen) who would work their passage home aboard the *Douro*.

It was Saturday. Weekend overtime was compulsory at sea, but not in port. The other JOS besides myself was a fellow they called "bonehead". Frank, I think his name was. The pair of us decided to go to the famous Copacabana Beach, because I had been to Rio four times now and had never yet got to see it.

So we took off in a taxi and spent the day lounging on the beach and trying to swim. This was unexpectedly difficult because the beach pitched steeply at the water's edge, and large south-Atlantic rollers were coming in with such speed, and gathering back to meet the next wave so rapidly, that we couldn't get beyond them.

I remember we were constantly hounded by people trying to sell us things. But we did buy two fresh pineapples, which the native vendor peeled for us, trimming the head and shaping it into a handle so that we could hold it easily to eat it. The pineapples were delicious. They only cost us the equivalent of 1d (one old penny) – nothing really to us.

The beach was pretty full of people, and in addition to some extraordinarily beautiful women, we sat and watched families relaxing in the sweltering heat – men, women and children: brown, bronzed and beautiful.

All once I chanced to notice a small girl of about five or six playing at the water's edge, within reach of that larger seventh wave which is often just a bit bigger than the others. Sure enough, a breaking wave knocked her off her feet. To my horror, the returning water, gathering into the next wave, dragged her back into the sea.

Instinctively I was on my feet and running towards her. She was along the beach from where we were sitting, so I was coming in at an angle. I was dimly aware of another man running in at an angle from the other direction.

The little girl stood up and lifted her arms to her eyes. Behind her the next wave towered above her – it was maybe six or 7 feet high. With perfect timing, the other man and I reached her at precisely the same instant and we both grabbed an arm each. Then we dashed frantically back up the beach with her dangling, closely followed by the huge wave tumbling after us. The little girl cried noisily, but she was safe and sound.

The other man, who turned out to be her father, smiled broadly at me, picked up his daughter with one arm and shook my hand vigorously with the other. *"Muito obrigado, senhor,"* he said, over and over again. *"Muito obrigado!"*

I've always been a strong swimmer and confident in the water, but I was really pleased with myself that day for what I'd been able to achieve, and how quickly I'd responded. Frank, on the other hand, had scarcely even noticed it all happening. I took pride in being an Englishman visiting a far-off country and actually doing some good instead of robbing people and exploiting the natives.

A little while later, two girls sitting at the water's edge caught my eye. One of them was absolutely gorgeous, it was love at first sight. Unusually for me, being a bit shy with women. I made a plan to position myself in such a way that, if I timed it right, a wave would help me to come closer, or even collide with her.

It worked. We laughed together at our little "accident" and got chatting. Luckily she could speak a little English, so we sat together at the water's edge for a while.?

Her name was Marabella. She had that dark Hispanic look, with long black hair and a body to die for. I could hardly believe my luck. With some sign language and a bit of pigeon talk, I managed to get her to understand that Sadly, shore leave ended at 4 PM and we were due to sail for Lisbon at 5 PM. So she said "Okay, come up to our apartment – it's not far away on Avenue Atlantico – have some food and I'll drive you back to your ship."

Our minds were boggling as we walked off the beach with the two girls, down into a car park and up in a lift to the seventh floor. She led us into the kitchen area, where I saw a woman on her hands and knees washing the floor. I assumed it was her mother. We went from the kitchen into the main apartment, passing paintings in the corridor each lit with its own little light.

It suddenly struck me that the woman in the kitchen was the maid. This was a very wealthy family.

She showed us into a huge bathroom and said "take a shower and we will meet you in the dining room shortly", gesturing towards a door in the hall. After we'd cleaned ourselves up, we entered a large room overlooking the bay and the beach. There was a dining table, big enough to seat 12 people, laid out with all manner of extraordinary food. They greeted us and we feasted together, chatting and laughing, quite forgetting the time.

Then I noticed it was 3:30 and I began to panic.

Marabella said "Come on, I'll take you back." So the four of us jumped into her VW Beetle in the basement and we took off, driving madly to the other side of Rio, then through the tunnel to the docks. The ship was on the long quay, but I struggled to recall exactly where. It was 5 PM – sailing time. I thanked her and kissed her – there was no time for anything else, although she managed to slip me her address.

We ran through the dock gates, glanced both ways – and saw the *Douro* further up the quay. As we ran towards her, we saw that tugs had been made fast to her and she was singled up on mooring lines. She was beginning to move slowly away from the quay.

As we drew closer I could see the bo's'un winding the gangway back down, and a man in a suit – the agent – was standing on the shore with our discharge books in his outstretched hands. We'd need those.

By the time we got to the ship the bo's'un was at the lower end of the gangway, making fast a rope, which he threw to the two watermen – the shoreside dockers – who were waiting to let go the last of the shore line. They caught the rope and pulled the gangway out on its swinging chain: a makeshift arrangement to enable the gangway to be swung out to cover any size of gap between the ship and the dock.

We hurriedly grabbed our discharge books from the agent and leapt aboard.

We'd only just made it. The bo's'un said calmly "you cut that a bit fine, lads." Smiling, he added "I hope they were pretty." We replied "Thanks, Bo's" and he said "Okay, bring the gangway back up and go to your stations."

So, having done that, we went forward, to a cheer and a round of applause from the crew. All in all, it had been a brilliant day, and a memorable end to our spell on the Coast.

From our conversations earlier, it turned out that Marabella's father owned the restaurant on top of the famous Sugarloaf Mountain. Obviously they were very wealthy. Sadly I never wrote to her, although I made several false starts at it. However my handwriting and composition were terrible as I was profoundly dyslexic, although that was something neither I nor anyone else knew back then.

Anyway I felt at the time that Marabella was way out of my league. Had she actually received a letter from me it would have been obvious that I was uneducated. Added to that, I was at sea, and where would she go in order to visit my family if it became serious? It seemed hopeless, so I just let it drift. That was the last trip I ever made to Rio, so I was inclined to write it all off to experience.

But in truth it was my lack of self-esteem that stopped me pursuing a relationship with her. I could tell she liked me by the way she looked at me. Had I followed my heart with greater conviction, it may have been a rewarding and inspirational experience in my life, not to say highly advantageous to my fortunes.

However it taught me a lesson for the future. Never walk away from what seems to be a genuine opportunity. It's always worth a try – you never know.

So now we were heading for home. We sailed out of Buanabara Bay on a beautiful South American hot summer evening, heading east out to sea. I remember standing aft on the port side for some time after we'd stood down and had dinner, mulling over my thoughts and memories of the visit against the backdrop of Rio de Janeiro. The sun setting in the west turned its mountains into dark silhouettes behind the city as it dwindled on the horizon. I watched it, wondering what could have been if we just have had a little bit longer. I thought about that girl a great deal. She was just so beautiful!

There were two other notable events on this trip. One took place on our first stop in Rio, on our way down the coast. I learned that the QE2 was in port on her maiden voyage round the world. I'd followed her career on the TV, radio and other media as she was being built and at last launched. So one afternoon after work I made my way up the long quay to take a closer look at her.

It was quite a trek along the great north-south sea dock, past ships loading and discharging cargo from all over the world. It was so hot too that even with my flip-flops on I still had to keep to the shade, slipping between the shadows of warehouses with the sun behind them.

When I arrived in the area where the QE2 was berthed I was amazed at how big she was. There were so many hatches in her hull for loading all the things she needed: linen, food and other provisions, passengers and crew. The painted finish of her black hull didn't look as new as I'd expected.

I stood for a while just looking at her, then I returned to the *Douro*.

—oOo—

It was hard to recall exactly what we did on our runs ashore. Often I did nothing except sit and get drunk or stoned, watching the strangest of scenes unfolding in front of me. Often I felt as if I was sitting beside myself, watching myself watching the others.

If I'm honest, I never really got it. I rarely drank or got stoned to the point of losing control. In retrospect I think of it as like the fear of flying. I guess it came from being thrown on my own resources and having to take responsibility for my own safety when I was still totally immature.

I do believe however that everybody should fly away somewhere, at some time in their lives, to learn what it's really like to be your own person. To live your own life according to your own values. To have the scope to be creative and lead a life discovering other cultures. Not to stay content to be one of the sheep at the back of the herd, following the others in front. Doing that for one's whole life can lead to great disappointment in later life. Be grounded in the present, trust to your own instincts and try to follow your own path in the making.

With the east coast of South America done again, we settled into our passage back home: another 16 more days at sea. It was back into the old routine of painting, chipping rust and sugeing (washing down) – essential maintenance. When the weather was bad we would find ourselves down below decks on the various flats, as they were called. We would clean out hallways, provisions stores, paint and chemical lockers. We would paint deck heads, bulkheads and ceilings or decks, whatever needed covering. There always seemed to be an endless supply of paint on all my ships.

I could never get over the wonderful diversity of change on a daily basis. Like those dark days of wind or rain and low visibility, sometimes only seeing the sea as it passed close to the side of the ship, or even just the glimmer of white horses in the scariest, densest fog. At the other extreme there'd be beautiful hot sunny summer days without a cloud in the sky. Sometimes you could see a clear horizon all the way around, sometimes dabbed with distant clouds like huge fluffy blobs of cotton wool. It imparted a sense of perspective that was completely different every day, which kept life fresh. There's a good line in the JJ Cale song *They Call Me The Breeze* – "ain't no change in the weather; ain't no change in me."

Most nights we would sit at the after end having a can or a spliff, watching ourselves moving across the sea towards the north-east, as the earth turned away from the sun until it disappeared over the horizon. The endless inner conversations which that wonderful scene inspired! Ever enriching my soul and my wellbeing.

Day after day at sea, life goes on. We were just like a little piece of England, bobbing our way across the ocean, doing our bit for the UK.

Although we were at the mercy of the sea – and it could and did turn bad at times and conditions did get dangerous - for the most part it was a carefree life. You could sit quietly for long periods and let your thoughts just wander. You could search inside yourself for the truth to be found within us all. You could learn to see within your own self and understand what you saw, which showed you the way you ought to be. All this is very difficult on land for people living normal lives, with society and its multifaceted systems keeping one forever busy, leaving precious little time or peace of mind to work things out.

Another thing: it's a blessing to be at sea in this day and age, with all our technology and channels of communication. With great numbers of ships at sea, search-and-rescue services are well-drilled and in an emergency the chances of survival are excellent. It is nothing like what our forefathers had to endure in the days of sail. They were in thrall to the wind and weather, with little or no chance of survival if wrecked by storm, fire on board, or uncharted rocks.

Yes, I had a great deal to be thankful for during my experience of being at sea: an experience which is very much part of what I am now.

So, northwards we went once again, sailing on our cardinal path north-by-east, clipping the eastern edge of the Caribbean, crossing the equator high above the sunken mountains of the Mid-Atlantic Ridge, coming out of summer in the southern hemisphere into a more familiar December, losing the hot summer sun as we headed towards winter days in Europe.

We arrived in Lisbon, Portugal, on Thursday 24 December 1970, and made fast. We had cargo to offload, but because the next day was Christmas Day we were unable to do that and leave until Saturday the 26th.

Spending Christmas Day at sea, in port on this occasion was memorable, for one thing: a curious seafaring tradition that the captain and his officers would serve Christmas dinner to the crew – and that was exactly what happened. It was the strangest experience for me and I felt embarrassed by it all. It seemed to upend the proper order of things.

We were all on our best behaviour – both officers and seamen – acting out our respective roles to a T, the officers making sure that we, the seamen, had everything we needed. We never spent much time with the officers, and as for the captain, we rarely saw him at all. So that was kind of nice, and I appreciated the sentiment.

When I was first told what was going to happen, I thought it was another seaman's joke, like the mail helicopter. So I was quite surprised when it actually took place.

All in all, it was a very strange day. But Christmas Day is Christmas Day, wherever you happen to be. And even with the absence of presents we enjoyed the day.

We left Lisbon on the Saturday night, and then it was back to continuous watches. This was because some two weeks before, soon after leaving Rio homeward bound, the autopilot stopped working. This is an electrical device physically attached to the helm and electrically linked to the gyrocompass which automatically holds a course. This would have saved having to maintain three-man watches solely for the purpose of steering.

As I was still a boy rating I couldn't work watches. However I did put in the odd hours to gain experience, or to cover for someone sick. The ship had to be hand-steered all the way up the coast and across the Atlantic on constant watches. This left us boy ratings to do all the day work. Chris, John and the rest of the crew were only there for the mornings or afternoons, doing some overtime depending on the watch they were on.

There was a lot of complaining among the crew about this, especially in bad weather. A ship is hard work to keep going in a straight line at the best of times. The constant onslaught of wind, wave, tides and currents determine the amount of correction needed on the helm. So you'd be constantly moving the wheel to port as the ship veered to starboard, or vice versa. In piloted waters you would be constantly receiving instructions with many changes of course. Following a compass course was a different matter. You had to use your own judgement to effect corrections according to what you saw on the binnacle or gyro in front of you.

The *Douro* was a bitch to steer, as she was flat-bottomed, twin-screwed, had square superstructure and was very old. All of this made her particularly hard to keep on-course. Her flat hull shape didn't allow her to cut through the water as well as conventional hulls, and the twin propellers confused the rudder by creating cavitation. This, along with her slow antiquated steering machinery, made her unpredictable in responding to the wheel. Additionally her square superstructure caught the wind, acting like a sail.

She had been built in 1948: most ships built after that time had more rounded features and a flared bow. This made them aerodynamically sounder, not to say more pleasing to the eye.

The upshot was you'd spend your spell on the wheel wresting it constantly port to starboard, the officer of the watch keeping an eye on the compass to see that you were never more than a degree or two out. It was really hard work, especially in bad weather if it was your stint on the watch, doing the first two hours with only a 15-minute break, which you had to do on one in every three watches. You would come off the wheel with your arms aching badly.

The electricians and some of the engineers were periodically back and forth to the bridge trying different things to rectify the problem with the autopilot. And sometimes, seemingly getting it to work again. On these occasions the watches went back to one man.

However, it only ever worked for a day at best before breaking down again, thus calling out the rest of the watch keepers once more. They failed to find the cause of the problem even in Lisbon, as there was nobody shoreside working over Christmas apart from a few: dockers. So we had to continue with men at the helm back to London.

We were now heading through the Bay of Biscay, with the weather getting colder and greyer. From months of wearing just cutaway shorts and a T-shirt, we went to several layers of warm clothing plus waterproofs, as we returned to winter in the brown waters of the Western Approaches.

At Gravesend we took up our pilot and our familiar SUN tugs, and tied up on the tide at G shed, the usual meat berth in the Royal Albert Dock. We were paid-off on 30 December 1970 – home in time for what was left of the Christmas holiday. With a total of £181 18s 5d earned, I was paid-off (less deductions) with £3 3s 7d cash and £70 in the bank.

We uncovered our hidden cigarettes – the usual routine – and with four of us to a taxi and the ten-bob note protocol to the police on the dock gate along with our customs baggage passes, we left the ship.

With about nine days' leave coming to us, what were we going to do? Most people would go home. Some would just book into the Mission and find another job. Some were company men – they stayed with the same company and waited to be notified of what ship they were going to be assigned to next. Some seamen like Clancy, didn't take any leave – they just stayed on the same ship and continued working. You would find a number of the old hands doing this – many sadly with no homes to go to anyway.

After my brief leave (well, nine days' leave is not a long time), where I spent my time in Watford, mostly with my mum, giving her heavily-edited accounts of my adventures in South America, I presently found myself back in the East End Mission and signed-on at the pool whilst looking for a ship. John and Chris were back too, plus some of the others. The usual affray of partying continued in the Mission, at local haunts around the East End, or up in town. We managed to get an ounce of some nice Lebanese hash, plus some acid.

My memory of those days is hazy, as we quickly fell back into the routine of arriving at the pool looking for a job and then going off partying. But you couldn't skip taking a serious look at the large board above the counter. Written on the board for each ship looking for crew was its name, its company, briefly where it was going, and the crew needed: EDH, AB, DB, JOS, Steward, Cook, and so forth.

Officers' jobs were never advertised here, as you'd guess. Officers tended to be on contract with a given company, which would sponsor them through their long-winded training involving college plus sea-time totalling three years. An officer's job on board was not only more responsible and accountable but also more technical – with a salary to suit, of course.

Having checked the board we would head off to the pub for our lunchtime session, spending the rest of the afternoon getting stoned or simply napping, then having something to eat before starting our evening session. This might involve the hostesses in the mission, going to see a film in a local cinema, or listening to a band in a nearby pub. Or else we'd head up to town to meet some of the girls, who had found their own flats away from the nurses' home, taking them to all-night rock gigs, generally after a few drinks and a bit of a taster of whatever we had with us to make it a bit more interesting.

This went on until we ran out of money. Then we had to move to the cheaper mission in Silvertown – the *Flying Angel* – where we spent more time playing snooker. We also spent more time looking for jobs, which were even then starting to go into decline.

MV Lock Loyal

MV Lock Loyal

However, just in time, we managed to find jobs for all of us, and on 25 January we signed-on with the same ship, the *Lock Loyal*.

Chris and John had made a deep-sea trip on her the previous year, running out to the West Coast of North America, where the ship called in at Los Angeles and Seattle.

We signed-on for the home trade, to discharge a mixed cargo from the States including beans, cheese and all sorts of things like that.

We had hoped to go deep sea on her, as it was a good run out there and she was a delightful little ship, very pretty, with all single-berth cabins midships. I say "little", but she was 10,035 tons grt.

It was good to have a job at last, plus free accommodation. We worked by for several days: berthed alongside E Shed, one of the usual Royal Mail berths in the Albert Dock. Still handy for going ashore in the evenings to the local pubs, or up to town.

It was good to be back on a ship again and focusing on a bit of work to help balance out the head a bit, as we were still recreationally taking various drugs at night, mostly smoking. But I never did whilst working, of course, keeping ourselves safe and those around us. It was strange how we could cut in and out like that. I think it was a good example of the strength of mind a seafarer needs to develop. You just deal with whatever comes at you.

Sadly, after nearly a week on board waiting to take her deep sea, she was put up for sale and our jobs proved short-lived. Our orders were to take her to Falmouth to be laid up. We left the Royal Albert Dock in ballast on 9 February 1971 and made our way down the South Coast. We went through the Straits of Dover, past Portsmouth, Southampton and the Isle of Wight, then Weymouth, Torquay and Plymouth, coming into Falmouth in the early evening of 10 February.

We made our way past Pendennis Castle off the port side, with helicopters buzzing around its naval base, then we passed St Mawes off the starboard side as we went into the Carrick Roads, past the estuary to the Penryn River, up to the Truro River. We were met there by tugs, to which we made fast as we turned into the River Fal. There the tugs turned us around and we dropped anchor just downstream of the King Harry ferry which links Philleigh to Trelissick.

It was very dark and cold, and getting late, so we all expected to be paid-off the following day. However, to our complete surprise, we were told to get ready to disembark and were summoned to the saloon, where we were paid-off. Then the whole crew were taken by a small boat to the quay at Philleigh where a bus was waiting to take us to Truro to catch the milk train to London.

It was a sad occasion leaving the *Loch Loyal* at anchor and wondering what her fate would be. She was built in 1957, so she was only 13 years old. Most ships have a working life of 25 to 30 years – some go on for longer. She was built by Harland & Wolff, Belfast, of Titanic fame, 11,035 gross tonnage, single-screwed steam turbine, double-reduction, with a 16 knots cruising speed. There was accommodation for 12 first-class passengers and a tiled swimming pool. She had been built specially for the North Pacific service for Holland America line. An engine room fire had disabled her in 1969. Some time after we'd left her, she was sold to the Aegis Group of Piraeus, Greece, and renamed *Aegis Loyal*. Sadly she was broken up at Shanghai in October 1974.

There is another story to tell about her, of how in 1964 one of her notable passengers was C.S. Forester, of Hornblower fame, quite aged and disabled, accompanied by his male carer. He became very good friends with one of the engineer officers. Coincidently on that voyage there was an explosion in the engine room that badly injuring the chief engineer. The ship spent the next three days floating around in the Pacific off the southern Californian coast until the tug arrived from San Diego. Under tow to Los Angeles, they managed to repair the engines and she entered the city under her own steam. Apparently Mr Forester regularly used the small swimming pool on the foredeck.

It was a long night, trying to get to sleep on the train. I suppose they didn't want to pay us or feed us for a single day longer than they needed to. The ship, whether up for sale or already sold, was no longer a productive unit. Containerisation was on the way, a much cheaper means of transporting goods, and new ships with new technology were now being built. Existing ships, with their labour-intensive cargo handling, were no longer profitable. Change was on the way: big and fast.

Another thing to consider, which I hadn't realised at the time, was that the impact of frequent dock strikes helped to propel the rapid changes that took place. Shipping companies were consolidating, and many were moving to the Continent. Britain no longer ruled the waves. The demise of the British Merchant Navy was in sight.

Out of curiosity I've been looking at my pay-off slip for this short trip. It was for 17 days, and after tax (£8.10), National Insurance (£1.71) and a cash advance, out of my total earnings of £25.25 plus £18.45 overtime I was left with £25.30 net.

From 1 January 1971 Britain had gone decimal, so underneath the total balance on the slip (£25.30) the chief steward had written "£25/6/-" in case We didn't get what that meant.

We arrived back in London Victoria station around six in the morning, making our way to the East End by tube and back into the Mission. Very few jobs were listed on the board, so things were slow. We'd gathered quite a few friends by now, all hoping to ship out together, which didn't make it easy finding work. The odd job might turn up, but we were looking for a ship to take on the whole crew, and preferably deep sea.

So we dropped back into the almost constant partying at the Mission, and it was another three weeks before we all got jobs. We were having a brilliant time, making new friends of the sailors arriving at the Mission at the end of their leave, looking for jobs. At one point there was about 17 of us.

Apart from Chris and John, a few notable characters I can recall were Digby, a really nice quiet calm sort of chap, who liked to be stoned and smiling; Big Ivan, a larger than life character of colour. He was a happy, confident, competent sort of man, who worked for Port Line; and Shaun, a nice mixed-race lad slightly unsure of himself.

Abby from the *Trebartha* turned up. And Tony Mullens, the steward from Ireland, a nice mild-mannered good man who had given us that fine portable stereo he'd bought in Singapore so we'd always have good sounds when at sea. He went his own way eventually and we never saw much of him again in those days. However, I did catch up with him some time later.

This all took place around the Seamen's Missions at Stratford, Silvertown and Woolwich. There were no end of people willing to entertain us. Quite a few were "queens" – lovely gay or cross dressers who contrived to look convincingly like women. Many had houses and flats round about the Missions, and threw parties for us. They were good people and never importuned. They didn't have to – there were plenty of men who'd quietly go off with them for a while. They offered a great service for those who liked that sort of thing.

We'd also end up at parties back on board ships in the docks, as those of their crew working-by or "rock-dodging" would come ashore and join up with us. I recall a few good nights on the *Aranda*. As the *Aragon*, a Royal Mail boat, she was one of three passenger cargo ships mentioned previously of around 18,000 tons, the others being *Aranza* and *Amazon*, taken off the South America run and put with Shaw Savill doing world cruises. They were later sold and converted into car transporters, eventually being scrapped in the 80s.

One story I heard, at a party on board *Aranda* in the Albert Dock, was that the Rolling Stones had been on board, heading out to do gigs in Brazil and Argentina. They'd spent most of their time in the crew's bar, where they'd been great fun.

Those were strange times – times of great change – as the American drug culture had started to develop in the UK and had been a scene-changer. The New Wave of young seamen had embraced this novel, emerging culture and fused it with what had hitherto been predominantly a drinking scene. Sadly this bright new departure for the merchant navy came just at the latter's demise. Generally speaking it was a more preferable alternative to becoming alcoholic (as most of the older seamen were) but it had its dark side. Some men fell into opiates, and if beached for too long would be lost.

In retrospect I recall that our group eventually broke up into smaller groups favouring different drugs. I think it was down to a man's character or temperament. We were the happy types and smoked hash with the occasional bit of acid. The darker, unhappy ones took to heroin, and we heard of a few dying badly from going down that route.

Alcohol was still to be had though, and represented by far the largest threat, as it does even to this day.

MV Pacific Ranger

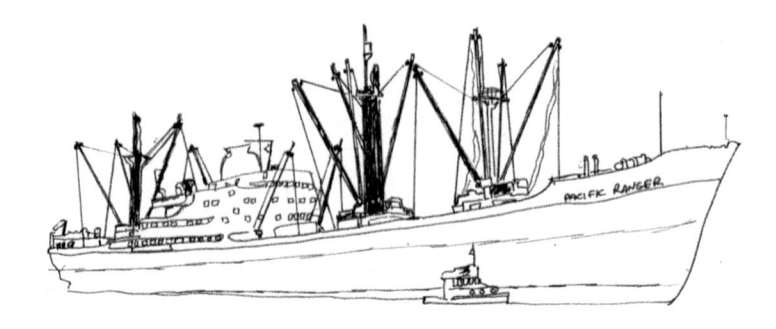

MV Pacific Ranger

Eventually we ran out of money. Fortunately we – or rather four of us – managed to secure a home-trade job on the *Pacific Ranger* (Furness Whitney), back from the Caribbean and the west coast of South America.

Her deep sea crew had been paid off and were now on leave, so we joined her in the Albert Dock on 19 February 1971, bound for Hull, Rotterdam then Hamburg to discharge cargo, Hull again, and back to London to load cargo.

She was a really nice little ship of 6,311 tons, quite small in comparison with my previous ships. But still with a good length, 475 ft, with a 44 ft beam. Built in 1956, she was just three years younger than I was.

She was a comfortable ship too, once again having single-berth cabins amidships: always preferable to stern accommodation, especially in bad weather. A cabin in the stern presents me with the problem of occasionally having to dash to miss the waves in order to get to the mess amidships. Just think about it – a ship bouncing around on a large running sea – and you realise that the bow and stern are going to move the most. In fact the best place to experience the least movement is in the lower part of the hull amidships, which is generally the location of the engine room. Here it is almost like a pivot point for the ship's movement.

After a day or two we set sail out of the Albert Dock into the Thames. I was in the foredeck again. Leaving our tugs and pilot at Gravesend as usual, we headed up north once more past The Wash and Spurn Point into the Humber estuary and Alexandra Dock, where we discharged cargo.

We had a few nights ashore in Hull, in the small dive clubs along the dock road, that led to the city centre approximately 2 miles away. There was also the Mission: that was worth a look-in as well.

When in port we were rarely if ever involved in the handling of cargo. And again we would be cleaning out the mass of rubbish left by the dockers, plus dunnage used to shore up the cargo by dockers in the Caribbean, or on the West Coast of South America. They would have loaded it on board in the various ports from the ship's earlier deep sea voyage, where the company picked up bits and pieces of cargo bound mostly for the UK and the continent, if viable.

Thus we were working around cargoes bound for Hamburg and Rotterdam. This was to be a 2-week trip, discharging and loading cargo for the ship's next trip deep sea.

This was typical of home trade jobs. A lot of seamen only worked on them so they would not have to leave their families for any great length of time. There would still be plenty of overtime, as you would be working watches: 4 hours on, 8 off.

So you would still pick up overtime during the daytime. Also "stations" could be at any time, so if this occurred out of your watch it counted as overtime.

Being the nightwatchman was also part of the equation, since the nightwatchman had to be available to deal with any emergency, fire watch and so forth. There would always be officers on watch on the bridge and in the engine room: in addition there would be a shoreside watchman provided by the port authority to safeguard partially unloaded cargoes and loading equipment, deter unwanted visitors on board or even stowaways.

Most European countries provided this service, within their ports.

So one cold February night we let go fore and aft and headed back down the Humber past Spurn Point. Then we turned east and sailed for a day and a half on past Neuwerk, the small island in the approaches to the river Elbe, and thence inland, heading up this huge motorway of a river to Hamburg.

What a mad place! I had been there before but hadn't really taken it all in. The Germans were certainly a very busy people. They worked fast and hard, and played even harder.

Presently we found ourselves in the red-light district: the world-famous Reeperbahn. We called it the Winkelstrasse – quite why I'm not sure. There is actually a *Winkelstrasse* in the Hamburg area (it means Corner Street), but not one near the city centre, so it was more likely a play on the baby word for penis.

Reeperbahn was a street full of hookers, who sat on display in row upon row of windows. If you fancied one of them you simply went up to the window, asked how much, struck a deal and went inside to enjoy yourself.

There was something there for everyone: all different shapes, sizes, genders, fetishes and orientations. As is the norm in these places, we went there just for the fun of it. We were all young and didn't need their services, even if we could have afforded them. European hookers are very expensive: it's all big business for pimps and club owners. Very few seamen would visit them, apart from one or two older ones who didn't have wives or were so institutionalised they didn't have the social skills to find someone and establish a relationship. There was also the time constraint: seamen were never in one place long enough for a leisurely courtship. On the other side of the coin. If you needed instant unconditional gratification, most ships had a queen or two, mostly stewards, Who would be quite obvious bye behave in a more feminine way who would be happy to oblige at any time if approved.

We passed through the red-light district enjoying the spectacle, but really much more interested in finding some acid. On our first night there we scored some, or so we thought. But we had been ripped off. We were charged 10 DM for each tab – about £1. But it wasn't acid, just saccharine or something of the sort. However we already had plenty of hash, plus money for booze, so we were happy enough. Rotterdam was our next stop, and we expected better luck there.

So two days later we were happy to leave Hamburg and find ourselves amidst the city of ships that was Rotterdam: the largest port in the world. After a couple of runs ashore we got hold of the acid trips we needed, and back later on out return to Hull we managed to swap some of them for a bit of hash.

As a rule you could get any amount of hash in Holland. But on this occasion we just chanced on a good deal. We had got to know some good people in Hull, who liked a bit of good acid, so it worked out fine for all of us.

It was easy but unmemorable sailing in UK and continental waters. I was now a JOS and stood a few watches on occasions, It was good to get some experience on the wheel, and also as lookout on the wing of the bridge.

At this time of year it was cold up there, and busy at times. As previously mentioned the basic task was to report lights, or (in daytime) items as they appeared on the horizon. You would report a sighting to the officer of the watch, who would note it on the chart, and more importantly (with always the possibility of quickly-changing weather conditions that could affect visibility) would be plotted on the radar screen. Here the reported sightings would be identified and marked with a marker pen on a plastic overlay on the screen. Each of the targets' positions would be updated and re-marked every 5-10 minutes or so. Joining the dots would then tell you the direction each target was travelling in. Targets that had not changed position were presumed stationary: they could mostly be identified by referring to the chart for that area.

All this would give the officer of the watch a comprehensive picture of what was happening in the immediate area, enabling him to plot our course safely. Sometimes this needed evasive action to prevent a collision.

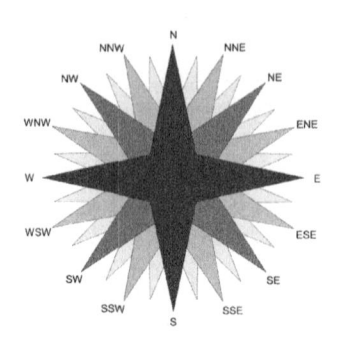

The sighting would be reported in a systematic way, which included a subjective judgement by the lookouts, using a division of the 360° of the compass into 32 points.

Examples:
1. Two points after of the starboard quarter.
2. Three points off the port bow.

Although your approximate target cited would be confirmed by the radar, being aware of new sightings was a skill. You needed to be ahead of the game and have your wits about you. Although it was confusing at first you did form general overview of what was going on in the sea around you after a while.

This was especially true in bottlenecks such as the entrances to large ports, rivers, sandbanks with shallow waters which gave you little room to manoeuvre, ferries and dense traffic. The English Channel ticks all the boxes: it is the busiest stretch of sea in the world.

On the quieter areas of the coast you would only have the officer of the watch, helmsman and lookout on the bridge. However, depending on the situation with traffic, weather conditions etc., you could find all the officers there, the captain and the deck cadets, plus two lookouts, one on each wing of the bridge.

Then there is conventional navigation to consider, especially the tide. Some tides run very fast: you can easily find your ship going ahead at 15 knots plus 6 knots sideways as you sail across the surface of a vast volume of water moving to its own rhythm, with its ebbing and flooding tides. The British have a formalised system for handling this, and under normal circumstances it works safely.

The weather of course is yet another factor. Wind, rain and fog bring poor visibility and present a consequent nightmare for navigation.

The last factor – and possibly the most dangerous one – is human error. You can't assume that all the other craft in the vicinity are being as diligent as you are. You must always expect the unexpected.

A good example of this occurred on the *Pacific Ranger* as we were leaving Hamburg. It was a cold bright February day. I was on the wheel, on the 8-12 watch. We had come down the Elbe from Hamburg. Like most large European rivers, the Elbe was like a motorway, with something like three lanes either side of the river. We were heading west just at the point where the river opens out into the estuary. A German ship of similar size to us had been slowly undertaking us for about 30 minutes. She was very close to us – maybe 100 yards. This is close when you think our ship was 475 foot long.

The second officer had been concerned about this, and the captain himself had been called onto the bridge. There was a constant movement of officers zigzagging across in front of me on the helm, from wing bridge to wing bridge, and sure enough, without any notice, and when she had passed us by only maybe 40 or 50 yards or so, she came hard to port right across our bow.

The captain ordered me, via the second officer, to bring her to port as he moved the telegraph to Slow Ahead Engines. The second engineer below repeated back the order, confirming it with the familiar clanging of bells. We started to slow as the bow moved to port. A more obvious move would have been to starboard. However we were on the northern side of the river, thus heading to starboard would have brought us into shallower water. Fortunately there was no other vessel coming up on our port side, so we had some room.

The ship hadn't even sounded its horn to notify a change of course (one blast would have meant to port, 2 to starboard and three dead ahead). There was a lot of swearing going on, I can tell you.

Once we were clear, I was ordered to bring the helm to midships, and then 20% starboard helm, bringing us back to our original course.

"That was close! What the hell was he thinking?" the captain said, referring to the ship now heading out more to the south.

It was all very exciting, and I well remember him saying "Well done, everybody".

The second officer had certainly done his job – he had called the captain to the bridge for support, he had called down by phone to the engine room to put it on standby, and kept on working, updating the general scene with the chart, radar, and visual both sides of the ship, so that in the event of something like that happening we would be ready for it, with several changing scenarios present in his mind.

As for me, I had just been a pawn in the game. I loudly repeated every order given, and confirmed it after I'd carried it out.

Thinking about it later, and ever since, I was struck by the feeling of exhilaration and total presence as I watched the head of the ship moving to port or starboard. I found, those few moments extremely confirming, followed by an overwhelming feeling of achievement. This was a huge step forward for my self-esteem.

I always loved being on the helm anyway. It was an incredible, inexplicable sensation that was pure Zen on one level, with the excited child still inside me with my heart beating quickly with excitement. There was also a strong sense of connection with the officers and the ship. Every ship has its own character or signature: each helm feels different and all ships move in a different unique way as you turn the wheel. I was amazed too at how a multitude of small moments added up to have a huge impact on me as a person, and my relationship with the people around me.

Arriving in Hull the net day, we spent two days taking on cargo, and had a bit of a run ashore.

Returning to London from Hull, I was on the same watch. It was somewhere between 8 and 12 in the evening and we were off the Lincolnshire coast. I was coming down from an acid trip I'd been on the previous night before leaving Hull, and still mildly feeling the effects. I was on the wheel, following a south-easterly course, glorying in the big-screen movie going on in front of me as I steered: the lights of towns on the coast, buoys ahead twinkling and flashing, a dark sea with a glow on the horizon and stars in the sky, plus the many lights of other ships. Frequent changes of direction drew my attention to the lit-up gyrocompass. I was relishing the whole situation, considering how lucky I was to be there experiencing it all.

A little later I overheard the second officer talking quietly to the third. He was saying "I can't wait to get to London. I have five weeks' leave coming and I can't wait to get back to the cottage and try out this supposedly lovely acid."

I couldn't believe my ears. But I was gradually becoming aware that in those days everyone was at it – people from all walks of life.

We arrived back in London later the next day. After picking up the pilot, plus the shadow of two SUN tugs at Gravesend Reach opposite Tilbury, we took the lines of the tugs on approaching the lock into our now very familiar Royal Docks. Later that night we found ourselves on the lay-by berth opposite E and F shed near the dry-dock and the swing bridge leading to the Victoria dock.

I was paid-off on 4 March 1971. In 14 days I had earned £28.15 and I received £10.99. I spent a few days' leave in London. It seemed hardly worth heading up to Watford for just two days, so I went back to the Seamen's Mission and plunged back into the never-ending party. I took the Friday and the weekend off and went back to the pool on the Monday.

Then the strangest thing happened. We were sitting in the lounge one afternoon when a familiar face walked in. I could hardly believe my eyes: it was Steve Peters, an old acquaintance, who had become my best friend in my final year at school. I had totally forgotten, he had joined the Merchant Navy some six months after I'd left Watford. He had passed through the training school and done two trips as a deck boy on the *Otaio*, a cadet ship of the New Zealand Shipping Company. He had just finished his leave, and walked out. He was now staying at the Mission too, and he sat down and joined us. It was really so good to see him.

I remember him having a few seizures at school, and at his home where I stayed with him for a while. He lived with his mother at her house in Bushey, near Watford. He was half-German on his father's side, but his father was not around. I do remember seeing a dark blue German uniform hanging in a wardrobe, but never understood its significance. I can only presume it must have been his father's uniform from WW2, or that of a relative.

MV Oroya

MV Oroya (formerly: MV Pacific Ranger)

On the Wednesday we all went to the pool and – *eureka!* – there was a PSNC (Pacific Steam Navigation Company) ship called the *Oroya* taking on a full crew.

We had a new friend, Sean, who had joined our happy group. He was a year or so older than me, of English West Indian origin. John, Chris and Sean all took EDH jobs whilst Steve and I took the two SOS jobs.

It was brilliant.

So we grabbed our gear and headed for the ship's berth at D shed in the Albert Dock. Lo and behold! It was the *Pacific Ranger* we had just done the home trade on, which had since been renamed.

She was owned by the Furness Whitney Group. Like many other such ships in those days, she was passed around the various companies within the group, being renamed each time.

Built in 1956 for PSNC as the *Pacific Ranger*, she was transferred in 1968 to Shaw Savill and renamed *Oroya*. In 1970 she was chartered to the Furness Whitney Group and reverted to being the *Pacific Ranger*, then in 1971 once again became the *Oroya*. The following year she was sold to a Panamanian company and renamed *Lamma Island*, being scrapped in 1984 or thereabouts.

It was a good run: Hamilton, Bermuda, Nassau, Bahamas, Kingston (Jamaica), Curaçao (for bunker fuel), then the Panama

Canal, followed by several ports up and down the Chilean and Peruvian coast, with some ports in Ecuador, and Colombia to the North. then back home via Panama again It sounded good.

We joined her on Thursday, 11 March 1972. We worked by for two days or so, and spent our evenings as usual drinking and getting stoned.

The day before we departed, we were treated to a curious sight. A gang of men arrived, some of them with scuba gear. They ran a thick cable from stem to stern and right under the ship from a vehicle on the quay, spiralling along the whole ship. The men in scuba gear went into the water to feed the cable. They then passed the current through the cable to de-magnetise the ship.

This was a procedure carried out on ships at regular intervals, especially those that would be using the great canals and rivers, such as the Panama Canal, the Suez Canal and the major European waterways such as the Rhine, the Meuse and the Danube, where large vessels travel many miles inland. I should note in passing that the Suez Canal was still closed in those days following the Six Day War in 1967. It did not reopen until 1975.

Metal ships are prone to acquiring a magnetic moment, and the process we witnessed – called "de-perming" – was intended to eradicate it to stop it causing problems affecting navigational equipment.

There is also another sort of magnetic variation to allow for, called "declination" or deviation. This is the difference between true North and magnetic North. The latter changes slowly over time: in the order of $0.05°$ to $0.1°$ per year. This doesn't sound much, but if your chart is 10 years old, then it is out by $1°$. Charts are dated for this reason. If you travel just $1°$ out for 24 hours at 13 knots, you will end up roughly 10 km from your target position. Multiply this by weeks travelling across large seas or oceans and you'd be in serious trouble.

Another reason for de-perming is somewhat dubious. I was told at the time that ships meeting in close quarters, one having come from the southern hemisphere, the other from the north, could be attracted to each other thus increasing the chance of a collision.

Shortly after de-perming we moved the boat across and down the dock onto the D shed berth with the aid of a tug. The next day was spent in dockers loading the last of the cargo, with us as usual following behind, dropping derricks, stowing and securing gear and making ready to leave.

The next day, on a very crisp sunny spring morning, we were turned to for stations and found ourselves being tugged away from the berth as we let go. I was with the foredeck crowd under the first officer, a strange round chirpy little chap with a high-pitched but surprisingly loud voice. We instantly nicknamed him Mighty Mouse. He always got us all smiling. He was either unaware of people's reaction to his strange persona, or chose to ignore it.

We mostly shipped out from the Albert Dock from the top end near the swing bridge at the Connaught pub, our regular for a pint. Sometimes on our way back from a night in town, that pint was strangely sobering. It brought us down-to-earth after the highs of the night before. It also served as the "hair of the dog", as in there somewhere, if not noticeable, would be a hangover from the vast amounts of beer that we always drank along with everything else we took.

Again, there was always something about moving down the dock, passing all the familiar liveries of the ships. Blue Star Line, grey hull and red funnel with its prominent blue star; Port Line, also with a red funnel; the buff colours of the Furness group (ours); the uniformly painted Shaw Savill, Royal Mail and PSNC, all slowly sailing under the one hat.

I loved going back to sea – the feeling of anticipation: what will this trip bring? Heading for new places I had only read about or heard tell of. I would always soak up confidence on seeing all the ships just back from their voyages, or just leaving, like us. Thousands of us, all moving slowly about the planet, taking the wares of our cultures and bringing back those of other countries, thereby enriching the world.

As we continued slowly down the dock towards the lock which led to the river and back to the sea, I found myself as usual thinking with guarded anticipation: what's the weather like out there today? Will we encounter storms this trip, or flat calm balmy days? Will we be safe?

It was early March, as we that morning as we moved out of the dock and down the river. Soon enough we were out of the Thames estuary and heading south-westerly down the English Channel. Whilst washing down and cleaning the decks we'd occasionally glance out over the starboard side to the Sussex coast. We'd pass other ships with a slow easy roll, slightly pitching over a brisk moderate sea, white horses waving us a fond farewell, with the occasional bit of salty spray refreshing our faces from a clumsy wave hitting the fore port quarter off the bow. Taking in breaths of good clean fresh air again, we'd know it was good to be back at sea.

We cleared the Dover Straits and the next day we were in St George's Channel off Land's End. We set a south-westerly course for our first port of call: Hamilton, Bermuda. Surprisingly enough, that was only an eight day voyage away, 3,000 nautical miles out and down across the northern Atlantic, crossing the current of the Gulf Stream to the edge of the Sargasso Sea. This is about 800 nautical miles from the American eastern seaboard, on a level with southern Carolina and northern Georgia. New York was about 700 nautical miles to the north West.

It never ceased to amazed me, how by simply heading across a very familiar ocean, only on a different heading, would completely change your perspective. The Polynesians of old were said to have navigated from the South Sea Islands to New Zealand thousands of miles away with only a coconut sextant, plus their skill and knowledge, which enabled them to read the sea and skies and feel the prevailing winds. I can well believe it.

Daily life at sea resumed. Ours was a happy ship. We had a lump of hash as usual that soon ran out, but we were not too bothered. There was always booze and we all got on and had great laughs together.

It turned out there was some more lads on the boat that liked to turn on – in fact eight out of us ten deckhands did. Well, with Steve now, and Sean, plus the three others we'd met on board, there were five of us at least.

I was not sure about the stewards. We never saw much of them, since they worked 12-hour days and we had a messman to look after us. There were three donkey men who shared our mess: they always seemed to be older men. It's strange how the different departments kept slightly apart.

The food on this ship was great and there was plenty of it. Some companies could be very mean with the food budget, but this would work against them as it would be reflected in the morale of the ship, and the quality of the crew's work. Our messman was great. He used to put a huge meat salad in the fridge at night. This was nominally for the watchmen but splendid for a bit of supper for us before turning in for the night.

I had a really nice cabin, amidships on the port side, with a wooden bunk, a daybed, a wardrobe, a chest-of-drawers with a pull-out writing table and an armchair. The ship was built in late 1957. In some of the ships of that period the accommodation could be really comfortable, and some not. It was all down to the designers, their specifications, and the company's budget. The *Trebartha* for instance, built in 1962, was extremely primitive, with its crew accommodation aft, with hospital-type metal beds. Although it was five years newer than the *Oroya* it was older in design. The *Douro* had been built in 1948, but based on a design going back to the early 1930s, with its angular box look with straight bow and cramped double-berth cabins. Therefore, as regards accommodation, it was just the luck of the draw.

The weather was hot on this part of the voyage, with temperatures increasing every day. Within three days we were starting to swelter, although there was still a bit of wind and lumpy seas, but the time went quickly, all in good form, until we spotted the island of Bermuda one evening.

The following day was beautifully sunny and hot, and we were called to stations early as we threaded our way through huge gaps in coral reefs with the sea breaking over them, and between small high-sided islands into the Great Sound. Sometimes we passed them worryingly close.

Eventually the beautiful view of Hamilton harbour was revealed, perfectly situated. We sailed into the inner harbour, and with the aid of tugs we drew alongside a smallish stretch of quayside right in the centre of town. We were next to Front Street adjacent to Cabinet Gardens, which surround the Cabinet Building.

It was a really beautiful place, with multicoloured shops and other buildings, all with upstairs verandas. The town had an Australian look about it.

It was still early in the morning, about 9 AM. We were only in port for two days, so the bo's'un gave the order for a "job-and-knock" – painting the funnel. Eager to get ashore, we set-to. Having done all the prep work previously, we rigged our bo's'uns chairs, then after heaving ourselves up to the top of the funnel, we quickly lowering ourselves down again, whilst painting a coat of Shaw Savill buff-coloured gloss. It's surprising what you can do if suitably motivated.

After eating our lunch most of us went ashore. None of us had much money, since we'd only worked for 10 days, so there wasn't much in the way of earnings to sub.

Hamilton was a sleepy little place, and very sheltered. There were no tall buildings but plenty of pastel-coloured houses heading up and over the low-lying hill surrounding the town. This was where many wealthy businessmen and Hollywood filmstars lived. Bermuda is a British colony and a tax haven that provides an office address for many groups of businessmen: syndicates that pool their wealth and make it available to banks and lending establishments all over the world, including Lloyds Insurance. It was a Bermuda consortium that underwrote the early civilian space programme for instance, plus the space shuttle. They could tackle any large project that no single person or organisation could afford to underwrite. Just another form gambling really.

The how island had a maximum speed-limit of 30 mph and drove on the left as in England. It was possible to hire mopeds, but we could not afford them. More's the pity, as it would have been good to explore that small but beautiful island.

After a few hours wandering around taking in the sights, we returned to the ship for dinner and to get ready for the evening's partying. There was no obvious drug culture that we knew of, or could see, so it was alcohol only for the anticipated fun ashore.

We started out in a club the lads who'd been here before knew of. There were about eight of us, all sitting at one of the large round tables. After a while it dawned on us that we were getting aggressive abuse from a neighbouring table of Americans. We rode it for quite some time, until they started to physically threaten us, calling us limey yellow bastards and such. There were fifteen or so of them, so we were well outnumbered. Just when it was all about to turn nasty, a crowd of big guys we hadn't noticed before came over from another table and silently stood by us.

That seemed to put the Americans off.

The newcomers were Canadians, as it turned out. They stayed to chat for a short while before leaving the bar – as did we. They told us the Americans had been making trouble deliberately and for no reason – it's something they haven't stopped doing to this day. Globally.

We then did a bit of a pub crawl, and were walking along the road laughing and joking when unbelievably we saw two English bobbies coming towards us, or so it seemed. What were they doing here? – I wondered. But as they came closer we saw they were coloured men – a thing you would not often see in England in those days. It grew even stranger when one of them stopped, looked hard at us all, then raised his hand and said in a broad American accent, "Hey! Cool it a bit there, you guys!" It was just so bizarre we couldn't help laughing. Quietly, of course.

By now we were all nicely drunk and on good form. Soon we found ourselves upstairs in another large bar. By this time I was feeling quite drunk and everything was becoming a pleasant blur. Suddenly shouting and crashing broke out. I saw John, with blood all over his face, fighting with another guy, fists and legs flying all over the place. Before I could work out what was happening I was pushed or knocked over and fell into a corner under a table. By the time I got to my feet again, a bunch of Americans were running down the stairs with our own lads in hot pursuit. I hurried after them, jumping over a few toppled bodies on the floor. Suddenly I heard "Run! Police!" – so I did just that.

Outside, I found myself alone. I wandered around aimlessly for a bit before meeting up again with Chris and a few of the others.

We went and had some more drinks, trying to work out between ourselves what had happened. Chris told me the trouble had been caused by some of the Americans we'd encountered earlier that evening. John had got into a slanging match with one of them, when suddenly the fellow put a glass in his face.

Instantly it seemed that everyone who'd witnessed the incident made a lunge for the assailant. His American pals started pulling and shoving, trying to get him out of the bar, with the rest of the customers throwing kicks and punches at them. They dashed off down the stairs, hotly pursued by our lads, who chased them off.

After wandering about for a bit, we returned to the ship to discover John fast asleep, with a large bandage on his face, crashed out in the messroom doorway. We stepped over him, still discussing what had happened, laughing over a big mug of tea and a plate of the wonderful cold meat salad that our wonderful messman habitually put in the fridge for us.

It turned out that John had been taken to the town hospital. He had a deep cut through his right eyebrow that needed four stitches. Luckily that was all. Knowing John we knew he could provoke a bit of trouble sometimes. However he wasn't a bad lad, and certainly didn't deserve that.

Next morning we all turned-to for work, John included, but it was clear he was extremely shaken and hung over.

That evening we were back at sea. We let go and headed from Nassau in the Bahamas, some 700 nautical miles away to the south-west: about 2 days' sailing.

The Bahamas are a string of islands to the east and south of Miami and the Florida Keys, and to the north of Cuba. Their capital is Nassau, on the island of New Providence. After an uneventful two days at sea, travelling down the eastern edge of the famous Bermuda Triangle, with good weather and no paranormal activity, unusual sightings or disappearances, we arrived at Nassau on March 22nd. It was well into springtime there, with temperatures of around 28°C – as hot as a scorching English summer, but very humid.

We entered the harbour from the north, passing some low-lying islands to the south of us – Long Cay and Crystal Cay – then Colonial Beach on the west end of Paradise Island with its town of Atlantis. We tied up alongside a long quay just before the ferry terminal and passenger liner berth.

It was a beautiful low-lying island. We were only going to be there for one night, but none of us had much money anyway. They accepted American dollars, as they did throughout the Caribbean. Six of us pooled what money we had and ventured out to see what we could find.

After walking around this busy town, we found ourselves in a strange club, or bar, full of smart-looking people all sitting at tables. On the stage was a small band of Hispanic-looking musicians playing Latin music, which I thought at that time was pretty repetitive. All the drinks were $3 or so, which was far more than we could afford, so we simply sat for a while.

It was impossible not to notice a crowd of very happy people at a table with large champagne buckets on it. Among them was a most attractive blonde. Presently, to our utmost surprise, she got up from her table and came over to us, grabbed a chair and sat down. In the silence that followed she looked hard at us and said in the broadest of American accents, "Hi there, call me Cocaine. I've got enough coke and acid to blow everybody's minds in here for the next four months."

We hadn't been sitting for long before John, after what seemed no time at all, said to her, "Would you like to come back to the ship?"

"Yes," she said.

As they left together, John said "Come back on board in about an hour." So we sat for a while and listened to the music, waiting for the guest artist – I think he must have been a local celebrity – who had been excitedly promised for some time. When he eventually came on-stage he sounded no different from any of the others, so far as I could tell. So, following John's suggestion, we went back to the ship, where we found John in his bunk with the blonde.

She said, "Okay, if you all line up I'll give you something nice." When it was my turn she held out a tin chock-full of pills and small packets. As I hesitated she looked at me with a smile and said "Okay, Purple Haze for you, I think." She took out a small purple pill and popped it into my mouth.

After we'd all taken an assortment of pills, we had a can of beer or two and went back ashore. It was hard to remember the rest of the night as this stuff was really strong. It was the first of the original American 450 mg trips, which went under a variety of names such as Orange Sunshine, Strawberry Fields, White Lightning and many others, all of which I was to take subsequently on various occasions.

I returned to awareness in the early hours of the following morning, and found we were all on the beach. It was an extremely beautiful dawn as we walked back to the ship. At this point everything had stopped moving, but still had an intensity of colour that was staggering. It was like being in a cartoon for real, and the ship looked like a toy model.

By this time my recall was back and I knew I had to turn-to for work at 9 AM.

So I had a most bizarre-looking breakfast, with lots of mugs of heavily-sugared tea, which helped me come down. Finally, after taking an extraordinary shower and sitting for a while on the poop deck at the after end, watching the city wake up and the dockers come on board to work our cargo, I heard the echo of a familiar voice. of the bo's'un, "Okay lads. Turn-to."

I don't recall being aware of the others. My feelings were intense and solitary. I was put to work on and around the outboard gangway, which was currently not in use. It was partially turned out, giving access to one side of the hull and the bulwarks for chipping and painting, to make it look nice for visitors coming aboard when it eventually got used.

First Impressions Count.

I spent a unforgettable morning sitting on the gangway, swung out and turned flat, chipping small areas of rust. Although I'm sure I was *compos mentis*, my senses were exaggerated and extreme. Rainbow-coloured sparks flew from my chipping hammer and each blow sent a shock through my whole body.

I watched as a passenger liner came in and tied up opposite us, on the other side of a small bay that formed the sea dock. The scene of the ship's docking manoeuvres seemed to move like a time-lapse film, as I must have lost brief periods in my sense of time passing, while my visual and thought processes drifted on a random journey of revelation. In retrospect, for me the return to normality as the effect of the drug wore off was the profoundest part of the acid experience.

It seemed scarcely any time at all before the chief's high-pitched screech cut through my waking dreams, shouting the unexpected order: "Stations fore and aft – make ready for sea, lads! Forward crew Start at number 3 hatch." After number four

So that's where I went.

Of the five hatches, number 3 is one of the three located on the foredeck nearest the bridge. On arrival I met up with all the other lads. Where had they all been? – I wondered.

As usual, the dockers had swung all the fore derricks out of the way of the shore cranes and just left them. So we were told to tidy them up and make them fast. The weather forecast was good, so we were just supposed to make them secure whilst leaving them topped. It's a lot of work lowering all 16 derricks only to have to top them again some days later.

For a minute we all just stood there in stunned silence, gazing at the mess of sticks, ropes, wires, block-and-tackle etcetera. I knew what was going on in everyone's minds, as I knew that everybody else had taken a trip last night: What the hell do we do with this lot? Where do we start?

Just then, on the other side of the hatch, a lad appeared who had been a night watchman and was just up and out of bed. He looked upwards, rolled up his sleeves and grabbed a rope. I'll never forget what happened next. The six of us, who'd been off our faces all night with no sleep, watched that rope as it rippled its way up to the top of the derrick head where it was attached. All at once it clicked in our minds, and everything we needed to do came back to us.

Chris and I jumped onto the winches. In no time at all we'd pulled in the derricks and positioned them neatly, fore and after. Then we secured them tightly with all the associated ropes, block-and-tackle, plus wires used to control their sideways motion, closed the metal hatches, then moved on to number 2 hatch, then number 1, the after-crew doing the same for hatches 4 and 5. Then we went straight to stations on the fo'c's'le deck, ready to let go.

This job would normally have taken two hours. Remarkably we'd completed it in 45 minutes. A miracle. I distinctly remember the chief officer arriving on the fo'c's'le head, staring at us all, then at the remarkably tidy and secure foredeck. He took his hat off with one hand, rubbed his other hand over his nearly bald head, put his hat back on and said with a broad smile in his squeaky voice, "Well, I just don't know about you lads, I really don't know!"

He looked around him, then said, "Okay then, let's get out of here." He pressed the transmit button on his hand radio and said, "Ready to let go forward, bridge." Next came the voice of the second officer, "Ready to let go aft." We then heard the familiar Geordie tones of the captain, "Okay, single up fore and aft."

"Roger that, forward."

"Roger that, aft."

We set-to, bringing in four of the five huge polypropylene mooring lines, made fast the tug standing-by off our starboard quarter, eventually getting the order to let go fore and aft. Then, with the deep throaty sound, and vibration of our engine, smoke pouring from the funnel, mixed with the roar of the tugs taking up the strain, we moved away from our berth. Within 30 minutes we were letting go the tugs and heading out into the open water.

We stood down, leaving it to the watch-keepers to rig the pilot ladder and see the pilot safely off the ship. We turned and stowed the gangways and headed into the mess for dinner.

I remember us all having apparently returned to normality, as we laughed and tucked into our food. However those of us who'd shared the experience of the night before looked around us and saw something profound in each others' eyes. It was an inexplicable feeling. I'm certain we all underwent some re-evaluation of our mental structures that night and in the days that followed, the effect of which would have an influence on the rest of our lives. It certainly did on mine.

The next port of call was Kingston, Jamaica. We were all looking forward to it. The weather was a bit unsettled on this leg of the journey, the wind occasionally giving us a running sea with some rain, and visibility was not so good. It was very hot and humid and we couldn't see the north eastern coast of Cuba, which lay to the south west of us as we travelled the 400 miles to our destination.

We passed the whole string of the Bahamas to our northeast: Great Exuma, Crooked Island, Acklins, finishing with Great Inagua off the port beam and the south-easterly tip of Cuba. Then turning to starboard we entered the Windward Passage, steering a westerly course between Cuba and Haiti to cover the last 250 miles to Kingston, Jamaica.

We were now in a region of the Caribbean Sea known historically as the Greater Antilles. The name predates the European conquest of the New World and refers to the phantom islands shown on ancient maps in random locations in the Atlantic Ocean. English, Dutch, Spanish and Portuguese explorers all coined variations on this word.

On the morning of the third day we found ourselves closing the east coast of Jamaica. We soon passed its thin south-eastern tip, past Port Morant, with its white sandy beaches and palm trees set against a backdrop of jungle-covered mountains rising in the distance. We kept well clear of Folly Bay, with its waves breaking on hidden coral reefs.

Along with the Bahamas, these islands of the Antilles are an absolute paradise. I relished the scene as we made our way along a channel marked with large buoys on the approaches through Kingston Bay, into the outer harbour of Kingston itself, passing between Port Royal and Portmore, with its aptly named Dream Beach.

We took our tugs as usual, came about and made fast on the sea wall. We were port side on to a long harbour wall just outside where the passenger liners berthed. There was one huge American liner with its stern on to ours, with its graduated rows of decks, moving in and up with hands of bloods (which is how a cruise ship crew refer to their live cargo). Liner crews are a different sort of seamen, but both are of equal importance to the welfare of the nation. We were bringing raw materials and manufactured items essential to its consumer, industrial and financial infrastructure; the tourists brought the hard cash to buy it all.

We'd arrived quite early in the morning, and were given a "job-and-knock" – topping the remaining derricks and swinging them all outboard away from the shoreside cranes once again. So we finished the jobs we had to do, had our lunch, then sat on the afterdeck watching the excitement taking place. Some of the local lads were entertaining the passengers by doing high dives off the stern of the liner.

One would stand on a prominent part of the superstructure while another collected dollars from the onlooking passengers. Then would come the spectacular dive. They worked in twos, taking it in turn to dive and take the money.

It was a dangerous stunt. Not so much for the height of the dive, even though it progressed to higher and higher decks, but for the fact that these waters were shark-infested, the sharks coming in to feed off the rubbish tossed overboard. Moreover the sea at that time was also infested with numerous types and quantities of lethal stinging jellyfish, the Portuguese Man-o'War being the best-known. So the swimmers had to judge their dives into clear patches of water, and their partners on deck then had to guide them to a clear path back to the steps on the harbour wall.

It was quite a climb back though, urged-on by loud roars and applause as he made his way back up onto the harbour wall, shimmied up the large after-mooring lines back on board, then make his way back up onto the upper decks for the next dive. We too enjoyed watching it and I think they did very well out of it.

That afternoon we went ashore for a while to take a look around. It was a strange place and we couldn't help feeling slightly vulnerable amongst all the hustle and bustle, with dark, strong-looking characters going about their business. Maybe I was just projecting my thoughts onto them as they looked at us with our long hair and white skins. I had the expectation they might harbour a grudge against us, for our ancestors possibly being the ones that brought their ancestors over here from Africa as slaves. However they all seem to be quite happy, with lots of music in their lives, living on this beautiful island. They may indeed have been thankful they were not in one of the many African states where life would not be as free for them. Sometimes it takes a while for blessings in disguise to become apparent. Which is not to excuse slavery in those days, which was horrendous and savage.

We did however relax when we came across a busy crossroads. Located in the centre of this was a large policeman in uniform, standing on a raised pedestal directing the traffic. Amazingly, he had a big smile on his face and, to our astonishment, a huge spliff hanging out of his mouth, with vast amounts of smoke belching out of it. He seemed to be dancing to all the different musical sounds coming from bars round about. I wondered if he might have been planted there by the Jamaican Tourist Board.

We realised at that point that we'd found our people, and really there was nothing for us to be afraid of. Thereafter we continued to look round the red-light district and tried a few bars until eventually we came across a likely-looking place. There we managed to score, or buy, a small bag of grass, which cost us next to nothing. It was lovely stuff with a lovely effect that just made you laugh, and it lived up to the reputation of Jamaican grass, being sweet-smelling and sweet-tasting.

We continued our walk, taking the long way back to the ship for our tea, having a shower, and heading back out on the town for the night.

During the hours that we worked during the day, it was a bit tricky to move around as the whole ship was just alive, with all the hatches being worked. Cargo for the UK was being loaded aboard and shoreside chains lifted out the cargo being discharged for Kingston.

One afternoon one of the officers asked me if I'd go down number 3 hold and be on cargo watch for a couple of hours. I must have looked at him in wonder because he said "It's okay – just a deterrent, really. You just make your presence felt down in the lower hold. Hopefully it will stop the dockers down there pilfering from the other lockers in the 'tween decks with goods for future ports of call."

So I went down there with the books I was currently reading, made myself comfortable and just read and watched.

There were six huge men handling barrels of lime juice that were being sent down, stowing them into the hold and shoring them up so they would not move. Periodically one man would stoop and pick up a scrap of paper from the floor, form it into a cone-shaped makeshift pipe, fill it full of grass and light it. They'd smoke these pipes together endlessly. I was getting high just from the fumes. Needless to say they didn't try to steal anything, and I couldn't have done anything about it if they had.

Some time later I was relieved by one of the deck cadets. I enjoyed the experience, and it helped me understand a little more about loading ships – the ambiance of those parts of the ship that the whole business is all about, but which you don't often get to see. Not to mention the working culture and work ethic of the Jamaican dockers.

We spent the next three days working happily in the sunshine during the day, and having a great time around the bars and cafes after dark. We were simply a load of happy people getting stoned, listening to music, dancing, talking to the beautiful women, and generally enjoying life. We just loved Kingston, and decided Jamaica really was a great place.

We were sad to leave this wonderful island, but before long we had to. But first we managed to secure a quantity of grass for ourselves. It came in the form of three tightly wrapped cylinders of newspaper which cost us $15 each.

We let go and headed out one afternoon, very sad to be leaving. It was nighttime before we finished tidying up and making good on deck. We had our evening meal as the ship headed south west into the night towards the island of Curaçao.

In the crew's accommodation you could hear a strange rustling noise, as everyone who had purchased grass were unwinding the tubes of the compressed stuff and separating it out on to the tables. Then, from a small mountain of the stuff, we sorted out all the small stalks, twigs, seeds, etc. and broke it all down to make it as small as possible. Then we put it into bags made from airmail envelopes by sticking them down and cutting one end open. The majority of it was stashed away somewhere, leaving just a small amount for general use.

Incidentally we gathered up all the little sticks and twigs, putting them in one small sack, which we gave to the messman. And from that day on there were always two large pots of tea on-the-go: one of ordinary tea and one of grass-twig tea.

Talk about "pastures of plenty" (Tom Paxton)! Every night we would pass the time sitting on the after-deck smoking, or in the party cabin in bad weather. I must add here that even though we did all this, we still never missed one minute's work on the ship and always did a good job. We all thought the captain kind of hated us, but could not fault us on our work.

From that day on we fancied that if you saw our happy little ship moving through the sea, and if you looked very closely, you'd see a blue haze floating astern of us. From then on, until the end of the trip – I'm not sure what it was exactly – but it just seemed to me that everybody on board had a bit of a smile after Kingston. Maybe others were at it as well. Maybe they were all at it – I don't know.

We moved on into that night ready for another day's work, yet more experience and the next big adventure.

The next stop was a little-known island off the north-east coast of Venezuela called Curaçao. It's a maritime version of your local cheap-fuel station. Trinidad and Tobago are not that far away to the east, and Curaçao is surprisingly close to the Venezuelan coast, these islands all being part of what they call the Dutch Lesser Antilles. It would be a two-day voyage across the Caribbean Sea, with only a short stop to pick up "bunkers", and we kept the engine on standby for the few hours it took us to refuel.

It was nighttime when we arrived. As they pumped aboard tons of fuel oil into our bunker tanks, we whiled away the hours trying to drop pieces of wood onto huge cockroaches the size of mice that infested the quayside.

Fuel oil is one of the major running expenses of a ship, therefore the price of it here must have warranted the extra day, plus a detour of a few hundred miles, before our next scheduled port: Barranquilla in Columbia.

We left Curaçao a few hours later, slightly disappointed as we have heard tales of a place called Happy Valley, for which the owners would organise coach trips inland for visiting ships' crews to what was claimed to be a fantastic experience. I was told you could have any type of sex you wanted there… at a price. We were intrigued by it, but not in awe as, having spent some time in South America, we fully understood the implications of that.

We headed back out to sea and into the darkness, and after stowing our mooring Lines we stood down, apart from the watch-keepers. Then we headed north past the island of Aruba, then east across the edge of the Gulf of Venezuela, rounding its northerly tip. Eventually we turned into the River Magdalina, very muddy, shallow and fast-flowing, sailing upstream to the city of Barranquilla. We tied up alongside a deep long quay on the west side, opposite low-lying jungle-covered hills to the west.

It was late afternoon, very hot and humid. We were only going to be there for one night. We made fast, had our dinner and went ashore. Six of us decided to stick together as this was a completely mad place, fraught with poverty and danger (you normally find the two going together).

There was obviously a great deal of crime in the city. The powers-that-be had to give the illusion of keeping it under some kind of control, I guess. So as we walked through the city that evening, we saw any number of policemen on the streets, armed to the teeth and wandering around, looking for trouble. It reminded me very much of Buenos Aires. We guessed that the police were probably poorly paid, and a bit frightened too, so it paid to be very careful.

We started talking to the taxi driver, who offered to take us to a cantina out in the suburbs run by a relative of his. He seemed okay – and there were six of us to one of him – so we thought we'd take the chance.

The driver drove very slowly through the suburbs – it seems to be a long way and we did begin to worry. However eventually we ended up at a very nice cantina bar. It was run by extremely nice people and we spent an unusually civilised evening with them, plus some locals – men and woman – drinking, eating, having a good time and swapping stories about Columbia and England. We shared our grass and they shared theirs, along with some lovely local wines. Eventually the taxi driver who'd bought us there returned, and after fond farewells we were driven back to the ship about 3 AM.

It had been a really good evening, and all relatively cheap. We'd seen the country and its people, and apart from the impression of a tense city they were just good normal folk going about their ordinary lives.

The next morning we turned-to for work. After the dockers had finished discharging our cargo, we were told to let go as quickly as possible. It seemed we were rushing to catch the tide at the estuary.

It was a close-run thing, but we just managed to make it. Not without some seriously worried faces on the bridge, though. We were literally scraping our hull on the sandbank as we left the port. I could feel the boat vibrating and slowing as we cut our own channel out, churning up the sandy-coloured mud. We all shared the anxiety, and everyone gave a sigh of relief as we finally cleared the sandbank into deeper sea and picked up speed.

We were now on a north-westerly course, bound for Colón and the Panama Canal. With a couple of days' sailing ahead of us – about 300 miles – we crossed the Gulf of Darién linking Columbia with Panama. Life at sea carried on as normal, working on our happy little ship, painting and cleaning. There was our usual evening light-show, watching the sunset on the after end, taking a drink and smoking a bit of grass to enhance the experience.

We found ourselves dropping anchor in Limon Bay outside Colón, awaiting our turn to enter the Canal. Now this area was quite renowned for sharks, so in our downtime whilst waiting we tried fishing for one. Someone had heard a story about catching one by using a meat hook on a fine wire, so we decided to have a go. One of the donkeymen cut a barb in one end of a meat hook for us, then managed to scavenge some raw meat from the galley. We dangled it over the side for hours, our wired end attached by a shackle. Sadly (but fortunately?) we never even saw a shark, let alone caught one. I do wonder what we'd have done with it if we'd managed to get one aboard.

Apparently sharks were attracted to this area by the number of ships at anchor at any one time, all waiting to pass through the canal like we were. After every mealtime lots of gash would be jettisoned over the side. So the sharks would come scavenging, but probably only at night. Once south of the equator, albatrosses would regularly follow ships for weeks at a time for the same reason, dropping back after every mealtime for a good scoff, then catching up again to await their next meal.

We were called to stations the next day and I found myself in the forepeak with another man, handling the long wire hooks used to coil the huge anchor chain into the chain locker as it was being winched in by the bo's'un. When coiling the chain down into the locker it's very important to do it properly. The metal hooks are used to push and pull it into position so it fits into the space provided, but does not kink when running it out the next time it gets used. It also helps secure the chain in extreme weather. It's totally amazing how this huge heavy chain, its links 2 foot by 9x9 inches, can lash around like a whip in heavy seas as the bow pounds rapidly up-and-down into troughs. At such times the chain becomes weightless, floating around in free fall.

It was a lovely day as we enter the narrows. Some of the crew cleared away seaweed and other debris, the deck boy as usual hosing down the deck afterwards: one of my old jobs. Soon we felt the vibration of the engines beginning to move us forward. We paused for a brief spell to bring up the anchor, then made our way slowly past Cristóbal into the channel approaches. At last, with jungle appearing on both sides as the waterway narrowed, we entered the first set of locks.

We had begun our passage through the jungle lakes and locks of the Panama Canal to the Pacific Ocean, en-route to Chile and the Peruvian coast.

It was early evening before we finished stowing away everything on deck and tidying up. After a late dinner we again took up our usual ritual: watching the beautiful sunset on the after part of the ship. We ran into the night, out of Panama Bay into the Gulf of Panama on a south-westerly course, passing between the Panamanian mainland and the island of Del Rey. I had a good night's sleep after another spectacular sunset of unimaginable beauty. I recalled the time I was last here the previous year. Once again I was impressed with the vivid, ever-changing colours, the birds and the sea life.

The next day we spent at sea. I was again aware of the complete change of perspective between the Pacific and Atlantic oceans. I recall it being a fairly uncomfortable sea in these shallow waters. From daybreak for the rest of the morning we could see the land of the west coast of Columbia rising ahead of us, towering up into the sky as we closed it. By lunchtime we'd arrived at La Guatra, a small town with a long thin quay, sheltered by a breakwater, on the edge of a vast jungle-covered mountain soaring up into the sky behind it.

We were only going to be in here for one night, and our one-and-only run ashore in this sleepy little town was uneventful, at least to begin with. Having a few beers in a few different bars, we had already learned from one of our fellow crew members, who was from Chile, that in the chemists here you could buy – perfectly legally over-the-counter – "blues". These pills, made in England, were known as Benzedrine, a trade name for an amphetamine. We called it "speed". You could buy them in packs of 200 for the cost-equivalent of roughly 10p per box. So we got some. This, together with the ample grass that we possessed, gave us a whole new perspective on life aboard ship.

Amphetamine's primary use was to help one stay awake. It was used by people in positions of responsibility during World War II, up to and including Winston Churchill. Then in later years it was reinvented as a slimming aid. This backfired to a certain extent, being highly addictive and giving a sense of euphoria. It started being used as a recreational drug in the late 50s and early 60s.

I was once told an interesting story by a London ex-heroin addict. At the end of World War II, benzedrine along with valium, prescribed to housewives to cope with life during wartime, left a great many people addicted. Sadly, and foolishly, the UK health authorities' approach to resolving this problem was to wean them onto heroin!

It was then that heroin, known as "smack", became freely available in cities throughout the UK, especially London. Knowledge of this fact attracted heroin users from America, Canada and other parts of the world to the UK. Eventually seeing the error of their ways, the authorities abruptly turned off the supply, closing all the affected clinics on the same day during the 50s. This launched the black market in heroin, starting probably in Chinatown, that continues to this day.

Makes you wonder how something that was inadvertently created by governments (the knowledge of which is eventually lost in time) eventually becomes the responsibility of the victims and they are penalised.

From La Guatra we literally sped off south down the west coast of South America, stopping off here and there at lots of stunningly beautiful ports both little and large. With fantastic backdrops of forested mountains. Sometimes we'd be only there for a few hours. It seemed we were forever taking in and putting out the shorelines. It was good to have just short spells at sea and short runs ashore. I really liked this coast: it was so different from the east coast, which was very cosmopolitan. It was far more interesting, with more indigenous people who seemed a lot happier. There was much more genuine cultural life going on here.

The furthest point south we reached was San Diego, the capital of Chile. After passing the aptly-named Ecuador ("Equator"), coastal Peru and Chile were hot and humid. After San Diego we turned and headed back north, calling at Valparaiso. We had a good few days here, since a substantial part of the cargo was discharged here, followed by cargo being loaded for home.

This gave us much more time to go ashore and explore in the evenings. Apart from the usual round of drinking, we flirted with all the beautiful women which, if you had the money to support one for the evening, you could get to gratify your young hormones in the appropriate manner. They were just so lovely: very natural and friendly. There was none of the hard-nosed business approach from the women you find in Brazil and Argentina.

We were going to be there for the week, with the weekends in port (for us deckies there was no compulsory overtime). So we took advantage of this, by visiting our local *Flying Angel* Mission, branches of which exist all over the world. They'd make an effort to keep our morals intact for at least a day or two by organising cultural trips. On this occasion they asked all of us if we would like to go horse-riding for the day, out in the jungle somewhere just out of town.

In due course, early on Saturday morning, a bus arrived to collect us. Quite a few of us from the ship went. We were driven through the city to a farm on the outskirts of town. There we met the owner, were each allocated a horse and given some instruction on how to ride it.

It was simply a brilliant day, one I really enjoyed. Definitely a refreshing change – a lot different from just going off to some bar, drinking and chasing women. We set off into a jungle in a line. I think we all were a bit nervous, with this guy leading us off along a jungle trail. It was really hot and humid, and the air teemed with insects.

Somebody from the Mission took a photograph of us at the time. Before we left Valparaiso we got a few copies of it from the Mission. It was a great picture. We fancied we looked like The Wild Bunch – or so we liked to think. Perhaps we identified with them because we'd been watching the film on the ship: it was out on current release at the time. We were a bit wild, and I must say the horses were very good with us. They must have known we were complete novices, and we were rather hard on them, so all I can say is that they must have had excellent senses of humour.

At the end of the day we got delivered back to the ship, with happy faces and sore arses. We had a late dinner – there was a little bit left in the hot press for us by the messman. Then after a quick spliff we headed back ashore for a few drinks.

It's very strange that, for all the ships I was on, we crewmen would never take too much notice of what actual general cargo we were carrying, as normally we would not have anything to do with its loading or unloading in port. We would just prepare the ship, then let the shoreside dockers and cranes take over, letting us carry on with our normal duties. This was true even when working the home trade. Invariably you would join the ship just 24 hours before sailing, and most crew paid-off immediately on arrival back in the UK.

Before leaving Valparaiso though, as we closed Number 1 Hatch lids, we couldn't help noticing that the hold was filled to the brim with tree bark. I understand it was used for the processing of soap. Ironically we had just delivered a large consignment of soap here. We only knew about this because a few cases of it mysteriously turned up in our washroom whilst we were in Kingston, Jamaica.

Eventually after making the ship ready for sea we were called to stations. We let go and left Valparaiso feeling refreshed, yet ready for some fresh air.

We headed north, calling in briefly at Lima, Peru, as we made our way up the coast. We stopped at one place which was memorable for the fact that, just for once, we were called upon to work the cranes ourselves, discharging our cargo over the side into smaller vessels.

It was a very small port in northern Peru, close to the equator. It had extremely limited access – so limited that we had to navigate very slowly into a tiny bay and drop anchor a few hundred metres from the shore, then go slowly astern towards the shore until we came up on the anchor. Then small boats carried our stern lines to the quay, where they were taken up onto the quayside bollards. Back on board, the lines were then turned up on the after winches and made fast.

Our ship was now held firmly between the anchor from the bow and several shorelines from the stern, letting us discharge a few large cases of cargo onto a smallish barge that came alongside. This procedure enabled us to work without being bothered by the turning tide or the wind.

I recall it being a hot sunny day with not much wind, so there was no problems on that score. However we kept to the procedure, as things can change very quickly with the sea and the weather.

Now came the tricky bit. Topping, lowering and making fast the derricks was quite familiar to us all. But actually lifting cargo out of the hold and placing it on a vessel off to one side certainly made an interesting first experience for me. Although men came on board from the shore and the barge to handle the cargo, the actual lifting and placing over the side was done by us. This was for insurance reasons, I understand.

I and two others on three of the winches were given directions by the bo's'un standing on the corner of the hatch coaming. This enabled him to see the winch-men clearly (us), plus what was going on in the hold and on deck. The first officer likewise stood by the side on the gunwale, strategically placed to see us, the deck and down into the hold of the adjacent barge being loaded.

Having topped the fore derricks at Number 3 Hatch and opened the hatch, we linked the two outboard derricks with a special block accommodating both lifting wires together. This doubled the lifting capacity of a single derrick to accommodate one of the three large cases to be unloaded. The derricks were placed directly over the hold. The two inboard derricks were linked in the same manner, but swung out directly over the hold of the barge below and secured.

I was on one of the two lifting winches that were simultaneously lowered into the hold. When the first case was ready, being secured by wire strops, the signal to lift was given from below. Then with a series of coordinated instructions we successfully lifted all three cases up out of the hold, swung them over and down into the hold of the waiting vessel.

After this operation was finished, without further ado the after-end stations crowd were called-to to bring in the stern lines. The rest of the fo'c's'le head crew, including me, de-rigged and dropped all the derricks and secured them. This we did in time to head forward and deal with the anchor chain, just as the ship came up on it. We washed the chain down and stowed it in the usual manner.

In no time at all we were free and making way, tidying up and washing down as we headed back out of the bay, eventually setting a northerly course to our next port: Buenaventura, back in Colombia once more.

Three things are characteristic of this coast: its diversity; its wondrous beauty with its jungle-covered mountains, occasionally with unforgiving rocks that you wouldn't want to go anywhere near in a boat; and in the equatorial region the uncomfortable heat and humidity.

The heat moderated as we travelled south, becoming more comfortable. I'm sure that if we'd continued heading south we'd probably have reached a happy medium, somewhat like the UK.

If we'd then continued on down the coast, the weather would have worsened to stormy at Cape Horn: the southernmost tip of this massive continent. And going on past the Antarctic Circle we'd reach the icebergs, ice fields, and snowy mountains of the South Polar region.

In a day or so, following the coast, we found ourselves moving into a large estuary, heading now east into more sheltered waters. Eventually we rounded the northern end of Cascajal, a large industrialised island, which led into Buenaventura itself under a bridge on its eastern side.

We continued on round the island, eventually coming about, then tying up alongside a long, straight, new-looking concrete quay on the northern side of the island. I remember the strange weather: very hot but very windy – it took the tugs a while to get us alongside the quay, with a lot of towing and throwing, horns and whistles. We needed to throw the heaving line several times before it was caught by the waterman.

Later that day I remember thinking, as I looked around at the shore from the monkey island: what will this place bring us now?

Poverty is ever-present everywhere you go, on both east and west coasts of South America. But the difference between the coasts is significant. On the east coast there seems to be more wealth around, yet still a great deal of poverty. Hence the far more obvious divisions between rich and poor give rise to anger and resentment, expressed in more prevalent crime. The poor are trying to better themselves, with little hope of prospering in conventional ways.

Here on the west coast however, everybody seems to be poor, but the people are much more accepting of their lot. I'm not sure why. Is it due to people's lives having a much stronger spiritual foundation? Or have they not been tempted and corrupted to the same extent by the trappings of capitalism, which on the east coast has constantly oppressed the poor over a longer period?

This is particularly noticeable in Colombia. The chaos we saw on the east coast did not exist here on the west coast. It felt completely different, although it was the same country: Colombia stretching from coast to coast.

As you move around in the different countries of the world, like outside the docks here, you do come across some good offers. There are many people waiting to sell you goods: they're generally very cheap, especially in South America. I'd buy presents to take back to my family. On this trip I had already bought a butterfly tray, some small paintings, plus a chromium machete in a leather scabbard, the last of which I bartered for three packets of Benson & Hedges cigarettes. These were from the ship's bond and had only cost me a shilling a packet.

Somewhere on the coast I had bought a pair of leather flip-flops. They were cool and comfortable. Although they cost me next to nothing – just pence – I was very attached to them and took to wearing them at every opportunity.

The following day I was finishing off a job close to the outboard gangway of the ship when one of my lovely flip-flops came off and fell in the sea. In panic I tried to work out how to recover it. I watched it for a while – it was still afloat and moving slowly towards the bow. I followed after it and eventually, from the fo'c's'le on the bow I could see it slowly moving in between us and the ship ahead of us, to drift under the quay.

With permission from the bo's'un, I went ashore and made my way to the end of the quay, some good few hundred yards away, climbed down under it and started back along the seashore towards the ship. Picking my way barefoot across the rocks I became aware of loads of Portuguese Man O'War jellyfish, stranded by the receding tide. I did wonder whether to turn back at this point, but spurred-on by the possibility of recovering my much-loved flip-flop, only another ship's length away, I carried on.

It was a grim journey, turning into a nightmare thanks to these scary decomposing jellyfish littering the place. It seemed to go on for ever. Desperately searching for my shoe as I went, I came across a tugboat with a man sitting on a small stage over its stern, repainting the name.

Then I saw my flip-flop floating gently on the water just an arm's-length away from him. I called out to him, "Señor!" He turned and looked at me in surprise. After a series of gestures and frantic pointing, I finally got him to understand that I wanted the flip-flop floating just below him.

He reached down. Then just as he was about to pluck it from the sea, he suddenly stopped. I could guess what he was thinking as he looked back up at me with a serious face. He rubbed his finger and thumb together to signal "how much?"

After a difficult negotiation, plus some hard bargaining in sign language that went on for some time, I being afraid that at any moment it could float away out of his reach, we finally agreed on the sum of... two packets of Benson & Hedges. I was becoming aware that around these parts English cigarettes were better currency than cash.

Now, both of us smiling, he retrieved the flip-flop for me and I made my return journey back to the end of the pier, climbed up onto it and walked back to my cabin aboard my ship. I got the cigarettes, went back ashore, found the tug once more... and completed the deal.

He was a nice guy: we both understood the situation. We shook hands with a smile. I returned in triumph with my lost flip-flop, once again reunited on my feet with its companion.

I was a happy man. It had been well worth the trouble. But all that had taken me around two hours, leaving me barely time to bolt my saved dinner before turning-to again for the afternoon's work. But I certainly got a good laugh from the rest of the crowd when I told my story that evening.

Graham's Great Adventure!

Buenaventura had been the last port of call before heading for home. Next morning we let go with the tide, this time sailing westwards back out into the estuary, and from there into the Pacific, heading north for the Panama Canal.

It was still very hot and humid as we went about our everyday work on board. It was the usual thing – maintenance – mainly painting. Working in the heat was always uncomfortable. It somehow seemed to drain my energy, and I think we were probably just out of our little blue pills by then, which certainly didn't help, One thing you definitely learn at sea is that it's all about change. One day is never the same as the next, and you never quite know what to expect.

It seems strange to think that we'd never get to hear the weather forecast. However we'd have a fair idea, and we'd guess if it was going to be bad weather. This apart from the obvious signs, such as darkening grey skies, plus the wind and the sea starting to pick up. We would find ourselves being given the job of checking the lashings on everything vulnerable on deck that was likely to come adrift, not to say stowing away anything that shouldn't be on deck.

If extreme conditions were expected, we'd also be rigging man-ropes around the decks. This entailed straddling long ropes fore and aft to give us some support in the face of waves breaking over the ship – that's if we had the misfortune to need to go forward in heavy seas. In the main, this would only be necessary if something came adrift, such as during the previous year when a lashing came loose on the fore derrick of the *Trebartha* during a storm in the Caribbean. So it was important to do a good job checking everything beforehand, as this could save having to risk someone's life to fix it later.

Changes can be very extreme at sea, from day to day or even sooner. The most spectacular change is a storm, of course. You can be sailing in flat calm conditions over a mirror-like sea, but within a matter of hours you might begin to see a few clouds appear on the horizon and the sea start to ripple as a slight breeze comes in.

After a while the sky grows dark with a canopy of cloud; and as the wind strengthens the atmospheric pressure goes down. Waves start to develop and pick up. Small wavelets turn into larger ones and continue to grow as the wind increases in speed, until within a few hours, the characteristic "white horses" start to appear. This generally happens at about force 5 on the Beaufort Scale.

Eventually the waves start to break. More and more white foam forms until the wind starts stealing it off the crests and spreading it out horizontally as spray across what has now become an uneasy sea.

What happens to you next depends on the severity of the storm, plus the course you are on with respect to the direction of the wind and waves. For example, if the wind is coming directly at the boat beam-on, the ship will roll from side to side as you sail along in the troughs of waves.

As the wind increases and the rolling intensifies, you could be forced into radically changing course in order to bring your head upwind a bit into the approaching waves. This would then make the ship engage in a kind of corkscrew motion. You are not only pitching up and down but simultaneously rolling.

If the storm intensifies, these measures become not only uncomfortable but even dangerous. Then you're forced to operate in survival mode, letting go of any idea of following your course. You'd just put the head up more into the wind, avoiding bringing her directly into the oncoming sea unless you really had to.

The sea can be very severe, threatening you with truly huge forbidding waves of varying sizes coming at you fast. You'd be literally sailing up the side of one wave, pivoting, then falling down into its trough, the bow digging into the bottom of the next wave. Another large approaching wave would then lift you back up again, and so on. This could go on for hours or days, depending on where you are inside the perimeter of the storm and the direction the whole weather formation is moving in.

Eventually the wind will start to moderate. You now look for an opportunity to set a new course bringing you back towards your original destination. This may need to be done gradually, a few degrees at a time. In conditions like this, your navigation officer (normally the second officer) will have been constantly recalculating your position, as very quickly the boat can not only go off-course but possibly head into danger. You might be close to the coast or heading into shallow water or onto sandbanks. A tide might be taking you forwards, sideways, or the stern, quicker than you can move over the surface of the water, since the whole expanse of sea would be on-the-move, and not necessarily in the direction you're heading.

For any of these reasons you could be forced into sailing with the sea. This is possibly the most dangerous position to be in. The following sea would invariably be moving faster than you. A wave will come up on your stern, lift you up whilst pushing you forward like a surfer for a few seconds, then drop you down again, to be picked up once again by the next wave. Imagine if you can a 500 ft long by 60 ft wide ship of 10,000 tons gross being picked up and pushed along by the sea in this way.

Storms can reach such an intensity as to put any ship in grave danger. If the wave frequency reaches the critical point where the stern is still down in a trough, the next wave could swamp or engulf the ship. Then you'd be right out of control. You need to have turned so as to be heading into the waves long before reaching this position, as in this sort of weather, turning the ship to come about would put you in the most vulnerable position. A ship of any size can simply be flipped over, or moved round and rolled over onto its side, or upside down (known as "turning turtle"). If fully laden, it can be dragged down beneath the surface in a matter of seconds.

Each storm has very different characteristics. How you fare in your encounter with it will involve many factors, such as the size of ship, whether with or without cargo, plus the effect of wind on the superstructure.

In the days of sail, on a sailing boat in such a storm, the wind could be so strong that even with no sails at all – just bare sticks – she could still be making speed. Driven solely by the wind on the superstructure she could still be sailing so fast that the crew would have to stream long ropes from the stern to act as sea anchors to slow the boat down and keep its head into the wind.

Your survival depended on the competence of the captain, the officers and crew, how experienced they were, the decisions they made and actions they took – and whether at the right time. The majority of seafarers are competent, experienced, intuitive, strong-minded people, some with a lifetime of experience. All know deep down inside that situations like this are within their control only up to a point. They are always at the mercy of the sea – and are humbled by that knowledge, treating the sea with the greatest respect at all times.

The lessons to be drawn? Change is inevitable; never presume anything; expect the unexpected; trust in your instincts and have the confidence to act on decisions made.

Fortunately we had fairly good weather, continuing northwest until we found ourselves coming to the north-east and so into Panama Bay. There we anchored as usual for a short while, once again awaiting our turn to enter the lock to bring us into the Panama Canal, then sailing north for our return to the Caribbean Sea – and Homeward Bound!

We weighed anchor first thing in the morning, washing and stowing the chain in the usual manner, then made our way slowly half-ahead into the Gulf of Panama and the approaches to the canal, with the rugged forested coastline off our port side, and the Amador Causeway to starboard. Once more we passed under the Bridge of the Americas, making fast to our tugs shortly after they had escorted us into the first set of sea locks. There we were delivered into the hands of the Panamanian management: pilot and crew coming on board for the duration of our transit, as ordained.

On this trip we transited the canal both ways; but on neither occasion did I get a spell on the helm since I was on the 4 to 8 watch. The timing of our passage through meant the task fell to the other watches.

Although it's usually very hot everywhere in this region, you could feel a wall of humid heat hit you immediately after coming out of the lock and into the first of the lakes. Hardly surprising, as these waters were tropical swamps before the building of the canal.

We sneaked our way through, savouring the exotic sensuality of this wonderful place. Although it was extraordinarily beautiful, with its changing, misty appearance, it was hard at times to figure out exactly what you were looking at.

Again we passed through that unforgettable avenue of rock through which I took the *Trebartha* when I was doing my steering ticket the previous year. I was unable to shake off the thought of those poor lost souls who'd built it long ago, especially in those afternoon showers that regularly occur on the east side. It must have been a living hell for the many who'd had to endure working there over a number of years in that damp, humid and dangerous environment.

Nevertheless the Canal was extraordinarily practical. It's the epitome of a short cut. It's also psychologically reassuring for a crew on a long voyage to know that, although the canal is only 80 miles long, once through you know you've just bypassed an entire ocean, bringing you much closer to home than you had been. You're now in a different world too, with Once again with the whole new perspective: that of the Caribbean Sea.

Once out of the lock, and back to sea level, we continued on our way, heading into the fading evening light and thinking of home. It felt as if we'd finished the trip, for all practical purposes, having visited all the ports on our agenda. Getting home was just a question of 4,000 miles – 15 days or so – back to England via Belfast, to be paid-off in Liverpool as we discovered some days later. Somehow it was not so exciting now, without the lure of the unknown. I now appreciate the poignancy of the saying: "Homeward bound".

We crossed the Caribbean, with Jamaica well to the north, passing through the straits between the Dominican Republic and the British Virgin Islands, close to the *Isla de Mona*. We passed through the south-eastern edge of the Sargasso Sea and headed into the North Atlantic, falling back into the routine of daily work after the irregular work patterns on the west coast. We'd been in-and-out of ports, sometimes on watch, sometimes on day work, not to mention the challenging changes of consciousness due to alcohol laced with herb and our various chemicals. It was rather refreshing to take it easy and get back into a work rhythm with a sense of reality.

Soon we started to leave behind the humidity of the tropics as we crossed the Tropic of Cancer. It was a much dryer heat here. It's notable for being not only the northern border of the tropics but also the most northerly circle of latitude at which the sun can be directly overhead at certain times of the year.

—oOo—

We were now in the Gulf Stream, taking advantage of its one-knot current once more.

We spent most of the time chipping and painting (of course), giving priority to painting the outside superstructure so as to give a good impression for the owners' sake of the ship on her returning to her home waters – and Liverpool: which happened to be the PSNC company's original home port. We, naturally, spent our spectacular evenings in our usual location on the after end, relaxing and having a few spliffs, others their drinks. No drinks for me though: I much preferred these evenings with the grass, as it was so much more profound, thought-provoking and enjoyable. I have to say I never quite "got" alcohol.

I definitely observed a social change going on in life at sea. The culture that had existed on ships for decades had centred on alcohol, which led to a lot of anger and violence. Now we were into the 70s. There seemed to be a New Age emerging of what you could loosely call "hippy sailors".

What had been in the past a macho, alcohol-pickled, closed social environment had now changed. The majority of us who spent those nights on the poop deck were now provided with more mind-expanding substances like mild hash, or grass, bringing you more into the Immediacy (what Buddhists refer to as the Present). More and more I felt, this effect allowed me to engage with other crew members on a more profound level, helping us to understand each other more deeply, unlike the superficial effect of alcohol. It helped to create bonds between us all: some that last to this day.

We maintain our track record of rarely missed a call to duty at any time on any ship we were on. By contrast, many of the heavy drinkers frequently would. A strange irony when you consider society's negative attitude to this emerging drug culture.

These drugs are not seen by many people as being congenial to everyday society. Yet, in practice, if you are able to find some middle ground with it and achieve some balance, as we did, it's fine and workable.

Provided, that is, you avoid heroin, barbiturates, cocaine and speed: the nastier chemical-processed compounds. The spirit-stealers, I call them.

Sadly, in towns and cities ashore this is hard to achieve. In those places you need to go through a lot of difficulty to survive and come out the other side.

It's such a shame that something so potentially good, which could promote creativity or even be used in a practical way as a medicine, is not more freely available.

It gets so readily dismissed by a society that doesn't understand it.

We had a mixed bag of weather for the rest of the voyage home. Slowly the days got cooler, with many sunny days, grey days, rainy days, some very calm days and some choppy days, until, at the end of June, we found ourselves entering St George's Channel.

As we approached the south-east coast of Ireland we went on to watches. I was still on the 4 to 8 watch and, after a day or so on the Irish Sea, heading north up the coast of Ireland past the River Liffey to Dublin, I found myself on the wheel at dawn, as we came about to the west and entered the beautiful approaches to Belfast Lough.

It was such a lovely clear day, with huge fluffy clouds. From the wheel you always had a fantastic view. This morning was particularly spectacular, with the added excitement of arriving home (almost) after a brilliant trip back: the end of two weeks at sea.

It was well into dawn as we approached the Lough, with all the lighthouses and navigation buoys twinkling brightly, their green and red flashes guiding us into a long avenue of channel buoys leading up to Belfast itself and slowly diminishing in strength as day took over night.

I was delighted at being on the helm, in these magical moments, following orders from the captain via the chief officer when making course changes. I relished the unique feeling again of being at one with 6,000 tons of ship.

After passing the power station on Carrickfergus we slowed to pick up the pilot, who came aboard and strode briskly onto the bridge with a cadet escort, just before I was relieved from the helm. I managed to snatch some breakfast before being called to stations.

I headed to the bow as we passed the famous Harland and Wolff berths, with their giant gantry cranes: Samson and Goliath, those used to build the Two Sisters side-by-side simultaneously – one famous, the *Titanic*, the other not so famous, the *Olympic*. Soon afterwards we were taking the tug's lines to bring us alongside our berth in East Belfast docks, where we tied up, secured and stood down.

So here we were in Belfast, Northern Ireland. We all knew we'd arrived at the height of what was then known as The Troubles!

After tidying up on the foredeck we made fast the anchor chain. This was always put into a ready-to-go position – gears disengaged and chain stop off – when coming into most ports to tie up. This was for emergencies such as engine failure or some such incident that might occur at such a critical time. We then spent the remainder of the morning topping derricks and opening the hatch covers of those holds from which cargo was to be discharged here in Belfast.

It so happened that it was my good friend and old schoolmate Steve's birthday that day, and we had plans to go ashore and celebrate.

East Belfast in 1971 was a troubled place. As we were walking off the dock that night we could hear a great deal of noise. We speculated on it being some kind of celebration with fireworks. However, on getting closer to the source of the noise, we discovered a full-blown riot going on, with gunfire, petrol bombs, people shouting, fighting, etc. We knew a little bit about history and what was going on, as we had seen it on TV and in the newspapers over the previous few years, after things had literally all blown up again in 1969.

We therefore guessed it was people fighting each other from different sides of the divide but also the RUC, and the British Army trying to contain it. It was a bit of a shock to us.

Needless to say, we beat a hasty retreat and decided to make do with the first pub we'd passed, which was right outside the dock gate. It was a very lively place, which seemed odd considering all the fuss going on just around the corner. Odder still, there was a party going on, with lots of singing and drinking. Stephen and I ordered a pint of Guinness each.

There were some large barrels on a shelf behind the bar. One barrel had a single X, another had XX and the third had XXX – this being the strongest of course.

The barman looked at us and said "Think you'd better stick to the 2X", so we had a few pints and began to enjoy the evening. And why not? It was Steve's birthday and we'd been at sea for two weeks, so we were determined to have fun.

Soon enough a man came up behind us, then putting his arms around our shoulders and his head down in between them, he said, in a deep voice with a strong accent: "Do you know, lads, that this is a Protestant bar?" Then he asked, "What might you be?"

I hadn't even heard the word spoken before then. Neither had Steve – but we gathered it was something to do with religion. We said, "We don't know – er – C-of-E, I think – is that ok?"

There was a great roar of laughter from the rest of the pub, which had ominously gone silent waiting to hear our answer. The man said, "Ahh – you'll do rightly here, lads" – and bought us the first of many drinks that just arrived for the rest of the evening: we never had to buy another ourselves.

Well, with us not being accustomed to the strength of the beer there, quite early on we'd had enough. Steve was close to passing out, and I thought I'd get him back to the ship before I had to carry him. So, with fond farewells from all those present, we staggered out the pub, following a zigzag course back to the ship.

Fortunately, it was not too far away. Back on board we made a half-hearted attempt to eat some of the usual salad that had been left out in the messroom for just such an occasion, and then fell into our cabins for a good night's sleep.

It was ironic to think of all the places in the world to go where you'd get caught up in a war zone and be potentially in danger, yet the only time it happened to me was really quite close to home.

As visitors we did not really understand the nature of the problems there at the time. But some years later I actually lived there for a while and it became much more understandable. But that's a story for another book.

We turned-to next morning after a hearty breakfast for another day's work. This was pretty much closing hatches and dropping derricks down. By the end of the day we were ready to sail. Somebody came up with the brilliant idea of posting some of the grass back home from where we were. I'm not sure who did, as we heard that people were then sending parcel bombs from Ireland to the UK, so the Post Office was being extremely vigilant. We did however jokingly speculate that they would know it was not a bomb if they could smell the grass.

All being good and ready for sea, we let go with the tide that evening. We headed back out of Belfast Lough and into the Irish Sea for the short hop to Liverpool, skirting the Isle of Man.

It was a brilliant feeling arriving in Liverpool. It was an incredible place in those days: really vibrant, with a lively Dock Road with its busy pubs and shops. There were ships of all nations in abundance throughout the whole of the docks.

We came in through the bay late in the evening and made our way up into the River Mersey with the tide. Supported by tugs, we came through the locks onto our berth. After standing down we had our last gathering in the bar and on the after end of the ship, before departing the next morning.

—oOo—

I paid-off the *MV Oroya* after two months and 15 days from leaving London. I had earned £260 gross, which after deductions of £158 meant I paid-off with £42 cash plus £60 in the bank.

So did we all, along with our discharge books duly stamped "very good" both for ability and conduct.

We left the ship in groups of four in taxis, giving the driver the usual 50p each with our baggage passes to hand to the dock police on the gate. Arriving at the train station in town, we presented our travel warrants for tickets back to London.

We smoked spliffs all the way to King's Cross, arriving four hours later feeling very wealthy and very stoned. We took a couple of taxis to the *Stella Maris* Seamen's Mission in Canning Town in the East End, and had a laugh with Father McGuinness as he checked us all in, smiling in wonder at the sight of a few little parcels waiting in the pigeonholes behind the counter at reception.

It had been such a great trip and the *Oroya* was a really good boat: undoubtedly the best ship I ever sailed on. Unforgettable. I'm not sure why we didn't think to try getting back on her for another trip. Though quite possibly the captain and chief officer wouldn't have wanted us back. I think we confused and worried them a bit, being so unconventional. But they surely could not fault us for our work on board.

We had a great evening in the Mission, catching up with some of the lovely Irish girls that were bussed-in from the nurses' training home in Victoria – the "Virgins' Retreat" as we called it. The girls were politely referred-to as "hostesses" by the Mission.

The next day was a Friday. Wondering what to do with ourselves, we thought it would be great fun to go to Devon for a few days, to Chris's home town, Dartmouth. We still had some of our grass, along with a large lump of hash, and scored some more acid for the trip (Purple Haze this time).

We found ourselves at Paddington Station after a long taxi ride from the East End in a red Jaguar. We'd smoked a few spliffs in the car and we left behind a very wide-eyed driver with a large tip saying, "thanks lads I think I'll have a cup of tea before heading back". Then, laughing away, we went off to find a compartment to ourselves on the train.

There were five of us: Chris, John, Steve and Sean, plus myself. A little while later a couple turned up with bags. A most attractive girl, smartly dressed, put her cases up in the rack, kissed the man goodbye and sat down. Shortly after that another couple appeared and the same thing happened.

The whistle blew, the diesel engine roared and we gathered speed, heading out of the station. It was the start of a five or six-hour journey to Totnes, where we were due to change trains.

Swiftly several joints got built with our lovely Jamaican grass, which is known for its sweet taste and popping seeds. To my surprise neither of the girls thought twice about partaking with us, and before long they had snuggled up to John and Sean, who looked a bit like Jimi Hendrix. We were all off our faces, laughing together in a smoke-filled cabin.

I couldn't believe what happened next. The two straight-laced looking girls at different times got to their feet saying, "God, I must get out of these clothes!" Taking a jumper and jeans out of her bag, each in turn stripped down to bra and panties and put on the jeans, then deftly popped off her bra while putting on her jumper.

It was a wild journey, with the two new temporary couples nipping out to the toilet every now and then, presumably for sex. At one point I think we all went to sleep. I do remember the girl opposite me kissing John passionately, at the same time putting her bare foot in my crutch and pleasuring me. A memorable occasion, interrupted at a high point in a delightful way, whereupon I had to leave the compartment for a while (on my own, alas) to avoid embarrassment.

This was 1971 – the tail end of the Swinging 60s: still a very permissive time. There were lots of young people hanging out in those days. I was just beginning to wake up to it all.

I don't know who those girls were. They weren't acquainted with each other. It was a Friday afternoon, so I imagine they worked in London and were going home for the weekend somewhere in the country. I don't recall them with us as we got off the train, so they must have got off along the way.

At Totnes we caught a branch-line train into Dartmouth via a small car ferry. We made our way to Chris's gran's house, stopping off at various pubs along the way, eventually crashing out on a couch somewhere. In Chris's granny's house the next morning we were up early for breakfast, lots of tea and spliffs, then we headed off to look around Dartmouth a bit before getting a bus to Kingsbridge, about 20 miles away. It was John's home town. He wanted to give his brother Graham some grass to try. It turned out Graham was looking after a pub in town while the owners were away.

As soon as we got there we decided to take some of the acid. Somebody said "here, take that", to graham, so he did.

As I've already mentioned, this American acid – Purple Haze – was very strong and took about an hour and a half to come up. Then things became very strange indeed. Fortunately the pubs closed at 2 PM in those days. We all simply had to leave, as John's brother completely lost the plot because of the acid.

For the rest of the afternoon I sat on a bench with some of the others and we quite literally watched the tide coming in up the river. For about three hours, or so it seemed, we couldn't move: we just sat there, experiencing psychedelia. That was all you could do with 450 mg of LSD inside you.

Next thing I know, we were sitting on a bus without the driver, waiting for John, who had gone off to see if his brother was all right. Graham had disappeared from the pub. He must have been in a right state, particularly as he had never taken acid before.

Now, it's widely believed that LSD is a truth drug, developed by the US military for interrogation purposes – I needn't go into more detail than that. The upshot was that John returned to the bus with some story about Graham, a young girl, a mother and an uptight father and husband. It all culminated in John's mother arriving at the driverless bus shouting out loudly "John, what have you been giving Graham?" The latter had just landed up back at home a gibbering mess, completely off his face.

Graham taking the acid had not been one of his better moves, but these were wild times. Though not in the backwaters of Devon.

The bus eventually left, and got us back to Dartmouth. Later on that evening we went to a disco dance after chilling out with a few spliffs and pints. But by then we had been traumatised by our adventures and were all getting a bit paranoid.

We were a wild bunch, very hairy, and having a good time in a small town in Devon. We had made ourselves conspicuous and the local lads were beginning to take exception to us, especially as their girls were finding us rather interesting. It dawned on Chris that there was big trouble brewing for us if we stayed there, so we decided to get out of town – and fast.

By now it was late, the pubs were shutting and the ferry was off. But Chris managed to get an old friend from the Rowing Club to take us across the River Dart to Kingswear.

It was a calm summer's night. So although Chris's friend complained all the way that he was too drunk to do this sort of thing, he got us across safely. We gave him some grass, said our farewells and found a taxi to take us to Totnes.

We were just in time to catch the milk train back to London. It took all night, but we slept extremely well the whole time, waking up as we approached Paddington station. There we ate a hearty breakfast, with gallons of tea.

It was quite an adventure, I can tell you. It only lasted 40 hours but it had felt like a week. We sat and reminisced about it, and laughed and laughed.

On our return from the Devon trip, Steve and I headed for Watford. I spent some of my remaining nine days' leave visiting my family.

I spent a couple of days with my mother as well as my father and his girlfriend, returning to the East End of London to meet up with the lads for the last few days of our leave. I also went to look for a job, only to find a strange set of circumstances. All the dockers were on strike. They were no doubt agitating for more money and better work conditions as usual.

The ramifications for us were serious: there were no jobs because nothing much was moving in the Royal Docks. With no cargo being loaded or discharged the berthed ships were unable to move. Yet with more ships arriving by the day, all the docks were filling up with inward-bound ships anchored in the Thames estuary, either waiting for the situation to change or for orders from the company to take the cargo elsewhere. With many ships arriving and their crews paying-off, plus seamen like myself arriving back at the end of their leave, all the seamen's missions were now filling up.

At the end of my leave I had been down to the Pool on the 5 June to sign-on as available for work. The Pool had a large board to show the jobs available. This would normally have had a list of ships written on it, stating what sort of crew were needed: working-by, home trade or deep sea. But the board was completely clear – nothing at all. There were simply no jobs: nothing was moving in the docks, therefore none of the companies were looking for a crew.

After a week or so, the missions were full – and the local B&B's as well. It wasn't so bad for those of us who still had some money left. There were however plenty of lads that did not. The money they got from the Pool was just enough to survive on – most of which would have to go on beer and dope anyway. They were now dependent on being snuck up to sleep on acquaintances' floors, or going to ships in the docks which had friends of theirs working-by on them.

It was hard to have any sympathy for the dockers, as their industrial action was messing us up too. We of course were in theory supportive of the strike because our trade union leaders supported it (our top man at the time being John Prescott).

On the upside, my friends and I were having a brilliant time, with many people milling about. It was party-party the whole time. Some of the older hands, and certainly a lot of the "queens", had flats or even houses in the area. They were very busy in the evenings. Therefore most nights we would go out somewhere or other to a pub or a club, in a house or a flat, or aboard one of the ships in the docks.

Somehow we all managed to get through the strike, thanks to the strong camaraderie amongst seamen – most of us sharing with those that didn't have very much. As they did for us later on, when we in our turn were getting low on resources. So we knew that the light-and-bitter would keep on flowing.

Even though there was an abundance of all manner of substances at that time, we still had quite a lot of grass. That made us very popular, and we used it for informal trades. If I'm honest, we didn't really need much ourselves, as we seemed to be easily gratified, content with getting high, listening to music, good company and laughter.

We also took advantage of our unscheduled time-off by heading out to gigs, plus the occasional rock concert, at various locations in and around London.

It was June 1971, and one day we discovered a free rock concert in Hyde Park in central London, with tens of thousands of people going to see Grand Funk Railroad, Humble Pie and Heads Hands And Feet. There was quite a gang of us: Chris, John, Steve, me and a few others.

At this time there were ongoing clashes between Rockers/Bikers/Hell's Angels and Skinheads. This we hadn't known about: being away at sea most of the time we tended to miss what was going on at home.

At one point in the afternoon we'd wandered away from the stage and were just sitting on a bench not far from the Serpentine, having a few discreet spliffs and taking in the day, music still audible in the background.

Suddenly we became aware of a mob of skinheads scurrying in front of us a short distance away, and disappearing into the cafe through the trees and bushes. Some even jumped in the lake. We then looked behind us to see that they were being hotly pursued by a bunch of Hell's Angels, 20 to 30 of them, wielding sticks and chains. Catching up with many of the bizarrely-dressed head-shaven skinheads, they dragged them out and away from the cafe, punching and throwing them to the ground, where they proceeded to kick, beat and poke them with sticks. I think the Rockers were supposed to be rock concert "security". More than likely they'd been provoked by the skinheads. We just sat there calmly watching the battle going on all around us. It seems as if we were invisible, nobody paying us any attention at all. The situation was completely surreal.

Later that day, as we looked out across the Serpentine, we saw one of the rented rowing boats full of lovely women, four of them dressed in hippy gear. We were now in our element (as were they), so we too hired a rowboat and set off across the lake in pursuit. We tried rowing close to them, hoping to get noticed, but they remained oblivious to our presence – probably stoned. So we came up softly behind them and for a joke one of the lads managed to unobtrusively tie our painter to their stern. Then we eased back slowly so that they were now towing us. This was fine for a while until somebody cottoned-on to what we were doing, came up behind us and did the same to us, securing their painter to our stern. They were followed by another, and then a fourth boat arrived.

It was great fun with us all attached to the girls, being towed along in a chain. We enjoyed watching them straining away, rowing harder and harder. All went fine until it occurred to them what was going on. Then all hell broke loose.

Shouting abuse at us, they cast off our line, brought their boat around and splashed out at us with their oars. We all thought it was great fun and started splashing back, which got them furious. We decided they must have thought we were just trouble spoiling their day. Needless to say, we didn't get anywhere with them. We did however spot them again a bit later – and they were smiling. I think that secretly they'd enjoyed the joke. It was a really hot day and it had helped to cool us all down.

After a few more weeks of partying, the strike was resolved and work began again in earnest. I was now 18 and had served enough sea-time to be considered a proper seaman. Stephen and I found ourselves at St Catherine's Dock in London for a week, doing our EDH (Efficient Deck Hands) certificate. This involves five days of instruction. I had an attack of dyslexic panic, but fortunately the exam at the end was a purely practical one. We were expected to demonstrate our command of all aspects of working life on board a cargo ship: helmsmanship; rope and wire work; handling derricks and hatches; plus all the paraphernalia you'd expect to find on a working cargo ship. We also had to demonstrate the launching, rigging and sailing – yes, *sailing* – of a lifeboat, since in those days there were still ships in service that had sailing lifeboats. We also had to demonstrate awareness of more modern types of lifeboat: those with paddles, oars or engines.

This was all carried out using an actual lifeboat in the confines of St Catherine's Dock. Alas, there was no wind that day, so we just floated around for a while. However we were deemed to have demonstrated our ability to sail the thing.

I gave silent thanks for all the dinghy sailing Stephen and I had done in our last year at school, and also to my father Erne, who had briefly owned one of these lifeboats when I was about 10 years old. Sadly the first time we tried to sail her – on a very windy day in Poole, Dorset – the mast broke, so the project had had to be abandoned. My father had done a fair bit of sailing on the lakes in occupied Germany at the end of World War II. He'd signed-up with the Army for nine years in 1938, the year prior to the outbreak of war, so when the war ended in 1945 he still had one more year to serve.

Anyway, with a small budget and little time for hobbies whilst building his business, he sold the boat on – and that was that.

We spend the five days of the course in St Catherine's Dock by day and partying up in town by night. At the end of each day we'd meet the lads in town and go off to rock venues, pubs and concerts. As far as we could see, London had not yet recovered from the Swinging 60s. That week I don't think Stephen and I got any sleep at all. So it was only by a miracle that we passed the course.

The miracle came with the production of sample wire eye splices, brought out of the cupboard and issued to each of us by the instructor at the last minute because he had forgotten to do that with us. We were not total frauds though as Steve had learnt the procedure at the training school, and I had done so with the lamp trimmer on the *Trebartha*.

So on 16 June, with no ceremony, we duly received our EDH and lifeboat certificates. (Incidentally I was commended for my eye splice!)

MV Essex

MV Essex

On returning to the pool at the East End, there was still a shortage of jobs, which made it very hard for us all to be together on the same ship. Therefore, being desperate now for money, plus the need just to get away, Stephen and I took the only two available EDH jobs on a ship docked at Liverpool called the *Essex*, owned by the New Zealand Shipping Company. It was only a home trade job and probably only for a few weeks.

So we said our goodbyes to the others, expressing our hopes that we'd all meet up again some future time. Steve and I went off with our bags to take the tube to Euston Station to catch the train to Liverpool.

Steve and I arrived in Liverpool, got a taxi to the docks and found the *Essex* on her berth. We went on board, reported to the chief officer and then went to our cabins, signing-on the next day, 6 July 1971. There were very few of us on board: forming the skeleton crew working-by on her as she discharged cargo from her previous voyage, as well as having some essential maintenance done.

The *Essex* was not unlike the *Trebartha*, having the conventional five holds: three forward and two aft, but with all her accommodation midships. She was built in 1954 for general cargo by the Federal Steam Navigation Company, weighing-in at just under 11,000 tons gross. Although now under P&O ownership, she was still painted black over the wall and had a red funnel with black topping, bearing the familiar quartered flag of the Federal Steam Navigation Company. Having more modern engines than the *Trebartha* – twin Salzbergers – her service speed was 16 knots, which was fast for a ship of her day.

I think Steve was really happy to be back on a federal again, as he often spoke affectionately of his first trip on the cadet ship *M.V. Otaio* of the same company. Maybe now he felt a bit more at home aboard the *Essex*.

Maybe it's a matter of nostalgia, your first ship being like your first love – the one you never forget. But I don't think I could say the same about the *Trebartha*, although I'm always happy to see a *Tre-* boat. It was the *Oroya* for me.

It's strange how you can form emotional relationships with ships. There's just something about them. Although they're made of solid metal plus a bit of wood, they're kind-of organic and alive. They each have their individual character: the way they smell, look, sound and move through the sea. Maybe it's to do with dependency as well, as on a voyage they do sustain you in every way. Consider how you might feel about your car, or your home. This may give you an idea of the feeling.

I think Steve was also happy to be away from the rest of the mad gang as well. We had been good friends in the last year or so at our secondary school. We were both members of the group that used to spend every Thursday afternoon dinghy sailing. I had witnessed Steve throwing a few epileptic fits on occasions. But he didn't have any in those later years that I was aware of. He was a lot stronger than me in many ways, so our support was reciprocal. Think it was a time for change, Our group of friends was so large buy now. I believe it would've been very difficult to have found one ship to accommodate us all. Also, I reckon that I had become a little dependent on John Chris especially, they had looked after me. literally showing me the ropes and looked after me well. But now although I love them both very much for that I was more mature now with my EDH ticket, I think it was the right time to move on.

We spent the next three or more weeks in Liverpool, working-by. Our duties were mainly cleaning out the holds after the cargo had been cleared outs ever. Many of the holds had fridges set into the "tween" decks, of which there were usually four to each hold. We were also tasked with sorting out small jobs around the boat, plus lots of painting of course, both on deck and in the accommodation – the latter especially on rainy days.

There were also a lot of contractors on board, doing jobs here and there: welding electrical gear and replacing some of the larger items like winches, etc. There were more contractors in the engine room. As they finished their jobs we would go in to clean up and make good.

That first week we mainly stayed on board, as we had earned very little money as yet. However we still had a plentiful supply of grass, so we were well content with that, plus the TVs in the mess.

Now we were EDHs, our basic wage had gone up to £56 per month. This seemed a lot of money to us, after the SOS's rate of only £36 per month. However it was different not being at sea – for one thing there was no compulsory overtime in port, so we were not making much more than our basic rate. We did however catch up with ourselves after a week or so, and began to venture out to sample the night life of Liverpool.

We spent many a night ashore, wandering around looking at the city and finding pubs to drink in. Some of them would have bands playing or just good music. I suppose also we were looking for female company, but we didn't have any success, or maybe we just weren't courageous enough. The local girls seemed to be so hard there, and already enjoying themselves well enough without us. It was difficult to know how to approach them.

One night we decided to get the Classic (ferry across the Mersey) to Birkenhead. As we were walking past the ferry terminal we passed a gang of about 20 girls. We looked over at them as we walked by, as you do. Whereupon they all turned towards us, looking really aggressive, and one of them shouted out, "Who the fuck are you looking at?" So we quickly shuffled off down to the ferry, hoping they would not be there when we got back later.

Liverpool is a very lively place, with loads going on. And the locals are a very special people who know how to have a good time, but I think we just did not fit-in somehow. Possibly all the mind-expanding drugs we'd been taking, plus not drinking much alcohol, had made us a bit too sensitive. Also at sea you have no opportunity to develop relationships with women, which is why most of the time ashore you find yourself in the red-light districts, where it's made easy for you. Maybe Steve and I had begun looking for something a bit more special in a relationship, but we didn't have the skills to know how to go about it, or to find other places than the bars, clubs and pubs where we were used to meeting women.

One night we went to the Hippodrome to see a band called *Sha Na Na*, an old-style American rock'n'roll band. They were playing in a venue that usually hosted boxing matches, and unusually the band was playing in the ring in the middle of the hall with the audience crowded around. The band were really good, though. We also managed to score a little bit of hash at the gig, just to make a change from our grass, also some speed in the form of strange capsules called "black bombers". It was an exceptional night-out – we really enjoyed it.

We decided to stay aboard the following night, and took one of our "black bombers" each. Steve was night watchman, but I just watched the TV and played music on my small portable record player.

Now Steve, who could be a little odd at times, came to my cabin later on, telling me that he'd just spent the last couple of hours sitting up in the crow's nest, contentedly looking out over the river and the city.

Not many ships had crow's nests any more as they'd been superseded by radar. I guess this boat still had one simply because it was there and nobody had thought to take it down. Or perhaps it had been used for training, as I understand the *Essex* had been a cadet ship at one time. Crow's nests are like small guard boxes, generally located two-thirds of the way up the foremast. They were made famous by the sinking of the *Titanic* of course, the two lookouts in the crow's nest spotting the iceberg just a bit too late.

It felt as though we were in Liverpool for a long time, but with limited resources and only Sundays off. We didn't manage to explore the city as much as we'd have liked. Finally after three weeks we received notice that we were sailing.

The day before we sailed the rest of the crew arrived and signed on. Then, one very windy afternoon in the first week of August we were finally called to stations. Making fast to tugs, we let go, moving off along the dock, out through the sea lock, into the River Mersey.

Though we didn't know it, we were heading out into an westerly gale, with the wind and rain slowly intensifying. We steamed directly into the wind as we navigated the relatively narrow winding channel westwards through the shallow sands of Liverpool Bay, heading out towards the westernmost tip of Anglesey.

We passed the northerly approach to the Menai Straits and continued until we made Holyhead, by which time the unsheltered waters started to attack us with increasingly large waves and extremely strong winds. We gave the Peninsula a very wide berth, heading out into the Irish Sea and eventually turning south.

Unfortunately, being in ballast and with very strong winds blowing directly on our starboard beam, we were now heading across the sea amid an uncomfortable onshore gale. Being on the 12 to 4 watch I made my way up to the bridge, not without difficulty in the wind and rain, to take my first stint on the wheel. This was to be for a two-hour period, with a 15-minute break in it when relieved by one of the other watchmen (the "farmer").

I was somewhat anxious as I made my way up to the bridge. For a start, I hadn't had a great deal of experience at the helm of a ship this size in conditions like these before – only whilst doing my steering ticket, and also whilst standing-in for the watchman for the last week or so on the *Oroya*. Also I had no idea what to expect on the bridge by way of procedure from the third officer, whose watch it was. The lower-ranking officers tended to be more relaxed on the bridge, but in this kind of weather, and in such close quarters, it could almost be guaranteed that the captain would be on the bridge too.

And he was.

I arrived on the bridge to find most of the officers present. With difficulty I walked uphill towards the helmsman, who was vigorously moving the wheel backwards and forwards from port to starboard, struggling to keep on-course. Then I had to wait for a relatively calm moment before I could relieve him in the usual manner; he telling me our current course: "steady she goes"; I then repeating it back to him whilst taking hold of the wheel.

The next two hours were exciting and extraordinary. That night I really learned how to steer a ship.

In the moonlight, looking out ahead through the spinning glass built into the wheelhouse, that kept a circle in the forward bridge window constantly shedding the rain for clear vision ahead, I could see the raging sea, with the head of the ship being struck from the starboard side by huge waves breaking over the bow and foredeck.

I not only had to keep a firm grip on the wheel, but also keep my left leg rigid and straight as I leaned to starboard. This was to avoid toppling over, thanks to the constant list to port that we had. The reason soon became apparent: with the ship being in ballast, coupled with the gale-force wind coming directly onto the starboard beam (the superstructure and the whole of the ship's hull acting like a sail), we were literally being held by the wind, causing us to constantly heal over to the port side.

Paradoxically this also had the effect of steadying the ship to a certain extent, as we were rolling extremely badly from side to side, with a slight pitching movement as well. This was the result of moving nearly along the swell with our head being slightly into wind, and so into the oncoming large breaking waves.

Initially this was quite scary at times, all exaggerated by being much higher up on the bridge. I remember some equally challenging moments when working at the top of the mast, or even worse: hanging off it on a bo's'un's chair. Periodically we'd fall down into a trough, and heal over further to port, to such a degree that it presented a wall of sea so close I felt I could reach out and touch it. Every time that happened my heart was in my mouth as I imagined the ship wouldn't stop but carry on and capsize.

Fortunately it didn't.

Occasionally I would received slight course changes, just a few degrees here and there. Keeping on-course was extremely difficult in these conditions. In practice you could only achieve an average. Also like the *Douro*, the *Essex* was twin-screwed, which is notorious for being difficult to steer at the best of times. Added to that, with the constant changing of the ship's heading due to the wind and buffeting sea, plus the pivotal effect on the gyrocompass, I was constantly bringing the wheel from port to starboard to keep her on-course. It was hard work and totally exhausting: I really had to focus and concentrate.

The commands would come to me from the captain via the third officer. The captain did his job by being fed information from a number of sources: continual position updates from the second officer; any sightings of lights from the look-out (our third watch-keeper, situated out on the starboard wing of the bridge); plus reports from one of the deck cadets also on lookout, the other monitoring the radar screen. All these enabled the captain to bring us to our destination in the most direct, safest and most comfortable way.

After being on the bridge for some time, your fears disperse as you gain greater confidence in the experience and expertise of the officers, especially when the captain is present, who ultimately shoulders all the responsibility. That night he stood the watch with the less experienced third officer, letting the chief officer get some sleep before returning to the bridge to stand his traditional 4 to 8 watch, and no doubt relieve the captain as well.

The responsibility of the captain is huge on board any ship. I was once intrigued to read an informal "Ultimate Oath" captains take: a kind of moral Order Of Priority for a captain whilst in command, going back many years. It ran as follows:

    1. TO GOD
    2. TO THE SHIP
    3. TO ANY PASSENGERS
    4. TO THE CREW
    5. *(then and only then)* TO HIMSELF.

After finishing the watch, I turned-in, exhausted and with sore arms. But I was up early for breakfast the next morning to take the opportunity of a few hours' overtime by working the morning before going on watch duty again at 12 to 4.

The weather had abated somewhat. It continued to do so throughout the day as we sailed down the coast of Wales. Eventually we reached the Pembrokeshire and rounded St David's Head into Carmarthen Bay. We passed the night sailing awkwardly around Land's End, and the following day we turned north-easterly into the Bristol Channel, carefully timing our arrival for high water at Avonmouth Docks.

The docks are located just to the south-west of Bristol in the estuary of the River Avon. This flows out through the Avon Gorge, under the famous Clifton Suspension Bridge which leads into Bristol proper.

The whole area is a nightmare to navigate. The vast rise and fall of tide here means that perfect timing is essential for negotiating the channels and shifting sands, with only a small margin of time either side of high water for bringing you safely in or out.

I was at the after end of the ship with the third officer for stations, when (as ever) we took in the lines of the tugs escorting us to our berth in the dock. There we made fast, tidied up and stood down.

As a deck hand, you don't get involved much with the technical side of navigation, apart from when you're on the helm, or as a lookout reporting ships or lights. Huge ships were constantly being taken to numerous locations all over the world, yet it never ceased to amaze me how we arrived at our destination as if by a miracle.

It wasn't until later in life, when I started sailing and navigating myself, that I came to understand the full extent of it. This incredible feat would be impossible to do safely but for several crucial pieces of equipment. They have been perfected over hundreds of years of constant trial and error by pioneering explorers and navigators from all over the world, including the great Captain Cook himself, by meticulous monitoring and recording of their use. The result is the highly sophisticated mapping system called the Admiralty Chart.

This chart lets you navigate anywhere you like in the world. It is basically all you need in addition to readily available local tide tables, Greenwich Mean Time, a basic geometry set and your current position. Together these tell you exactly what should be happening at that time in any position on the globe. Admiralty Charts give you both the sea depth and the direction the sea is moving in at any given hour on any day anywhere in the world. They are absolutely fantastic.

Armed with this equipment, plus a system of calculation, our second officer and the pilot managed to bring us safely into Avonmouth Docks that day, at exactly the right point in the tide cycle to accommodate our ship's size and draft. They did it simply by governing the speed of the ship on its given course, with slight adjustments for local weather conditions.

Time is of utmost importance on a ship, which can be likened to a small factory with 30-70 employees afloat on the sea. Its earnings come from what it carries in its holds. Therefore any time wasted through delays adds to the overheads of running the ship, and so reducing profits. Therefore the company exerts enormous pressure on the captain to plan the voyage with great care to guarantee minimal time loss. Dock fees, pilotage and fuel oil are extremely expensive items, as are wages, food and maintenance. When these are factored-in, you need to be in and out of port as quickly as possible. Shortening the voyage increases the profit.

Insurance plays its part in all of this, as errors or mishaps such as running aground or colliding with another ship cause considerable losses to both the ship itself and to third parties. Therefore the highest degree of professionalism is entailed and the people taking the big decisions are to be admired, as sometimes they have to take them in the most desperate conditions and circumstances.

So here we were in Avonmouth, continuing to work-by, all the time wondering what would happen next. Steve and I hoped to stay aboard and go deep sea on her. However these hopes were dashed when we learned that the ship's future was uncertain. Nothing was planned for the present, so disappointingly we were all to be paid-off.

This duly happened on the morning of 9 August 1971. We took a taxi to Bristol Station with the balance of our payoff, plus our baggage passes, and boarded the train to London.

With little leave to speak of, we went straight to the KG5 pool to sign on. There were not many jobs on the board, so we headed off to the Mission and checked in.

We encountered a few familiar faces, but most of the crowd had dispersed by now, mostly shipping out. After spending a quiet night we went back to the pool the next day.

It seemed we were entering a time of great change, with not so many ships coming into the Royal Docks – especially in the wake of the dock strike. I learned later that many shipping companies had had enough and had begun to take their business elsewhere. I imagine this was partly due to the prevailing economics, and not just because of the recent industrial action.

With containerisation looming, many companies were under pressure to scrap their conventional labour-intensive cargo ships, replacing them with larger, more technically advanced container ships which only needed a third of the crew. The traditional UK companies were slowly disappearing: Holder Bros, Royal Mail, PSNC, Blue Star, Port Line, Furness Witney, Elder Dempster, Clan, Glenn, Blue Funnel and many others were compelled to sell out to Shaw Savill, who were then in turn to sell out to P&O.

The writing was on the wall. The days were numbered of all the famous ships that for many years had sailed from this dock, and sadly for the seamen's jobs too. There were 57,000 British seamen at this time, but it was planned to reduce them to 40,000 in the near future – and that was only the beginning. Over the next few years nearly all the ships of the previous era of conventionally handled cargo would be sold off, mostly to be broken up.

I have to say Steve and I were not really aware of the politics involved, being very much in the immediacy of things and still in thrall to the romance of the sea. In a carefree fashion we'd go down to the pool each morning looking for jobs.

The drug scene amongst seamen was now well established and starting to show its effects, with a range of drugs now available and in use by many of us. There was a drug, it seemed, to suit every person's character.

Drug-takers fell into three main categories. Speaking for ourselves, we liked to smoke grass and take a bit of acid occasionally, with no desire for anything stronger – we were the Romantics. Others were getting deeply involved in smoking, but also using barbiturates, known as "downers". These people were looking for sedation, I think. The sad ones. Then there were the lads who had heavy childhood backgrounds which had badly affected them. It was heroin and cocaine for them: they needed seriously strong drugs to blot out the past and suppress their anger.

When returning to sea, most of us were happy to come down and clean out. But doing that could be a steep learning curve for some, or possibly even a cure for their addiction. However if you fell back shoreside, you could be in for a ride. You might come out the other side, but some people from the last of our three categories just met their fate and sadly died in their quest for freedom from their pain and anger.

It is so sad and disappointing that society blames people for getting into this situation who are actually escaping from that same society's malign influence via institutional or family abuse. These are victims of our society that successive governments are ultimately responsible for, even being created by them in the institutions that have abused them.

My own experience of drugs in those days turned out to be generally positive, I believe. With some of the stronger drugs I fought demons at times, yet none of them ever got a total hold over me, or took over my spirit. In retrospect I consider my use of drugs to have opened my mind and taught me lessons that have been of the greatest value to me: bringing illumination, intuition, a sensitive awareness and an understanding of myself and others.

But I was fortunate in having had a decent, balanced childhood. My nature is not addictive, there is very little innate anger, and I have the ability to seek solutions, to change and to explore new experiences without getting bogged down. My father called this a love of nine-day-wonders. I thought at the time his opinion of me was a bit of a put-down. It must have been very frustrating for him trying to lead me out of adolescence. But this propensity of mine has turned out in adulthood to be on balance an asset.

Whatever the case, the early 1970s were strange and unusual days that posed a great many questions to which I needed to find answers. It would be a long and winding road.

MV Rio Cobre

MV Rio Cobre

As required, we reported to the KG5 pool each day in search of work. With very little local work available, more often than not it was jobs at other ports that were posted up. Eventually after a week or so of this, Stephen I took EDH jobs on a boat called the *Rio Cobre* running out of Southampton.

Following the usual routine we found ourselves heading there, from Victoria station this time. Arriving at the docks we discovered her in dry dock.

Bought by Fyffes Line in 1969, she had been built in 1945 for United Mail by Gulf at Chickasaw as the *Junior*. She was painted white over the wall and was quite small, having a gross weight of just under 7,000 tons, with two steam turbine engines having a service speed of 18 knots. This was fast.

She had a most appealing itinerary, loading general cargo for Jamaica, once there loading bananas for the west coast of America, then returning to Jamaica to load bananas for the UK. We arrived on board on the morning of 17 August 1971 and signed-on articles in the saloon that afternoon. Stephen and I were told we'd need to share a cabin.

Having found our cabin, and not being required to start work until next morning, we settled down for the rest of the afternoon with a few spliffs, thinking happily to ourselves that this was all great and was going to be a very interesting trip.

Later we met another EDH called Brian, who had also joined the ship that day. It was obvious he liked to smoke too. We had a little bit of acid left, so we decided to take half each and go ashore for the evening. It would be one last trip before heading back to sea for a clean-out.

A short while later the three of us were walking off the dock, when two police officers on the dock gate stopped us. They asked us who we were, what ship we were off, and so on, then started probing further. They asked us to turn out our pockets. At that point to our complete surprise, Brian suddenly took off, running out of the dock gate and down the road. One of the officers sped after him in a car, calling back over his shoulder as he left, "Hold them two."

We stood in a small office for what seems like forever until eventually the other policeman arrived back at the gate with Brian, handcuffed, in the back of the car. We wondered what was going to happen now, as the effects of the LSD were starting to kick in.

Soon enough we were taken on foot to the police station. It was only a short walk as it was right there near the gate. My memory of the rest of the night was extremely sketchy, but I think we spent the whole night just sitting in the police station. Occasionally people would come in and peer into my eyes. There's be a garbled sound of people talking but making no sense. We knew where we were, but without knowing why. LSD is the only drug that makes itself irrelevant.

It wasn't until early next morning that we started to come down from the effects of the drug. Dawn brought the realisation of what was happening to us.

The policemen gave us lots of cups of sweet tea, and after a while we were given permission to make them ourselves, once they were happy that we were sufficiently coherent. Then later they proceeded to search us under caution. We were confident we had nothing incriminating on us, until one of the police officers, delving into my money pocket, found something small that must have looked a bit strange to him. He said, "What's that?"

I said, "I don't know, but quite honestly it looks like a small piece of wood."

He took out his lighter and proceeded to burn it. Sniffing the smoke, he said, "no, that's hash, I recognise the smell."

Steve, sitting next to me, stood up, pointed at it and said loudly, "you planted that!" He was certain we didn't have any hash.

At that point I recognised it. I recalled sitting on the floor at a party and somebody handing me something small with the words, "here's a little piece of Nepalese for you, Graham." I had wrapped it in a cigarette paper and put it in my money pocket for safekeeping.

That had been months ago. If I'd remembered I had got it, it would have been smoked by now. The jeans must have been washed umpteen times since, but unfortunately leaving that tiny trace. So I said, "It's all right, Steve, calm down. I remember it now. It's ok."

The policeman told us later that we'd simply been unlucky. The second policeman had only been there briefly to bring him a cup of tea, and they'd just happened to be talking about drugs and that kind of thing as we walked by. He admitted he'd only recognised the hash because he used to smoke it in his younger days, before joining the dock police. Truth to tell, in those days he and many other policemen in the ranks probably still did.

I asked him, "What next?"

He said, "We are waiting for permission from the captain to accompany you back on board to search your cabins."

Our hearts sunk. We knew they'd find the remainder of our grass. Sure enough, returning to the ship and our cabin with the dock police, they found the unmistakable debris and paraphernalia for a spliff-rolling. After rolling one, we had left it all out in full view before going ashore the previous night. Along with cigarette papers, tobacco and bits of ripped-up cardboard, they inevitably found our last remaining bit of grass: the merest half a gram.

Having found nothing else, they left the ship and took us to the police station in the centre of Southampton. We were formally charged and then bailed, pending forensic analysis of the substances found. If it proved positive, we'd be summonsed to court in approximately three weeks' time.

Steve and I were charged with joint possession of the grass found in our cabin. I had an additional charge for the hash found in my pocket. We were then released, the dock police kindly giving us a lift back to the ship. Once there, we went straight to our cabin and tried to get some sleep.

Later we were summoned to the chief officer's cabin. He told us that we would be unable to sail, as the case would take too long to come to court – the ship would be sailing within a week.

So that was that. We were paid-off there and then, and issued with train passes back to London.

We had barely been on the ship for 18 hours, but it felt A lot longer. We were still rather high on the acid we'd taken the evening before, but harsh reality was starting to sink in. Though at the time neither of us fully understood the implications of all that had happened to us.

After a very glum hour spent packing, we left the ship and headed for the station. Getting the train, we returned to London's East End and booked back into the Seamen's Mission. There we slept until the next morning, when we reported to the KG5 pool, only be to be greeted by some very serious faces.

They told us that we would continue to be paid pending the results of the drug analysis and possibly a subsequent court hearing. If convicted, we would need to attend a disciplinary hearing. They also told us that if convicted, in view of the current shortage of jobs, coupled with Federation policy on the use of illegal drugs at sea, the chances were we'd be dismissed from the industry.

In the clear light of day, and now fully grasping the consequences, Steve and I were totally shattered. How could this have possibly happened? And after just achieving our EDH status, too.

We knew our job – and we did it well. We'd been looking forward to a long career, sailing the world, fulfilling our dreams. After all my perseverance, how could this be happening at this late stage? Even though the industry was contracting, and we'd lately become aware that we'd probably need to sign a contract with a company to remain at sea, it was still a devastating blow.

Having a few weeks to kill before the court case, we pretty much fell back into the East End scene – the pubs, the clubs and the missions. We were still being paid by the pool, so we'd have enough money for accommodation and food, but we were well short of money for leisure activities. However, as ever, our circumstances were understood by the other lads waiting to ship out or arriving back after pay-off, and they cared for us to a certain extent. So we were never short of a pint or two and a bit of blow.

We spent part of the time back in Bushey, Watford. Steve would go and visit his mum for a while and I would visit mine, plus my father. It was not a good time, though after the initial shock we'd cheered up a bit. There was a chance we might just get through it ok, with added possibilities of going with non-Federation shipping companies, back on the coasters, or even with the Scandinavian merchant navy. So we remained hopeful.

We still enjoyed being part of the maritime scene. We spent many nights on board various ships in the Victoria, Albert and KG5 docks. We could pretty much come and go as we pleased, as we were mixing with fellow seamen and never being checked, since docks are busy places. As visitors we would invariably eat on board some ship as well.

Many a night was spent all crammed into a 4-berth cabin, partying after a good evening listening to bands. We also visited friends who had flats and houses around the area, including some of the nurses who were hostesses in the missions – those who had made their flight of freedom from the nurses' home by taking flats in and around London. Some of these were now in more serious relationships with seamen.

Eventually Stephen I received a summons to court, forensic analysis of the drugs seized having been positive. Well – we could have told them that. So we had to return to Southampton on the morning of our court appearance to answer the charges.

On our arrival the appointed solicitor asked us if we'd be pleading guilty or not guilty. We'd plead guilty of course. Our solicitor also told us that he had managed to separate our case from Brian's. In the first place he had been in a different cabin. Secondly, the nature of his charges were far more serious than ours. It would be distinctly to our advantage not to be associated with him in any way.

Unbeknown to us, when the police had searched Brian's cabin they had discovered morphine – and not just any morphine but in an easy to use form, something only to be found in the first-aid kits of emergency services or survival equipment.

We were appalled. Not only were we completely unaware of the existence of such a thing, we never indulged in drugs of that nature ("spirit stealers"). We were also absolutely disgusted by the knowledge that it could only have come from one of the various sorts of first-aid kit. This we considered inhumane. We tried to imagine any one of us finding ourselves in terrible circumstances, seriously injured, in an isolated place, or adrift at sea maybe, only to discover there was no morphine in the first-aid kit. It was unthinkable!

It greatly shocked both Stephen and me. It made us seriously re-examine the boundaries of the drug culture we'd got involved in.

We never saw Brian again, or ever found out what happened to him. But if he really had been responsible for stealing the morphine I can only hope he'd never in his life be permitted to do that sort of thing again. And if addiction had driven him to it, I sincerely hoped he'd find some therapy that helped him out of his dreadful predicament.

Steve and I were each fined £20 for possession of cannabis and I was fined a further £10 for the fragment of resin. All for a mere half a gram of grass and a quarter of a gram of hash.

Two days later Steve and I were summoned to the KG5 pool for a disciplinary hearing. Not much was said at that meeting. For some time there been a small poster on display in the pool office, as well as on noticeboards in various ships. It let it be known that anybody found with an illegal substance on board ship would be dismissed from the industry. Obviously we'd not taken this poster all that seriously. But as we sat opposite the Federation representatives, one of them silently slid the very poster across the table under our noses and said, "Have you seen this before?"

"Yes," we replied.

"Then there's nothing more to say. That's it: you're off the pool – as from today."

So there it was. I hadn't believed it would really happen, but it just had. What were we to do now?

We went back and hung around the Mission for a day or two. Then out of the blue Steve simply said, "Well, I'm off – I'm moving in with my girlfriend in South East London."

He'd kept that quiet!

His girlfriend turned out to be Irish – one of the nicer hostesses-cum-trainee nurses from the nurses' home in Victoria. I saw Steve very briefly sometime later. where he told that they had a young baby and he had a job now as a sales rep with Ever Ready batteries.

I was pleased for him that he'd found a direction to go in. I wished I could have said the same for myself. Sadly, I couldn't.

Have you ever found yourself literally standing at a crossroads, with no plan? With everything you are and you own in a rucksack on your back, trying to decide whether to turn left, right or go straight on – with going back not an option? All in the knowledge that whichever way you turn you will be sealing your destiny for the rest of your life?

In the past few years I'd found myself in this position many times. I had hoped never to be in it again. Yet here I was, having to start all over again. Which was the way I ought to go?

It was a familiar feeling for me, as I had been in this painful position before. And bounced back. However this time I had no vision and no direction.

Who would have thought it?

Back To School

I have begun this book in January 1970 when I joined the *Trebartha* as a deck boy for the first time, on that wonderful voyage that turned me from a boy into a man. But this story actually begins earlier.

Let me go back to that day in 1966 when, at the age of 13, I went to the Albert Dock with my brother to meet his old school friend returning after eighteen months at sea on the *Port Montréal*. The magic and romance of it all had caught my attention, and embroiled me for the next two years in making plans to start my career at sea.

Searching for any information about life at sea, I began to collect books on the subject, along with a huge map of the world upon my bedroom wall. It became a bit of an obsession. I had many interests in those days and jobs at different times, such as delivering papers, doing a milk-round, even working in pubs early-mornings putting bottles on shelves, earning money to support my hobbies.

I kept and bred tropical fish, which I sold to the local pet shop. This in turn funded my interest in photography, for which I needed equipment and chemicals for my darkroom, where I developed and printed my photos.

After my father's bankruptcy and thereafter, in the final year of his marriage to my mother, and having moved to several different houses, we found ourselves in a Council-owned house that sadly turned out to be the last family home as such I knew.

It was in the centre of Watford. It was only a temporary arrangement as the house was scheduled for demolition, along with the house I was born in, which lay close by. It was part of a scheme to build a new road through the centre of town.

I had left school in June 1968 at the age of 15 – this incidentally was the last year you could leave school at so young an age. I couldn't go into the Merchant Navy until I was 15½, so I spent the filling-in time working at various places such as: a supermarket, a hotel, tyre fitters, a boatbuilders, and at the marine engineering company where my brother worked. Eventually after applying for and going through the interviews and medicals, I had a date set for leaving home.

Naturally there was a shortage of money in the household at this time. Therefore, with what little money I'd saved from working, coupled with the sale of my tropical fish tanks and my darkroom equipment, I had the £30 needed for my keep, plus £30 as spending-money for the 14 weeks I'd be at the Pre-Sea Training School in Gravesend, Kent.

The very same day I left my family home was also the day that my mother and father, who had been living separate lives in the house for some time, would also be leaving and finally going their several ways.

Early that morning I took the train to London, and then on down to Gravesend. I knew the route well, since I used to regularly visit the pilot/tug station on the River Thames near there in my ship-spotting days.

I arrived at Gravesend Station at 9 AM, in the winter of 1968 with a crowd of other boys. We were bussed to the school for our induction. The building itself was four-storeys high, large, boring and uninspiring, built of concrete that had been custom built and opened in 1965. It was on three sides of a courtyard, with the open side looking out over a playing field leading down to the bank of the Thames, where there was a small practice wharf with derricks, hatches and a lifeboat hung on davits.

I was billeted in the catering boys' section, along with about 20 other students, in one of many large dormitories with bunk-beds located on the top floor.

We spent the morning and most of the afternoon being introduced to the school. After dinner I headed off down to an event in the main hall. I'd got talking to the lad who slept on the bunk below me. We went together and discovered that Monday night was boxing night.

The officer running this regular event announced for the benefit of us newcomers that all arguments were settled in the boxing ring on Monday nights. Fighting elsewhere, at other times, was strictly forbidden. He continued: the reigning champion was looking for a challenger – did anybody fancy their chances?

To my complete surprise, the lad I came in with, who was sitting next to me, said "Yeah" and stood up. "Me, I'll have a go". He went up onto the stage and got beaten after 3 rounds. He did however earn a lot of respect from everybody for doing that. A shrewd move, I thought. He'll be okay here.

Sadly not for me, though. I left the school early the following Monday morning after only one week. There were a number of reasons for this. In the main, I was not accustomed to this kind of establishment. At the time it felt as if I had no support from home, but no home to be homesick about, if you understand that.

Every day that went by was like a classroom situation. It reminded me of school, and brought back all the fears of failing academically, finding myself blocking up, and panicking in the classes just as I'd done in all those tormented years at school. I also felt from my reading that I had an understanding of life at sea, and I believed naïvely that this was nothing like how I imagined it to be.

Yet in retrospect I think the real reason was that my profound dyslexia and my inability to communicate in the written word would eventually lead to me failing. After all the time and effort that I'd put into getting there, I couldn't bear the thought of failing at the end of it. Even though all the officers and other lads who I had got to know tried hard to talk me out of it – the chief officer of the school telling me that if I left I would never be able to get away to sea – I knew in my heart I just had to get out of that place. I was blind with emotion – fit to burst.

You must understand that my schooldays had been a living hell for me. I was a bright, intelligent child, but unfortunately I couldn't grasp the fundamentals of grammar, or the spelling skills needed to progress and achieve any academic qualifications. Even reading was difficult, though it improved in time through necessity. I couldn't understand why. Nobody else at the school understood it either. My poor school reports would end with every teacher stating: "I do not understand why he doesn't do better". Dyslexia was not recognised as a disability in those days and the general feeling was that people like me were just thick, or a bit slow at best.

Years later I was pleased to hear that my old school in Leggetts Way in North Watford had been demolished some years before to make way for a housing development. I'd have paid good money to watch that useless seat of learning destroyed.

As I left the Pre-Sea Training School that morning, looking back at the building I said to myself, "thank God that's over" – promising myself I'd never let myself be humiliated like that again, come what may. I remember getting on the train to London from Gravesend, looking out of the window and saying to myself, "There must be another way!"

I spent the rest of the journey to London trying to work out what the hell I was going to do now. I felt as though I'd burnt all my bridges when I left home, unable to imagine what I was going to say to my mother or father now. They'd moved on, thinking they would not have to worry about me any more. I had got myself into this mess, but how was I going to get out of it? I felt a hopeless failure. Only in retrospect, many years later, did I fully understand why I'd walked out that day.

I wandered around London all day, and eventually found myself in the evening at Euston Station, still undecided what to do. Eventually I called my mother and explained to her what had happened. She said (bless her heart), "Well just come back here and we'll see what we can work out."

Unfortunately by that time I'd missed the last train, so I spent the night on Euston Station and got the early train to Bushey and Oxley Station near to where she now lived.

I spent a few days staying with her and her boyfriend, sleeping on a temporary bed in the living room.

I got in touch with an old school friend, Steve Peters, and his mother very kindly let me rent a room in her house, also in Bushey. I worked away at printers. for a few weeks and tried to come to terms with the fact that I'd spoilt my chances of fulfilling my dream of going to sea. I was however checking newspapers and periodicals, looking for adverts to see whether there were any jobs even distantly related to being at sea.

I soon discovered that unfortunately most of the major British shipping companies were affiliated to the British Shipping Federation. This organisation, funded by these companies, acted on their behalf to recruit their labour force. They had offices in most ports at which members would be able to find jobs at the end of their official leave, plus a kind of unemployment benefit would be paid to them until they found a job. Unfortunately the Federation also ran the Pre-Sea Training School that I'd just left.

However not all shipping companies were part of the Federation. There were small unaffiliated companies that only operated around the British Isles and the closer parts of the Continent. So there was hope for me.

Barge Diction and Barge Blatence

I continued my search, sometimes travelling to different places in the hope of finding a job. I found myself back at the London docks, Harwich and Felixstowe, phoning and (with help) writing to various companies such as Trinity House to see if I could get a job on their ships and boats that serviced lightships and lighthouses, channel buoys, etc, around the coast and harbours of Britain. But it all proved unsuccessful.

Part of the problem was that I was not yet 16.

Then, on one of my Saturday adventures, I was up in London looking around, when I noticed a string of barges alongside the ready-mix sand and gravel silos at Nine Elms Lane, close to Vauxhall Bridge. They were typical of the boats and barges you saw in those days endlessly sailing up and down the River Thames, with the crew looking up at you whilst you looked down at them from the London bridges.

I went exploring and came upon one of these barges alongside a small wharf. On-board I found the skipper and just asked him, "do you know of any jobs going here?" To my surprise he said "Yes, we're looking for a third hand on this barge".

He explained that they spent their time running sand and gravel from Harwich, up on the east coast, back into London, supplying the ready-mix concrete company.

"We do 2 or 3 runs a week. But the job needs to be arranged through the company, so you'll have to go down and see them in Kent. They're called the London & Rochester Training Company and their office is in Rochester, Kent. If you're serious about the job I'll let them know I've spoken to you. Call them to make an appointment and go and sort out the details with them."

Can you just imagine the incredible sense of excitement as I returned on the train back to Watford that day! What potential this held for me.

On the following Monday, after contacting the company, I organised a day off-work and found myself travelling back down the same line towards Gravesend again, but this time to Rochester on the River Medway. The interview was successful and I secured a job as a third hand on the barge, which was called the *Diction*.

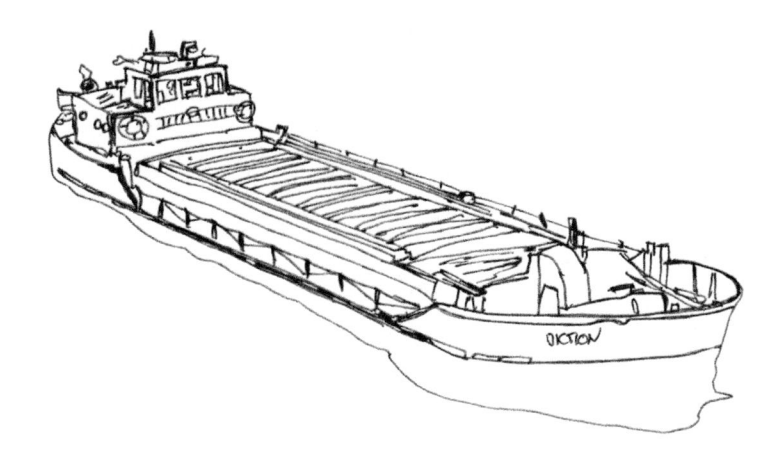

Barge Diction

This was one of the company's fleet of smaller barges, it also having a range of vessels from 188 ton to 600 ton coasters, all painted in pinky-red livery. They mainly operated around the coast of England but also to the nearby parts of the continent. The *Diction* was built in 1963, with one cargo hold, secured by sliding beams, small thick boards and tarpaulins, with battens, lugs, and wedges. I could not believe my good fortune having finally got a foot in the door. It just goes to show: perseverance brings success.

I gave in my notice at my existing job, then, with the help of a lift from my father with all my gear, I joined the barge at Nine Elms Lane and got settled in my cabin – it was up in the bow of the boat yet comfortable.

Early next morning, now Afloat at hight water, we sailed with the tide. We slipped our mooring lines and came out stern first to mid-river. Then, moving ahead and slowly picking up speed, we headed down the Thames under Vauxhall Bridge. It was a fantastic moment in my life to be finally part of what I'd been watching for all those years, now looking up at the people on the bridges I'd gazed down from on numerous occasions.

The Thames in those days was a very busy working river with a constant movement of boats of all shapes and sizes, from large vessels to small waterman boats manoeuvring hundreds of lighters: engineless barges placed alongside ships to load and discharge cargoes. These were then towed by tugs to the smaller accessible creeks and wharfs to be found all the way up and down the river.

It was wonderful passing down through the Pool of London – there were still cargo ships moored opposite the Tower of London in those days, to which they needed Tower Bridge lifting to gain access.

We continued under Tower Bridge and downstream, gazing at any number of vessels tied up on both banks, north and south. There were many tugboats towing streams of lighters of up to ten at a time. Then we went down to the lower reaches where all the major docks are located, passing and manoeuvring between the larger seagoing ships entering and leaving from all over the world.

It was absolutely fantastic, quickly moving with the tide, on down the river. We passed the tug station at Gravesend: there was a feeling of horror in my gut, mixed with other feelings as we passed the Pre-Sea Training School further downstream. Then out into the estuary itself, turning northwards to make our way to Harwich to pick up our cargo of sand and gravel and take it back to London.

It was a fantastic feeling to finally get to sea at last. It was a taste of reality, a bit challenging at times in bad weather. The meandering up and down the Thames to the centre of London, with all its bustle, was the most enjoyable part of the journey. It was a constant reminder of my ultimate goal of going deep sea some day.

We were all paid in the following way: the company would take 60% of the gross earnings of the boat, the captain then taking out all the overheads of the running of the boat per week, with the balance being paid to us in proportion to our seniority. This worked out at approximately £5 per trip for me. How many trips we did in the week however depended on the tide, weather, and shoreside working hours for loading and unloading. The most we could do in one week was three trips, but, subject to these factors, this would occasionally be reduced to two.

The tide was the trickiest factor. Although Harwich was a deep-water port, and freely accessible at any time, our boat would take the ground at low water on the Thames at Vauxhall. At the northern approaches to the Thames estuary were a number of sandbanks that dried out at low-water. One of the larger ones on our route was The Spit. If that dried out we needed to sail around it, adding 10 hours to our journey. Timing was of great importance.

One night after leaving Harwich on our return trip with a full cargo of sand and gravel, there was considerable discussion about whether we would make it across The Spit or not. The skipper decided to try it anyway. He and the first mate worked watches between them, but I only worked during the day, so I took to my bunk, not knowing whether we'd make it across or not.

I woke up next morning to an unusual sound – the sound of silence. I went up on deck to see what was happening, and was met by a very strange sight. We'd obviously not made it across The Spit as we were completely stopped and high-and-dry on the sandbank. Looking round about me, all I could see was sand. I couldn't even see the sea and, with no horizon, it was like being in a dead flat desert. Completely bizarre.

We spent the rest of the day doing maintenance on the hull, rudder and prop, plus a bit of painting with the ladder over the side, walking about on the sand. Eventually the tide came back in, lifting us until we were afloat once more. We continued our short journey into the Thames estuary, turning into the river and up to Vauxhall Bridge to discharge our cargo.

It turned out that I'd only been covering for the skipper's son, who had been away travelling for a couple of months. So after about five weeks it was announced I'd have to leave. However the skipper had been on to the company and given me a good reference. So to my delight they offered me another job.

It was now May 1969. After spending a few days at home with my mother. I received a letter enclosing a rail-pass asking me to travel up to Hull, on the east coast, to meet the skipper and crew at the Merchant Navy Hotel. We'd all be staying there for a short while before joining the *Blatence*, a newly-built 660 ton coaster. I was to be the fourth hand. This I did, checking into the Merchant Navy Hotel next to the Central Station, where I met up with the skipper, mate, and third hand.

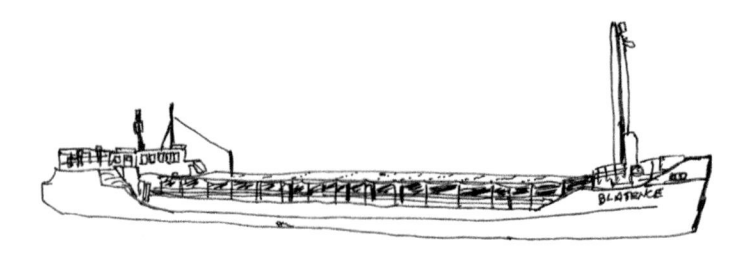

Barge Blatence

The *Blatence* had been built and launched from the boatyard in Paul, just a few miles down the River Humber. Now she had been brought up into Albert Dock, where all manner of service engineers were putting the finishing touches to her and checking all the on-board systems. This led on to sea-trials, which involved regular moves in and out the dock's lock, and sailing up and down the Humber, just to make sure that all the on-board systems were working correctly before she was handed over to us.

Finally after staying in the hotel for 10 days, being taxied or walking back and forth to the dock, we were finally given the go-ahead and moved aboard. Then after signing on ship's articles at the local Board of Trade office, we left on the tide the next day, with orders to head further up the Humber into the River Trent to the South and onward to Gainsborough to pick up our first cargo of grain bound for Amsterdam.

She wasn't a pretty ship. She looked like a scrubbing brush with a matchbox stuck on one end. Her wheelhouse was low in order to negotiate low bridges. You could hardly see over the bow for the huge motorised winch stuck on it, used for opening the hatches and operating the anchor.

Incidentally, it was because of that winch we had to get a new third hand. Unfortunately, while we were learning to use it, the swing handle needed to start the beast slipped off, hitting him on the head and injuring him so badly he had to go to hospital: the infirmary, as it was known in those parts. Fortunately his replacement arrived a mere two days before we left.

The *Blatence* was one of six boats commissioned for the company at that time, three being built in England and three in Holland. It wasn't a particularly good design of boat, especially the accommodation – very cramped and small. The skipper and mate had single-berth cabins, but the third hand and myself had to share a really small cabin. It was so small that only one of us could stand up to get dressed or undressed at any one time.

The whole boat was cramped, square and difficult to work. Even its modern McGregor hatches never worked smoothly.

Many years later I found myself sailing on one of the Dutch boats, built at the same time to the same specification. It was a beautiful little ship. Everybody on board had single-berth cabins, everything was spacious, worked properly and made for a very attractive boat. I was amazed how two ships of exactly the same weight and dimensions could be arranged so completely differently. The Dutch have always been ahead of the game when designing ships.

We left Hull on the tide that morning, headed up-river, turned south into the River Trent and made our way upstream, to tie up that evening alongside the grain silos in Gainsborough.

We arrived there on Friday evening, and as the mill workers didn't work on the weekend, we had some time to have a look around. On the Sunday somebody brought the *News Of The World* newspaper, where it was plainly stated on the front page that Gainsborough was the one place in the UK where you were most likely to be able to have sex. Sadly this didn't happen for me on that occasion – probably because I was unable to frequent the local pubs as I was still only 15 at that time, and looked about 12.

The River Trent being tidal at that point meant that we took the ground a few times throughout that weekend. But this was not an issue, as she was built for that very purpose. Then on the Monday morning we opened the hatches and took aboard our cargo of grain. Then with the next high tide we let go and headed back down the winding Trent to rejoin the Humber. Then turning to the east, following the charted course but navigating the ever-changing channels around the sandbanks, we passed Hull off our port side, where we'd started from some days before.

We continued down and out of the river, leaving the pilot and the lifeboat stations to our stern at Spurn Point. Then we sailed into the estuary and out into the North Sea, setting a south-westerly course towards Holland and our destination, Amsterdam.

Cooking on board was mainly shared by all the crew. However the washing-up, cleaning the galley and the messroom, along with all the cabins and the associated companion ways, descended firmly on my shoulders. Only after all my chores were done in the accommodation would I be working on deck, with the exception of leaving or arriving in ports, when I was needed for mooring lines etc.

We arrive at our destination late the next evening via the locks and the Nordzeekanaal, tying up alongside a lay-by berth on a still mild evening.

Two notable events took place here. First of all I was required to jump onto the harbour wall to take the lines and place them over the bollards. Somehow in this process, to the great delight of the rest of the crew, I managed to fall into the harbour. Fortunately the water level was very high and with assistance from the mate, who was on hand very quickly, I was got out of the water onto the side of the quay, soaking wet.

It took a few days to live that one down, I can tell you. Secondly, customs and immigration officials arrived the next morning to check us out, which was normal procedure. However I was summoned to the skipper's as there was a slight problem. My passport, which was in his possession, stated that I was still not yet 16. The Dutch immigration officer had taken issue with this, because in Holland the school-leaving age was 16 and, as he understood, it was the same in the UK. I only needed to explain that when I had left school in June the previous year, according to UK law it had been 15. Only since then had it been changed to 16. I also mentioned that I would be 16 in about two weeks' time in June. This seemed to satisfy the officials, and as I left noticing a look of relief on the skipper's face as well.

This is one of those moments I clearly remember. In my bunk that night my thoughts turned to the officer of the Pre-Sea Training School saying to me on the morning I quitted the place, that if I was to leave at this stage I would never get away to sea.

Yet here I was, at sea, and in my first foreign port. I was learning on-the-job what they'd proposed to teach me at the training school, but in a way I could understand. What's more, I was being paid for it.

I slept soundly that night, with a heightened feeling of confidence. For the first time I began to believe that everything would work out okay for me after all.

Later the next day we moved the boat to the berth for discharging our grain. After opening the tin-lid hatches we watched as huge flexible tubes like those on a vacuum cleaner were passed down into the hold and quickly sucked out the grain. When nearly finished, several men with shovels were sent down into the hold to dig out the last bits for the suckers. It was all done in what seemed no time at all, and in a matter of hours our hold was empty. After closing the hatches we timed our departure to catch the ebbing tide. We moved back along the Nordzeekanaal, back out through the lock into the Estuary and through the breakwater. Then we turned south for our next destination, Ghent in Belgium, for a cargo of steel to take back to England, up the River Humber to Goole.

Normal routine prevailed as we made our way down the West Coast of Holland, riding high on the sea as we were now in ballast. There is never a dull moment aboard a ship. There were always plenty of jobs to do on board this boat, especially as she was new. We were constantly sorting out all the little jobs that had been overlooked whilst being fitted out.

Continuing down the coast we passed the Hook of Holland, then the many inlets and islands to the south of it, until eventually we reached Belgian waters and the port of Zeebrugge. We then entered the Boudewijnkanaal, that took us up to the port of Bruges where we found our berth in this very busy port and awaited being loaded with our consignment of steel, mostly large RSJs of H-shaped cross-section, brought on board by large shoreside cranes and secured.

After closing the hatches and making ready for sea, we let go and returned to the canal and the North Sea, moving west across it to close the English coast. Then we turned and headed north, passing along the East Anglian coast and Lincolnshire, eventually reaching Spurn Point. We passed it once again going into the River Humber, back past Hull on the north side, then continuing upstream to the port of Goole.

I did experience some sea-sickness in those days, never being physically sick, but I did have varying degrees of nausea at different times, especially when I was working in the accommodation. I was always much happier out on deck. Smaller coastal barges that are flat-bottomed will usually have an uncomfortable roll to them, unlike conventional-hulled boats that ride the sea and the waves in a much more comfortable way.

You couldn't help noticing that the coastal waters were extremely busy in those days, with many vessels of different types, sizes, and nationalities. This I found most enjoyable. I could have almost done the job for nothing but the pure pleasure of just looking at all the wonderful ships as we made our way along the river.

After discharging our cargo in Goole, we were ordered to return to Gainsborough for another load of grain, this time bound for Ipswich, back further down the coast. That wasn't so far away, but it involved quite a lot of work as we had to completely wash and scrub out the hold from our last cargo of steel. It had to be clean to accommodate our cargo of grain.

I remember the skipper remarking at the time, "Just consider yourself lucky we didn't have coal for our last cargo, as the dust gets everywhere on the boat and it all needs to be thoroughly cleaned."

Once loaded we returned down the river into the North Sea, followed the coast, passing Felixstowe then sailing around into the estuary of the River Orwell. I noticed a familiar sight on its northern shore as we passed large piles of sand and gravel. This was where we used to regularly visit on the *Diction* some weeks before. Continuing up the river, we went through the sea lock and into the relatively small docks of Ipswich, eventually tying up alongside the grain silos there.

We had hoped to start discharging our cargo the next day. However, to our surprise, the company that was to receive our cargo of grain was on strike. We ended up having to wait for two weeks before we could eventually discharge the grain. We'd never imagined anything like that affecting us in this way, and took us a few days to work out what exactly the implications of this were to us.

I soon discovered that there was insurance in place for circumstances such as this – it's known as demurrage. This meant that for the period of time that we were waiting for the situation to change, we would be paid a wage based on our average earnings over the previous few weeks. As our company had a system of paying the crew a percentage of money that the boat was earning, this worked out at around £30 per week for me. This was a fortune in comparison to the £10 a week or so I had been earning on the *Diction*.

Incidentally, going deep sea as a boy rating at my age with the British Shipping Federation at that time would only have earned me £24 a month. One reason for the heightened level of earnings was that the skipper did not have to pay for fuel or harbour dues, as had previously been reckoned.

It was a bit boring not being at sea. There was however still plenty of work to do during the day, though not much for a boy of my age to do in the evenings in Ipswich. We joked among ourselves that we'd all do much better financially by just staying there for a few months, as there was no guarantee that future earnings for the boat would be as lucrative as they had been the previous few weeks – as we would soon find out.

I think in retrospect perhaps I should have stuck with that boat. I would probably have done quite well. However in those days money was not a priority for me. I was still stuck in the romantic notion of going deep sea whatever. The money side of things was unimportant.

After two weeks the dispute ended and we managed to discharge our cargo shortly afterwards. Sadly, due to the delay we had lost the next few cargoes on our schedule, so we had no work to do. We were therefore ordered to head out of Ipswich, back down the Orwell, back out into the North Sea, head south into the Thames estuary and up the river Medway to Rochester, Kent. This we did and picked up a mooring boy adjacent to the Company head office. On arrival we also learnt that the company had been taken over, and our new employers were now Crescent Shipping.

I left the *Blatence* there. With no work for her in the immediate future, she looked a poor prospect. Moreover I'd been worried by the mate's attitude in the last two weeks or so. He'd been giving me strange looks and had started conveniently coming to the shower room just when I happened to be having a shower. He'd also been making remarks that worried me, my having just turned 16 (the age of consent).

At around that time too, I'd received a letter from my father with some interesting information. Therefore, having secured my wages and the all-important discharge document, I decided that this was a good time to move on. So once more I found myself on the train back to Watford.

The *Blatence* continued on with Crescent Shipping until 1984, when she was sold to Derek Paraby Shipping. Then, sadly, two years later in 1986 she sunk in bad weather off Ronaldsay, to the north of Scotland.

On my return I went to stay for a few days with my father and his girlfriend, who also lived in Bushey.

The letter I'd received from him had not only told me about him and his girlfriend, it also mentioned that he'd been in contact with an old friend from his freemasonry days, a director of a small shipping company called Combe and Longstaff Ltd. This friend had been a member of the same London lodge as my father. But after his bankruptcy, father had been unable to keep up the fees and sadly had had to leave his lodge. This had disappointed my father as he was very much into it and had been a member for a long time, at one point having been Grand Master. I always saw freemasonry as a businessman's and capitalist's insurance policy for heaven when smitten by feelings of having been disowned by God for the greedy pursuit of wealth.

MV Westminsterbrook

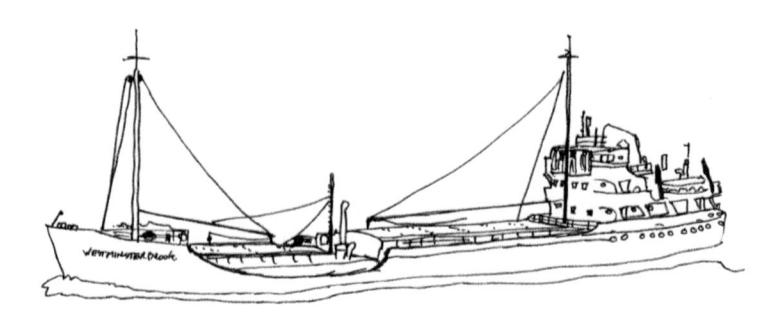

MV Westminsterbrook

I called and made an appointment to go and see this friend of my father's at his company's office in Leadenhall Street, London. After a long discussion he offered me two options, the first being that he could probably arrange for me to go back to the Pre-Sea Training School in Gravesend, something he strongly recommended. Otherwise he could give me a job as a cabin boy.

It was No Contest: I accepted the job immediately.

Once again, it was not a large foreign-going ship, but I'd gone one rung up the ladder as she was about 1,000 tons. She worked around the coast of England and the nearby continent and her name was the *Westminsterbrook*.

I joined her on 9 September 1969. She was tied up at Deptford Creek just upstream from Greenwich on the south side of the river in London, in a strange little corner of wharfs and warehouses used by many small companies including Crescent, and Everard's to name but a few. The creek mainly dried out at low-water, however there was a berth at the end where some boats could stay partially afloat.

She was 66.1 m by 10.3 m and drew 4.7 m, having two forward decks at different heights, with all the accommodation aft. Weighing in at 1,000 tons gross, she had a black painted hull and a crew of about 10, all having single berth cabins, including myself.

I had had to wait two weeks or so for this position to become available, and had spent time staying sometimes at my father's and sometimes at my mother's. As I knew this would only be a filling-in job to gain some sea time, I had still been trying to find a way to get deep sea. Therefore I had spent that time going back to searching through adverts, heading up to London, walking round the docks talking to people, still searching for that elusive backdoor in. I even applied for a job with the Antarctic Survey company, to no avail.

Sadly I only lasted a week on this quite nice Dutch-built boat. It was a very unhappy ship however, with a really miserable skipper. As with most of the ships I had sailed on to date, my job was to help the cook do all the washing up and of course clean all the accommodation on a daily basis, especially the officers' cabins, galley, messroom and washrooms etc.

The next day after joining her we let go. With the ebbing tide headed down to the Thames Estuary, around to the north up east coast and into the Humber to Goole once again, this time to load coal for Avonmouth. This was all be coming so familiar now, it seemed as if I was stuck in a loop between London and the Humber River.

I may have lasted for a little bit longer if it hadn't been for the rather unpleasant drunken Scottish cook. During the voyage to Avonmouth he decided to disappear into his cabin drinking for a few days, leaving me to do everything alone.

Therefore, on top of my cleaning duties, I was now expected to cook breakfast, lunch, and evening meal. I protested to the skipper on a few occasions, saying this was a bit unfair. He just used to say "Never mind that, sonny, just get on with it." And that's exactly what I did.

The only two saving graces were these. Firstly, I used to help my mother cook at home some years before, therefore I did understand the basics of cooking. Secondly, there were four deck hands on board. They had an unofficial rota *in situ*. At any given time one of their wives would be allowed to stay on board for a while with them. The current wife on board took pity on me and helped a great deal, especially in organising myself for the evening meal which was the most challenging, having to cook for 10 people or more. Somehow I managed.

I could not understand how everybody just accepted that the cook locked himself away in a drunken stupor, not responding to knocks on the door, and that the captain just expected me to take on his duties as if it was a normal thing. He even complained about the quality of the food at times, the ignorant bastard.

Needless to say I left the boat when we reached Avonmouth. I headed off the ship with my week's pay, discharge papers, and to my surprise two other crew members came too (probably because of the food) – plus the cook! We even had to share a taxi to the station with him. He tried to be friendly with me, making out that nothing was wrong. But when I complained to him for doing what he'd done to me, he just told me to "shut your face, laddie", or he would part my bollocks.

The *Westminsterbrook* was sold by Coombe and Longstaff in 1973 and passed through many British companies with various name changes, eventually being sold to a Honduran group of companies in 1976. Sadly she ended her days in 1999 by running aground and getting wrecked in the Mediterranean off Greece. By then she was named *MV Nawara*.

So here I was once again out of a limb, heading back on the train to London, wondering what to say to my father and how he would feel about it after involving his friend and me having let him down.

The next day I went up to see the very man again, who was shipping superintendent for the company at their London office. He was very understanding about the situation I'd found myself in, but although I had explained to him that my preference was to go deep sea, he suggested to me once again that maybe it would be better if I was to go back to the Training School.

The very thought of it gave me great pain, but after discussing it with him some more, and out of respect for him and for the sake of my father I agreed and asked him if he could try and arrange it for me. He said he would, but it might take some time to organise. I went on to explain that I had a problem with accommodation. He thought for a while and made a phone call, after which he gave me the name and address of a friend of his who was the manager of the *Flying Angel* Seamen's Mission in Silvertown Way, close to the Royal Docks in East London, suggesting I go down to see him as he might be able to help me.

I headed straight on down to the Seamen's Mission where I met the manager. His name was Jeff, a really nice chap. He accepted my story and agreed to let me stay there and work my bed and board until I returned to the training school. This was a large Victorian building with my work mainly involved cleaning the toilets on about seven different levels in the mornings, for which I'd be given a room and my food. This would be great while I waited for a date to return to Gravesend.

I moved in straight away and within a week a letter from the British Shipping Federation gave me a return date to Gravesend on 17 November. So I had a couple of months to wait. I felt glad that at least I had somewhere safe to stay whilst I did so.

Although bed and board were covered, I had to think about earning some spending money, not only for now but also to cover the time when I was once again back at the Training School. Therefore during this interval I had to find temporary jobs. The first of these was in South Woolwich, it was a short bus ride away across the Themes via the Woolwich Ferry (not so very far away), constructing security fencing. This was hard work but well-paid.

When that job finished I found another at Tate & Lyle sugar refinery back across the river in North Woolwich. This was a terrible job that involved large boxes containing smaller boxes of cube sugar, taking them off a conveyor belt and putting them back on again whenever the machine for sticking down and labelling the boxes broke down and was being repaired. Besides doing these two jobs I still had to clean the toilets for my keep.

The Mission itself was run by the Church of England. It was a brilliant place. From the upper floors where my room was situated I could see all over the docks. There were also many seaman staying there as they looked for jobs, or just spending their leave there if they had no homes to go to. Some of these became good friends and we spent many an evening drinking and playing snooker or pool whilst I listened to their stories and exploits across the world. I even got to know the Chinese who lived in the basement – they worked for the British companies that employed Asian and Chinese workers on their ships and were spending their leave there too. These folk were simply brilliant – they taught me not only to write my name in Chinese but also to play table tennis, for which I use their techniques to this day.

Eventually the big day came, and I was back at the Pre-Sea Training School at Gravesend as a catering boy. I had kind-of convinced myself I was a bit older and a bit tougher than I had been, and that maybe this time I'd be able to cope. But it was not to be: on this occasion I only lasted 24 hours. I very soon realised it was all a terrible mistake and on the following morning, Tuesday 18 November, I found myself once again on the train heading back to London from Gravesend. The echoes of the chief officer's voice rang in my ears: "Nobody ever gets back in here a second time – I don't know how you did it. But one thing's for sure: you'll never get away to sea now."

Looking at the countryside passing by outside the window, I thought to myself, what the hell do I do now?

Here I was once again following my heart and not my good sense. There was really no way that I could go back into that school again – I just couldn't do it. But what would I do now? I didn't feel I could go back to the *Flying Angel* – I'd said all my goodbyes there. And what was I going to say to my father? – "I really appreciate all you've done for me"? I didn't think he'd see it in a good light and would feel I'd let him down yet again. My mother of course would take it all in her stride, but it was difficult staying at her flat for any length of time, due to the obviously confused attitude towards me from her new partner Rod.

But then by burr chance, a very strange but significant thing happened.

As we were pulling out of Strood Station a youngish man came into my compartment and sat down. We got talking after a while and exchange stories, Brian, that was his name, said he could identify with me, because coincidentally he had done his time at the same school. And he agreed it was a desperate place.

I then heard his story. After getting into some kind of personal difficulties in Singapore he'd got in a fight with another crew member who had been rather badly beaten as a result. Brian had then been sacked, paid off, and flown home immediately. A further coincidence was that he was on his way up to the company office to see the superintendent there, to try and recover some wages that he'd felt were owing to him. He then suggested that I should go with him up to the office and ask whether they have any jobs. He added, "You have nothing to lose by it, and there's no harm in asking." I agree with that and said, "Okay let's go for it".

We continued our journey by Underground and went to Leadenhall Street, the home of all the major shipping companies in the UK. We went into a building and up to the office of the shipping superintendent who was in charge of crewing ships for the Hain-Nourse Shipping Company.

Just before we went in, Brian stopped and said, "Look, I'll go in first to sort out my business, then you come in shortly afterwards and act as if you don't know me. I don't think it you would do you any good if they thought you were associated with me in any way." So I went in shortly after him.

I politely asked if I could see the shipping superintendent. A man said yes, he was busy at the moment, but free soon. He pointed to a seat and asked me to wait. I could hear a heated discussion going on in office nearby i guessed it must be Brian.

Shortly after they both came out of the office, with Brian, looking very angry, storming out the door. But as he closed it after him, with a quick look back he gave me a sly wink.

The superintendent composed himself, taking a few breaths, looked around at me, smiled and said, "Now what can I do for you, young man?"

I said, "Do you have any jobs going for a catering boy?"

"Do you have any experience?"

"Yes," I replied. I told him what I'd done and, in the absence of a seaman's discharge book, produced my two paper discharges which had been issued independently from the two coaster jobs I'd had, on the *Blatence* and the *Westminsterbrook*. I added that coasting was not the life for me and I was looking to go deep sea.

He said, "Well, we do need boys – can you do the job?"

"Yes," I said, "of course I can."

To my complete surprise he said, "Okay then, but you need to be Federated. Just hang on in there for me and I'll go and sort something out." I sat there for a while, not quite believing or understanding what was happening at that moment. The superintendent returned with a piece of paper, saying, "Okay, tomorrow morning first thing go around to the British Shipping Federation office in Dock Street, just around the corner. Ask to see this man, take your paper discharges with you and he'll sort it out from there. And I'll speak to you again after that."

I thanked him, we shook hands and I left the building, heading for Euston in a daze. I called my mother, explained what was going on and arrived back at her flat that evening.

It had been quite a day. I slept well that night.

First thing on Tuesday morning I headed up to London, arriving at the Prescott Street building. I was really concerned about what was going to happen there, as this was the British Shipping Federation, where I'd originally gone for an interview for my first spell at the Training School. These were the very people who managed all the crewing for federated shipping companies, and ran the associated Pre-Sea Training School at Gravesend – that I had left for the second time scarcely 24 hours earlier.

I decided not to mention anything about it unless directly asked. I took a deep breath and went inside and up to the counter, explained I'd been sent by the Hain-Nourse superintendent, showed the piece of paper he'd given me and asked to see the person named. The man behind the counter made a phone call and said "If you'll just wait there, he will see you in a minute."

The minutes felt like hours as I waited, I was almost bursting. I was scared stiff that at any moment somebody would say "Just a minute, don't I know you?" and get literally thrown out of the place on my ear.

But no, what happened next was totally amazing. The man I'd been sent to see appeared and asked, "Are you Graham Durrant?"

"Yes," I said.

"Okay, what you need to do now is go round to the dentist. I've made an appointment for you this afternoon. You must get your teeth checked out and have any work done that needs doing. Then, tomorrow morning I've also made an appointment for you to see a doctor close by, where you will have a medical and have your inoculations done. Then come back here tomorrow afternoon with four passport-sized photos to sort out the rest of your paperwork."

All this I did. I had five fillings done without delay at the dentist that afternoon, then next morning (Wednesday) going to the doctor's surgery. I was declared fit and given my inoculations plus the supporting paperwork. Upon returning to the Federation office I was then sent round the corner to the Board of Trade in Dock Street, where I witnessed a remarkable thing.

After waiting for an hours or two I was ushered into a small office where an elderly man took the photographs from me and disappeared for a while, returning with two books in his hand: my seaman's discharge book and my Board of Trade ID book. Then, in what seemed like slow motion, he carefully wrote out on a sloping desk all my details in both books, remarkably using a small ruler underneath all the wording to form a perfect straight line. I could hear my heart beat in the silence. Armed with these two items, I went back to the Federation office, where I had to pay One Shilling to become a fully paid-up member of the Seaman's Union.

MV Trewidden

MV Trewidden

That afternoon I walked out of the building in Dock Street as a fully-fledged British seamen: registered with the Federation, the Board of Trade, and the Union – with a rail warrant accompanying the instructions to report to a certain hotel in Victoria on the Friday evening with all my gear and spend the night there.

Then, with the rest of the crew, catch the flight from Gatwick Airport to Antwerp, Belgium on the Saturday morning, to join one of the Hain-Nourse ships named the *Trewidden*. She had been built at Newcastle-upon-Tyne in 1960 and weighed-in at 6,469 tons gross.

I went back to my mother's that night, not knowing what to think. I couldn't believe what had happened that day, nor could anybody else. I sat there for hours, looking at my seaman's book, I.D. book, train pass and aeroplane ticket. It was beyond belief, especially as I'd only just got off the train back from Gravesend a little over three days ago.

I'd finally made it – just. And it had all happened in such a strange fateful way. It was as if somebody, or something, had been looking down on me from above and had simply decided to give me a break as a reward for all my efforts, not to mention the difficulties I had gone through during the previous months.

It was a sheer miracle, and could almost have turned me religious. However intelligence and good sense prevailed.

Having made my way up to the Victoria Hotel in London on the Thursday and checking in, I briefly met some of the other lads in the bar. But soon I went to bed in anticipation of our early start. I could hardly sleep with excitement.

We were picked up by coach early the next morning and taken to Gatwick Airport where we took our short flight to Antwerp. We were met at the airport by another coach and taken to the docks where we were dropped alongside the large dark blue hull of the *MV Trewidden*, with its even darker blue funnel emblazoned with the large letters HN.

We went on board and found our cabins. I would be sharing with another catering boy in a two-berth cabin within the midships accommodation. We were then summoned to the saloon, where we signed-on ship's articles.

We returned to our cabins, turning-to for work almost immediately to do the lunch. Afterwards we had a siesta, then turned-to again at 3 o'clock to prepare for the evening meal.

After a good night's sleep I turned-to at 6.30 AM to do breakfast, only to find us moving away from the berth, still in the dark. We made our way through the docks, through the sea lock into the River Scheldt, continuing on down into the North Sea. Then we turned south, sailing down the coast past Belgium and Northern France, heading for the Bay of Biscay, then the Straits of Gibraltar. There we turned east into the Mediterranean towards our destination, Marseilles, in southern France.

—oOo—

It took us about ten days to get to Marseilles. After a day or so at sea we soon fell in into a rather regular routine. As this was the first time I'd been on a proper large seagoing ship, it was all a bit new to me and I hadn't really realised the extent of the work involved, and how completely different it was in comparison to the coasters I had working on previously. It really was full-on work from 6.30 in the morning until about seven in the evening, 7 days a week.

Every ship would have two catering boys, one would be allocated to the saloon and messroom for officers and crew. The other would be working in the galley. Whichever you did it always involves a great deal of cleaning and washing-up. I was allocated to the pantry, this involved getting up first thing in the morning to set out all the places on the officers' tables in the saloon, with knifes, forks, spoons, plates, and condiments etc. The stewards would serve the breakfasts, then I'd clear it all away, washing up, hoovering and washing the floors. This was then followed by washing down the floors and bulkheads of all the companionways in and around the accommodation.

When that was finished I was expected to help the stewards clean the officers' cabins, from the first officer down to the third engineer. Then it was straight back to start all over again for lunch. I'd normally have all the strapping-up done and dusted by 1 o'clock. I would then have from 1 PM until 3 PM off. Most people slept during this time, taking a kind of siesta. Then I'd wake up and start all over again for the evening meal. I'd normally be finished by 7 PM. This was long hard work and not particularly interesting. Also the chief steward, who was not a happy man, took a dislike to me and had me frequently going over work again, saying I had not done it properly.

It was an uneventful journey down to Marseilles, with the weather only reaching a state of early spring in the UK. It was still getting dark early, which left no time for going out on-deck and seeing where we were going. I spent most evenings with the deck crew. There were a few good lads there plus one really interesting man called Sparrow, the bo's'un.

I think the biggest problem for me was that whereas previously on the coasters I used to spend time on the bridge steering, plus working on deck, this wasn't going to happen as a catering boy on a big ship. As time went by, I came to realise that maybe I was better suited to life on deck.

Sparrow the bo's'un, well-named because he was a slight man, was probably in his late 50s, almost definitely an alcoholic, but well-liked and trusted by the crew. Although little, he was as hard as nails. I spent much time in the evenings talking to him and slowly getting to understand what the job on-deck was all about. Also I realised I knew more about the job from my previous experience than I'd guessed.

I did my job every day but I was certainly not happy in it.

We soon arrived in Marseilles, known as the Chicago of France. We were to spend about five days there, loading various cargoes, but mainly a large consignment of Sandeman's Port. I found that out as presently the ship was awash with the stuff, nearly all the crew having several bottles stashed away in their cabins, including myself.

I didn't get to see much of Marseilles, though I did have the odd couple of hours taking a look around. This was partly due to my working long hours every day with no days off, and partly because I had little money to spend. Also being so young I was restricted in what I can do. This meant that most of my free time was spent on board the ship – drinking port in fact – and for the most part bringing it back up.

The pilfering soon came to the attention of the chief officer. One afternoon I was taking a short break on the afterdeck chatting to Sparrow when the officer of the watch turned up. The bo's'un turned to face him and I overheard their conversation. The officer was saying to him: could he be on the lookout for pilfering of port out of the holds as it had come to notice that quite a few cases were missing. Now Sparrow always wore a grey jacket when he was working. He stood there with his hands in his trouser pockets saying, "That's terrible! I'll certainly keep an eye out and let you know if anything turns up." I was standing behind Sparrow, so I could see that he had his hands in his trousers pockets in order to hold his coat back so that the officer couldn't see the bottle of port in each of his jacket pockets.

The *Trewidden* was a tramp ship, therefore no one really knew where she was going until it happened. So on the day that we left Marseilles, news spread around the ship that we were heading back to London.

I had mixed feelings about this. On the one hand I was disappointed because we weren't continuing the voyage and going to more exotic places. On the other hand I was pleased as I could pay-off the ship in London and do something else; maybe change to working on-deck. I was more and more of the opinion that the catering department at sea was not for me.

It was just so boring! You are confined to the accommodation of the ship for 12-14 hours seven days a week. You never got to see where you were going or experience all the wonderful places you may be visiting around the world. I spent the rest the voyage home thinking that I may have been better off even staying on the coasters.

I had quite a few runs-in with the chief steward, on one occasion all but throwing a bucket of water over him one day.

So here we were, heading back west along the French coast, then the Spanish Mediterranean, emerging into the Atlantic through the Straits of Gibraltar. We turned north and made our way back through ever-colder weather in the English Channel to the Thames and into the Royal Albert Dock, arriving early in the morning of 16 December 1969.

After breakfast it was announced that everybody who wished to pay-off, was to report to the saloon now. The chief steward already knew I was leaving, so I went straightaway.

Arriving in the saloon I discovered there were quite a lot of the crew doing the same as me – paying off, with others arriving to sign-on – so it was rather busy. After signing off and receiving my payslip and money, I turned around to go – and to my surprise came face to face with the very man who'd got me the job: the company shipping superintendent.

He asked me why I was paying-off, and I explained myself as best I could. He stared hard at me and said, "Look, just what do you want?" In my embarrassment I heard myself saying to him, "I want to change jobs and go on-deck."

He was silent for a moment and then said to me, "Okay then, here's the deal. If right now you go straight down to Tilbury and work-by as a catering boy on the *Trecarne* over the Christmas period, I'll put you on a ship leaving here for Australia in the beginning of January as a deck boy. How does that sound?"

I replied it sounded brilliant. "Will tomorrow do?" I asked. He said, "That's fine."

I shook his hand firmly and said, "Thank you very much." I really wish I could remember his name: he was a good man, and in some curious way bound up with my fate at that time.

I said farewell to the other members of the crew and headed off to the station and back to Watford, spending the night at my mother's before heading back to London and down to Tilbury on the train. There I found and joined the *MV Trecarne*. The next day I was told to go ashore to the local Board of Trade office at Tilbury to sign-on-articles, as their officers would only come aboard the ship to do this job when there was a whole crew signing-on or -off.

The *Trewidden* incidentally remained with Hain-Nourse until 1975, when it was sold to a Cypriot shipping company called Eahteos and renamed the *Serena*. She was disabled with engine damage in Somalia in 1978, eventually towed to Taiwan in 1979 and broken up in December of that year.

MV Trecarne

MV Trecarne

The *Trecarne* was a bigger ship than I'd yet been on, weighing-in at 8,523 tons gross, 471 ft long, 61 ft beam and 26 ft draft. It was built in 1959 in Glasgow a year before the MV *Trewidden*. Although only a year older she seemed to be of a different design, an earlier one, with much squarer features, steam winches on deck and in a far rustier condition. Maybe she'd been built of inferior steel, or just hadn't been maintained so well.

So I started work straightaway, but happily I was put in the galley this time. This made a change for me – it was completely different from stewarding. It was still very demanding though: I still had to work the same long hours, seven days a week, and I just spent more time washing pots and pans, scrubbing floors and cookers, plus collecting and carrying food from the food lockers on the fridge flat.

I also worked on the preparation of vegetables: potatoes – lots of potatoes. It was hard work and very hot. Probably it would have been unbearable in the tropics. I was at the mercy of the chefs as well, whatever their temperament, although I have to say they were fairly decent on this boat.

I think I preferred the galley to the stewarding side. In the long-term I guessed it would prove to be very restricting, though moving up the career ladder would eventually lead to becoming a chef. That was not my forté, but it was worth a thought.

However I had made my decision a while ago to change to the deck department. I was happy in the knowledge that I only had a couple of weeks more to do now, during which time I'd know for sure if changing to the deck suited me, and whether this was really the life for me. I do think that, at the end of the day, it was those invaluable jobs on the coasters that helped me to realise it. My only misgivings were: would I have the self-confidence to deal with the extremes of being on deck in bad weather and avoid letting myself or others down? I also had a fear of heights. Sparrow, the bo's'un on the *Trewidden*, had assured me it would pass with practice once I got working aloft.

So the days went by as the ship discharged her cargo, ramping up to the few days before Christmas, when the company was having a large party on board. This involved a lot of preparation, so we were all very busy. I however, with my usual tenacity, managed to wrangle Christmas Day off by swapping days-off with a lad who needed the extra money for working that day. As for me, I needed to nip home to say goodbye to my mother before I went deep sea, just in case I didn't get another chance. So that all worked out well.

Time flies by when you're busy. Christmas came and went, and it was coming to the end of the year, when suddenly we discovered that we were leaving Tilbury and sailing out of the Thames, then heading north up the east coast of England once again. Where to? You've guessed it: Hull of course.

I remember the Geordie donkeyman on the *Trebartha*, after hearing the story of my experiences prior to arrival on that ship, laughing scornfully and saying, "Yeah, you must be the London-to-Hull Kid!" I think he'd read too many of the westerns that filled ships' libraries in those days.

Arriving in Hull, we came in through the lock, tying up alongside a berth in the Alexander dock at around 11 PM on 31 December, just one hour before the New Year began.

We had all been drinking when, at midnight, all the ships sounded their horns. Fireworks went off in the docks, thrown and launched from the many ships there. Fireworks were also going off all around the city, as we could clearly see from where we stood on the upper decks. Being the youngest on board, I had to perform a ritual which entailed me taking off all my clothes, running down to the foredeck and up to the ship's large and very loud bell on the fo'c's'le head and ringing it. This I did: it was freezing cold but I enjoyed doing it. I did however cheat a bit by keeping my shoes on.

I worked by for a few more days on the ship, occasionally going ashore, mainly to the Mission to Seamen on the dock road. Then, some nights, afterwards we'd go on to one of the dodgy late-night clubs or dive bars not far away, where the proprietors were not too fussy about your age, especially if you were obviously a seaman. They were not licensed, of course, therefore not responsible for the consumption of any alcohol you might discreetly take in with you.

Eventually on 6 January 1970 all the home-trade crew signed off, myself included. Those wanting to remain on board would then sign-on again for the next deep sea voyage, along with the new arrivals.

Armed with my payoff money, I left the *Trecarne* for the station in a taxi with three other crew members. As had been promised me, I'd been given a rail warrant back to Watford, and another to return to the Royal Docks, together with a letter from the company requesting me to join the *MV Trebartha* at F Shed, Albert Dock, on 8 January 1970, signing-on for the position of deck boy.

Brilliant!

On the train back to London I decided not to see my mother, as it was a difficult house to stay in, besides which I'd seen her on the Christmas Day just past. Therefore I headed straight for the Royal Docks, checking in that evening at the *Flying Angel* Seamen's Mission on Silvertown Way – the place where formerly I'd been working for my keep. It was handy for where the ship I was joining was tied up. Also I thought it would be nice to see

Jeff and all the other inmates in that salubrious establishment, so I could tell them all how I was doing, plus saying goodbye before shipping out.

I stayed there two nights, as a resident this time. It was good to see everybody again, and I had a good few games of snooker and table tennis with my Chinese friends in the basement. I said all my farewells and left the Mission late afternoon on 8 January. Taking the bus down to the swing bridge near the Connaught pub, I walked through the dock gate on this cold, dark, murky night. Next-door to G Shed I found F Shed and the large hull of the *Trebartha* on the next berth.

I walked up the gangway, and at the top there was a board stuck in the taff rail with the message chalked upon it: *Depart 18:00 hours for Las Palmas*. I didn't know where the fuck that was, but it sounded wonderful.

The rest of the story you know.

—oOo—

It really had been a long hard slog to bring me to that point. Due to my circumstances I had arrived by a most unconventional route. My inability to learn in ordinary ways forced me to find another way, and it was only thanks to that dream when I was 13, the lack of a proper home to go back to, and my sheer determination that got me through.

Epilogue

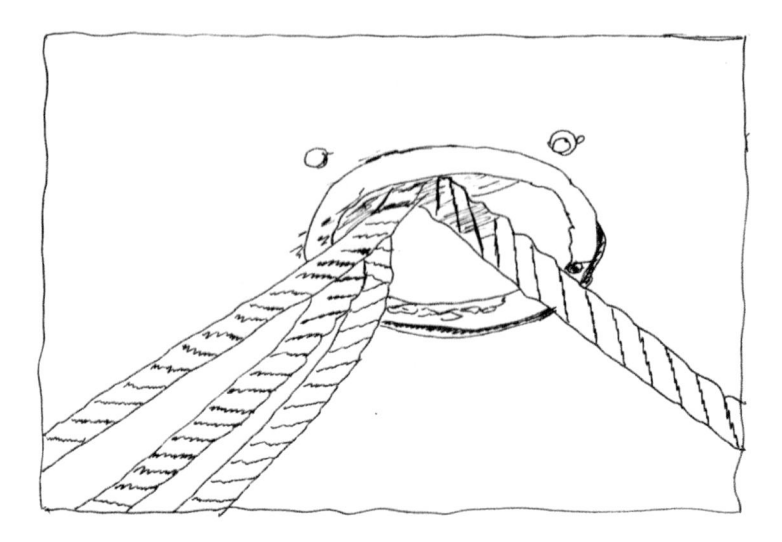

I left home a young, naive, uneducated boy, unable to cope with conventional life. For reasons I could not then grasp, I had to take this path so that I could gain knowledge, become stronger, and learn to have confidence in myself. This gave me the gratification of reaching the limits of my potential, by embarking on the career I'd chosen for myself years before.

Had I not spent those precious weeks on the coasters, discovering that I was much more suited to the outdoor life, I don't believe I would ever have realised that going on deck was the answer for me.

In those early days of planning my future I didn't imagine I'd be able to deal with the extremes of being continually out in the elements. Also my early researches had told me that one could make far more money on the catering side with all the compulsory overtime – if money was one's priority. I now knew I was perfectly able to deal with the work entailed in being on-deck, and that in fact money was not my priority. My inner feelings of satisfaction and happiness were far more important to me.

The deck crowd on merchant ships are a very tough bunch, and obviously it was going to be far more difficult to prove myself to them. You must be fit to do any job you're given, in any circumstance, at any time, whatever the weather – and ensuring that every other member of the crew have confidence in your abilities. Furthermore, to achieve this you must have total confidence in yourself. This knowledge has been my signpost in life. It has enabled to me to succeed at whatever I've chosen to do.

As for my dyslexia, I've endured and managed its incapacitating effects throughout my life. Sadly, when I was at school, it was an unrecognised condition. As a result my teachers found no effective way of teaching me anything very much. Ironically, the one lesson of value that I gained from my schooling and have never forgotten, was the single consistent comment made by all teachers, whatever the subject, at the end of every failing low-grade report. It said, "I cannot understand why Graham doesn't do better".

In some profound way, that single sentence gave me *hope*.

—oOo—

I'd love to believe that those same teachers eventually started to look deeper into the problem, which in time would lead to the identification of *dyslexia* as a treatable condition, so triggering the development of new procedures and attitudes to help people like me. In recent years, technologies unimaginable in those days have been developed which would certainly have helped me back then. Technologies such as the one I'm using at this very moment (speech-to-text) that I have learnt during the process of producing this account of my early years: something I would not have been able to do otherwise, or only with the greatest difficulty.

I do wonder however what might have become of me had I not suffered from dyslexia. I might well have done better for myself; led a more secure life; grown richer; become famous – or even infamous. But, as we all know, we can't re-live our lives to see how things would have been different had we chosen another road to our future.

One thing I know for sure, however. It's unlikely I would have had half the extraordinary experiences – the interesting, adventurous, or creative life I've led – nor would I have had nearly as much companionship, joy, fun and laughter.

END

Printed in Great Britain
by Amazon